GENDER

MILITARY OCCUPATION

AND THE AMERICAN CIVIL WAR

Occupied Women

Edited by LeeAnn Whites *and* Alecia P. Long

LOUISIANA STATE UNIVERSITY PRESS

BATON ROUGE

Published by Louisiana State University Press
Copyright © 2009 by Louisiana State University Press
All rights reserved
Manufactured in the United States of America
LOUISIANA PAPERBACK EDITION, 2012

DESIGNER: *Amanda McDonald Scallan*
TYPEFACE: *Whitman*

Library of Congress Cataloging-in-Publication Data
Occupied women : gender, military occupation, and
the American Civil War / edited by LeeAnn Whites and
Alecia P. Long.
    p. cm.
Includes bibliographical references and index.
    1. United States—History—Civil War, 1861–1865—
Women. 2. United States—History—Civil War,
1861–1865—Social aspects. 3. Women and war—United
States—History—19th century. 4. Women—Southern
States—Social conditions—19th century. 5. Women—
Employment—Southern States—History—19th century.
6. Military occupation—Social aspects—Confederate
States of America. 7. Sex role—Southern States—
History—19th century. 8. Occupations—Southern
States—History—19th century. I. Whites, LeeAnn. II.
Long, Alecia P., 1966–
    E628.O33 2009
    973.7'1082—dc22
                                    2008042281
ISNB 978-0-8071-3717-8 (pbk: alk. paper) — ISNB 978-
0-8071-4394-0 (pdf) — ISBN 978-0-8071-4395-7 (epub)
— ISBN 978-0-8071-4396-4 (mobi)

Contents

Occupied Women

Introduction

LEEANN WHITES AND ALECIA P. LONG

In the spring of 1861, tens of thousands of young men formed themselves into military companies and offered themselves up to fight for their country, whether they saw that as being the Union or the newly formed Confederate States of America. Their families and local communities assisted them, sometimes by sewing uniforms or company flags, other times by providing arms or supplies. Perhaps the most critical way in which the civilian population assisted these men was by providing them with encouragement and moral support. After all, these young soldiers represented the flowering manhood of their communities, and they were volunteering to fight and die for their country and their community's cause. Each side had faith that its boys would be quickly victorious on the battlefield and would return home in a few months' time. On both sides of the conflict, understandably worried mothers, fathers, sweethearts, wives, and siblings, as well as the newly minted soldiers, consoled themselves with the thought that it would surely be a short war.[1]

Of course all these parties were very wrong in their calculations in many ways. Perhaps their first and most serious miscalculation was that the war would be short, when, in actuality, it would drag on for four long years. As those years passed, more and more men would be called away from their homes. By the war's end, nearly half of the adult male population of the North and a staggering 90 percent of the age-eligible white male population of the Confederacy would enlist or be taken into military service. Local communities, which gave up many of their best and brightest young men at the outset of the conflict, found the demands of the formal field of battle reaching progressively deeper into their populations, lives, and hopes. As patriotism and, later, conscription forced towns and individuals to part with ever more husbands, sons, and fathers, many places were transformed into cities of women with only small populations of elderly men and young boys left among them. Indeed, by the last year of the war, especially in the Confederacy, adult civilians were basically women. It is the often unacknowledged role these civilian women played as direct factors in the conduct and outcome of the Civil War that is the subject of this collection of essays.[2] To date, the central question posed by historians who have explored the relationship between women and the Civil War has been whether the war changed their status as women. In answer to this question, some historians have suggested that nothing was more important to the changing position of women than the extended and unexpected loss of so many men, some of them forever. Many historians of women have suggested that this long-term absence of men "opened every door" for women. From this vantage point, women seized the opportunity to run their households in their men's absence and to widen their public presence and activities as well. Other scholars have suggested that the wartime necessity of attempting to compensate for the absence of so many men had exactly the opposite effect on the women they left behind on the home front. These scholars conclude that rather than carving out new and enduringly independent roles for themselves as a result of their wartime autonomy, women learned from the war-born necessity of filling in for their men that they most definitely were *not* men, were not able to *be* men, and did not *want* to be men.[3]

While historians of women would readily acknowledge the starting point for this debate in the war-driven absence of men, their interest has focused primarily on the issue of the impact of the war on women and their social standing, rather than the role of women as direct players in the conduct and outcome of the war. Instead of focusing horizontally on the relationship between the home front and the battlefield, historians have tended to look laterally down the corridor of time in order to discuss the long-run political and cultural implications of what the war set in motion for women. They ask questions like: Did women make lasting gains in the home or in the public realm of paid employment? Did they receive legal and political rights as a result of their need to compensate for their men's absence at the front? Were there lasting changes in the relationship between men and women as a result? Did marriages, for instance, become more companionate in the war's aftermath?[4]

Women's responses to the absence of their men may always be debated because the war undoubtedly generated a vast range of reactions that varied in no small part based on the class, race, region, or personal inclinations of different women. Despite the range of existing historical discussion, however, no one has suggested that the female civilian population as a whole was not burdened and made busy by the absence of so many men. Increased workloads could be buffered somewhat by slave labor or hired male labor, or even mitigated by the purchase of market goods, if one had the wealth and these things were available. But not even wealth could eliminate the need to step up to the responsibilities of household direction and public representation that were normally the purview of white men. It is this sense of being occupied and its consequences for the gender order, particularly for the relative power and standing of women in relation to men, that historians have debated most intensely.[5]

Women's enhanced workloads and responsibilities were a given in the absence of so many men, but there was a second and related way that civilian communities miscalculated the consequences of the war and women's occupation. Not only would legions of women be preoccupied with additional duties; many of them would also be literally occupied by the presence of enemy men. In point of fact, adult men were present on the streets of towns and villages as a consequence of enemy invasion or success on the formal field of battle; they just were not men of the local community. And because the war's significant territorial gains generally went to the Union, this experience of being occupied by enemy men was most commonly a Southern one. Certainly the Confederacy also made a few brief forays into Union territory, most notably during their advance into Pennsylvania, which culminated in the Battle of Gettysburg in July 1863. As Margaret Creighton's contribution to this volume on the Confederate occupation of Gettysburg suggests, the experience of being occupied held certain common structural characteristics for women regardless of which side of the conflict their male occupiers were on. In the war of occupation, the home front and the battlefield merged, creating a new kind of battlefield and an unanticipated second front, where some civilians—many of whom were women—continued resisting what they perceived as illegitimate domination.[6]

As our map indicates, the experience of the war of occupation began early in the war for many women. By the end of 1861, the Union had established areas of occupation all along the northern perimeter of the slaveholding border states. During this same period the Federals were able to use their overwhelming naval strength to throw up a maritime blockade around the eastern seaboard and then to establish occupied areas in key coastal regions, especially in the low-country area of northern Virginia. This was a vast sweep of territory, stretching

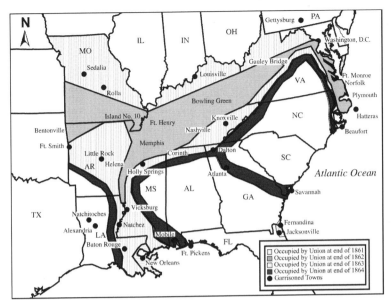

Areas of Union Occupation, 1861–1864
Map by Aaron Sheehan-Dean

all the way from the states of Missouri and Kentucky eastward to Maryland and Delaware, basically from the upper Mississippi River to the Atlantic. The Union was aided in this effort by the divided loyalties of the inhabitants of these northernmost slaveholding states. Those divided loyalties also meant that this initial occupation was just the beginning rather than the end of the war in those areas. It is this contingent, continuous, and critical war of occupation that we detail in this volume.

By the end of 1862, the Union had made little advance in terms of expanding the area of occupation in the East. The armies of McClellan and Lee fought seemingly interminably over a limited area in northern Virginia. In the West, however, the Union was more successful in expanding its control southward from its initially occupied border-state areas of Missouri and Kentucky. The combined successes of naval and ground forces resulted in the Union occupation of both Memphis and the strategically important city of New Orleans by mid-1862. By the end of the year, the Union also made inroads into the low-country areas of South Carolina and Georgia.

With the fall of Vicksburg in July 1863, the Union consolidated its occupation of the West, establishing a corridor of occupied territory that ran the entire length of the Mississippi River, while in the East the gains in occupied territory were still limited. Indeed, the greatest interior expansion of Union occupation in the East came late in the war, when the Union marched its men out of the West and, under the command of General T. Sherman, cut a wide and infamous swath through the states of Georgia and South Carolina. Thus, by the last year of the war, the Federals had established areas of substantial occupation across the entire Confederacy, from the Mississippi River to the eastern seaboard.

For Confederate-identified women, this occupation often had difficult, even tragic, aspects. For other women, Unionist women and slaves among them, Union soldiers represented liberation from Confederate occupation. For enslaved women in particular, Union advance most clearly offered the possibility of opening a third front, their own war against their now occupied owners. These multiple meanings of occupation for women constitute one of main themes we will explore throughout this volume.[7]

In mapping the gradual expansion of the Union occupation of the Confederacy, we mean to give a basic chronological outline of the formal Union military advance while at the same time alerting the reader to the alternative forms that replaced it in some areas—the informal wars of occupation. Historian Stephen Ash has aptly termed these kinds of areas "no man's land," where neither the occupying army nor the occupied civilians had any clear control. The essays in this volume will illustrate that, while the Union was able to establish military posts in urban areas throughout the Confederacy, areas we call "garrisoned cities," they were never able to completely dominate those cities. Nor were they ever able to securely control the surrounding countryside, the "no man's land" of guerrilla warfare. Perhaps nothing is better testimony to the efficacy of this second front than the way it was eventually adopted even by the formal Union military itself as a way to close off the war in the East. If we map the course of the war from the point of view of occupied women, Sherman's March through Georgia and South Carolina appears on our map as the moment when the war of occupation merged with the formal field of battle or, conversely, as the moment when the war of occupation finally overwhelmed the formal field of battle in the East.[8]

Looking at the war from the position of the occupied helps us to understand why this war of occupation has been so nearly invisible in all accounts of the military history of the Civil War to date. The prevailing focus on the evolving status of women on the part of historians of women may have diverted our attention from the extent to which women and the home front came to be directly involved in the military struggle itself. Similarly, the focus of many military historians on the formal field of battle has also contributed to the relative neglect of the less formal fields of battle that developed in the course of the war and shaped both its conduct and outcome. The proposition that women should be considered as direct military factors in the war is particularly difficult to envision if we assume that the war took place only on battlefields as traditionally defined. Using that approach, the beginning of occupation signifies the end of military conflict rather than reconfiguration of the field of battle itself.

Certainly the recognition of the agency of slaves, sometimes referred to as the war's third front, has complicated and enriched our understanding of the military history of the Civil War. Using this perspective, historians have begun to document the critical contribution that slaves and former slaves made to the Union advance through occupied territory by contributing information, supplies, and labor. We think that a wider consideration of the civilian population, one that includes all women and the structural significance of gender, will serve to expand our understanding of the conduct of the war even further.[9]

Our core point is rather simple: women in occupied areas during the Civil War were not simply preoccupied, that is, basically rendered either inert or of little structural consequence by their domestic status in the face of military force. Rather, they were occupied, as in busy and responsive, in the face of an occupying military presence. It is this second form of being occupied—not as the hapless victims or collateral damage of Union occupation or as the occasional and atypical politicized woman but as the critical bottom rail of the war of occupation—that provides the central focus of this collection of essays. In order to begin this task of expanding and transforming the way we think about the borders of the battlefield in the Civil War, we focus on everyday, "occupied" women whose history has only begun to be considered from this perspective. In doing so, we begin to see the occupied South as a field of battle in its own right.[10]

Fortunately, some military historians of the Civil War have already begun to look beyond the formal field of battle, a few by focusing attention on the significance of guerrilla resistance to Union occupation. They have identified the decision to pursue civilians as combatants as the turn to a "hard war," one conterminous with the recognition of the importance of guerrilla war and the issuance of General Order No. 100, or Lieber's Code, in the spring of 1863. Yet even those military historians who write about guerrilla war have assumed that "no man's land" was in fact a man's land, indeed a hyper man's land, where women, who are most often collapsed into the supposedly gender-neutral category "civilian," mattered primarily for the way they were rendered the hapless victims of men on both sides.[11]

We see this approach to the place of women in a "hard war" as describing the effects but not the roots of guerrilla war. Much as the massive slaughter of the battlefield and the large death toll from disease have not clouded our appreciation for the basic importance of the role the soldier played on the formal field of battle, we should not allow the abuse of defenseless women by marauding guerrillas or Union troops, which certainly did occur, to obscure the basic and critical role women played in the very existence of ongoing resistance to occupation. Although historians have begun to realize the importance of women's domestic contribution to the formal field of battle, many continue to suggest that guerrilla warfare was carried on almost entirely at the expense of women, rather than with their support and active participation. We offer evidence, however, that women were an integral part of the war of occupation. Lieber's Code, which provided the theoretical legitimization for the Union military's pursuit of "hard war" against civilians, was clear in identifying the significance of the provisioning supply line. According to Francis Lieber, the guerrilla was supplied by civilians. As this volume will document, a significant number of those troublesome civilians were women, a point that has not always been made explicit by historians.[12]

Guerrillas were therefore created by their domestic line of supply, whether that supply was food, clothing, shelter, or information and emotional support. So while some women were indeed robbed by their kin or neighbors in the bush, many more worked as the quartermasters and orderlies of this war of occupation. Without them there could have been no effective guerrilla resistance. From a gendered and domestic location, it mattered very little which front—the home front of the occupied war or the more distant formal field of battle—their men were fighting on. The difference for women was that in the home-front war women themselves came to be defined as combatants by Lieber's emphasis on the supply line as critical to guerrilla activity—and to the very concept of what it meant to be a guerrilla.

Several of the essays that follow will demonstrate that women sometimes were surprised and offended by this public, partisan criminalization of their normal domestic relations to their men. And if Confederate women were unprepared for this merger of home front and battlefield, they certainly were not alone. On the Union side, soldiers encountered the occupied enemy in forms they had not expected either. Union soldiers were not prepared to cope when they encountered aggressive and militant behavior on the part of Confederate women. These encounters quickly generated descriptions of occupied women as "She Devils," "She Adders," and just plain "Pukes."[13]

It was, after all, a third widespread but mistaken assumption at the outset of the war, especially in the North, that most white Southerners did not really support secession. Many Northerners were inclined to assume that the war was really the responsibility of the narrow, power-hungry slaveholding elite in the South whose members had monopolized the political process. Many Union soldiers believed that it would not take long for the majority of whites to defect from the secessionist banner once they were free to assess the bigger picture and to realize their true interests. In this miscalculation, no one gave much thought to the possibility of serious civilian male resistance, much less to the possibility of active or effective resistance on the part of rebel women. This assumption faded away quickly any time Union soldiers had on-the-ground experience with Confederate women.

We know that guerrilla war was most intensely associated with areas where the Confederacy had less control—for instance, in border areas like Missouri or Kentucky that were under Union occupation for most or all of the war's duration. We are less likely to see, however, that "irregular" warfare was as constituent a part of the war as its well-known battles and a facet of the conflict that moved with the Union military wherever it went. Historians have not been inclined to see that, although the Union secured a beachhead in Southern territory through victory on the formal field of battle, its battle continued in the roiling sea of resistance surrounding the occupied area (or even within it).

However, once we approach occupied areas armed with the assumption that war can be driven by the occupied, as well as through the policies of generals on the formal field of battle, we can begin to see these areas as truly occupied, in the sense of being densely populated with historical implications, rather than as postscripts or insignificant locations that are analytically dead. The failure to recognize the agency of women and the critical structural role of gender has created a blind spot that obscures the significance of the war of occupation, particularly the war of the second front, as having legitimate roots in the civilian, female population. In considering women during the war, most historians have seen only violation and victimization. We argue that agency and the structural roots of authentic local resistance to military invasion are also present if one is willing to look.[14]

In most military histories of the war, women really appear only twice in the conventional battlefield narrative: first, with regard to General Butler's infamous "Woman Order" issued in May 1862, and second, in relation to Sherman's infamous March to the Sea in the summer of 1864. The broad historical interpretation of these two events reinforces our understanding of women's apparently "noncombatant" status. In the case of the Woman Order, Butler's response to the troubling resistance of Confederate women was to threaten to treat them like prostitutes and leave them to the mercy of his men. According to Butler, the Woman Order "executed itself" because women simply folded in this challenge to their social status and respectability. This is a claim that most Civil War historians have accepted at face value.

And then there is Sherman's March, generally viewed as a desperate gamble that paid off for Sherman but seen as vile precisely because it crossed the combatant/noncombatant line and made war on women directly. Because we generally accept the view that women were respected as noncombatants until this period in the war and were thus "victims," Sherman's March is considered by many to be an outrage and an exception to the rules of engagement generally observed on the formal battlefield. But what if women experienced engagements with opposing troops more numerous and ubiquitous throughout the war than has commonly been recognized? What if the Woman Order and Sherman's March stand as tips of an iceberg rather than as a first course and the dastardly dessert reluctantly served up by military men to unruly women in the course of the war itself? What if women were not simply occupied by the advancing Union forces but rather were active and their resistance to occupation was their form of battlefield engagement? We recognize this kind of irregular warfare already in the guerrilla activities of dissenting white men and see it in the self-emancipation of many slaves. Here we hope to extend those analytical insights to women in order to understand how occupation activated and was often fought as a gender war.[15]

The volume is divided into three parts, reflecting three approaches to thinking about occupation: first, as an incubator of military policies that reflected the exigencies and activism of occupied women; second, in terms of the locations in which these military policies were enforced and evaded; third, in terms of the occupations within occupation along the complex and overlapping axes of race, class, and cultural difference.

In the first two essays we tackle the two points of the occupied war that are clearly visible in the literature as it now stands: Benjamin Butler's Woman Order and Sherman's infamous march through Georgia and the Carolinas. In her essay "(Mis)Remembering General Order No. 28: Benjamin Butler, the Woman Order, and Historical Memory," Alecia P. Long critically interrogates Butler's own account of this order and suggests that rather than "executing itself," as he claimed, the order was in its very origin a reflection of a war against female opponents that the soldiers did not know how to fight. She concludes that the Woman Order was more of a defeat for the general rather than the complete victory that he claimed. Lisa Tendrich Frank's gendered interpretation of Sherman's March continues this exploration of women's activism by suggesting that when men transgressed onto women's space—that is, entered into the domestic sphere—rather than solely victimizing women, as much of the literature suggests, they encountered intractable resistance.

In "'Physical Abuse . . . and Rough Handling': Race, Gender, and Sexual Justice in the Occupied South," E. Susan Barber and Charles F. Ritter consider the emergence of new military policies that frankly acknowledged sexual violence against occupied women and girls. Although the Civil War has been considered a "low rape" war, Barber and Ritter's survey of the Union military court-martial records suggests that such violent encounters were prevalent enough to require the development of the first explicit military policy on the issue. Some women doggedly pursued their rapists through this new policy of sexual justice, not unlike the way that escaped slaves, by voting with their feet, helped to initiate the military policy of contraband.

This discussion of military policy in Part I of the volume opens the door to Part II, just as the tip of the iceberg alerts us to something much larger below. Although most military history stops when a given battlefield objective is achieved, the essays in this section start to make the contours of other contested terrains visible in their explorations of the quotidian but critical aspects of occupation in practice. By examining the key tactics and flanking maneuvers used by occupied women, this section begins the work of outlining what the war with occupied women looked like from the perspective of the women themselves. In "Gettysburg out of Bounds: Women and Soldiers in the Embattled Borough, 1863," Margaret Creighton considers the war's most famous and widely commemorated battle from an unfamiliar, women-centered angle. In the social geography she reconstructs, Creighton argues that Gettysburg has a "wider cast of characters, . . . a longer chronology, and a bigger field of engagement" than has traditionally been understood. She makes the case for a more inclusive battlefield and a more human set of soldiers whom she observes as their lives intersected with the local women with whom they engaged in the "social battle of Gettysburg." Because this secondary battle violated the traditional understanding of separate spheres and took the focus off the noble exploits of soldiers as men, it has largely been forgotten, despite its important and enduring effects.

Moving back south to the Confederate border, Kristen L. Streater's "'She-Rebels' on the Supply Line: Gender Conventions in Civil War Kentucky" makes visible the work of women on the domestic and logistical supply line of guerrilla war. While much has been made of the logistical difficulties inherent in the Union's invasion of the South, especially its long supply lines through enemy territory, less has been made of the guerrilla supply line and how it helped to fuel the informally organized war that was particularly internecine in the border areas of the South. Streater's essay echoes Creighton's discussion of how women's domestic labor, particularly cooking and provisioning, was politicized and how critical it became in supporting and facilitating Southern sympathizers' resistance to Union occupation in Kentucky.

LeeAnn Whites extends this discussion of the politicization of women's domestic duties in her essay "'Corresponding with the Enemy': Mobilizing the Relational Field of Battle in St. Louis." Women in St. Louis, who defied Union occupation in variety of ways, might be charged and then banished to Confederate lines for a crime that came to be called "corresponding with the enemy." Whites shows how women's attempts to stay in contact with their loved ones, and to facilitate others doing the same, became politicized, crucial to the war effort on the Confederate side, and grounds for banishment. Because their activities, which were gendered female and therefore generally considered unimportant, came to have an enormous impact on the Union's ability to control "a border area critical to the northern war effort," we have sometimes failed to understand how these women's actions drove the development of Union military policy in Missouri.

Finally, we turn to the character of occupation in the Deep South. Along with the defeat of the Confederates at Gettysburg, the North's victory at Vicksburg in July 1863 is frequently emphasized as a turning point in the war. Yet in her essay "The Practical Ladies of Occupied Natchez," Cita Cook considers the particular resources the women of Natchez employed after the formal military victories had been won in their region. Cook's essay also focuses on the human side of the occupying men and reveals how their own self-images and class aspirations shaped their interactions with the occupied women around them. In Cook's rendering, the domestic resources of women were as integral to this war of occupation as were the personal aspirations and feelings of the men who confronted but sometimes also admired and indulged the women whose city they held.

The first part's focus on policy and the second part's focus on place are complemented by the final part's insistence that we remember the social fissures of class, race, and gender through which the war of occupation was complicated and ever more deeply enjoined and engaged. In her essay "Between Slavery and Freedom: African American Women and Occupation in the Slave South," Leslie A. Schwalm suggests that the deepest social fissures were opened and made comprehensible in the occupation of enslaved black women, a "multilayered" occupation as she puts it, since slave women were occupied three times over: as slaves in slaveholding households, as slaves in the Confederate military, and, finally, when they were occupied by Union forces. Schwalm's focus on female contraband is echoed in Victoria E. Bynum's emphasis on conscription and the politics of class in her essay "Occupied at Home: Women Confront Confederate Forces in North Carolina's Quaker Belt," which elucidates the experience of Unionist women in North Carolina. Like many slave women, Bynum's subjects experienced an occupation within an occupation as they fought the Confederacy's efforts to draft their (often reluctant) men into the service of the formal war effort. In her essay "Widow in a Swamp: Gender, Unionism, and Literacy in the Occupied South during the Civil War," Joan E. Cashin reconstructs the story of an individual widow in the backcountry of South Carolina who remained loyal to the Union. Despite her patriotism and political beliefs, her property was raided by Union troops. Her attempts to recoup those losses were not resolved until the end of Reconstruction. Her own experience as a Unionist dissenter in the South and her later attempts to secure recompense suggest just how complex, contradictory, and enduring the saga of an occupied woman could be. Historian Judith Giesberg brings the collection to a close in an epilogue that demonstrates how important postwar congressional debates were driven by the need to address the wartime disloyalty and resistance of occupied women before the nation could be fully reconstructed.

In early April 1865, a worn and weary Robert E. Lee called the Army of Virginia together for one last time and advised his men to lay down their arms and to return to their homes and to lives of peace. The only remaining alternative, given the shattered state of the Confederate military forces, was full-scale guerrilla warfare, and Lee was determined to avoid this outcome. Formal surrender to the Union military forces, even in the face of the huge losses of men and arms over the previous four years, was clearly preferable to this alternative in his mind. He refused to advocate continuing the war by other means. In a field of inquiry drenched in counterfactual suppositions, there has been little extended discussion of the possibility of guerrilla war or what might have transpired in the South if Lee had refused to lay down his arms and had instead urged his men to take to the bush. We are left instead with our eyes firmly fixed on the last formal field of battle, even as the shattered, defeated men began trudging slowly homeward, back to the women they had left behind.

While Lee and his officers may have refused to reconsider the field of battle in 1865, this did not mean that myriad forms of alternative warfare had not existed throughout the conflict. Whether along the axes of race, class, or gender, the formal field of battle was always deeply intermeshed with these wider, more diffuse, and subterranean informal wars. Guerrilla warfare by what military officials termed "irregular" troops was the alternative field of battle that Confederate politicians and military men had in mind when they did consider the possibility of carrying on the war by other means. Even this irregular field of battle, which Lee ultimately refused to endorse, was only one possibility among a mobilized population that had both experienced and shaped these alternative forms of warfare. This collection of essays constitutes an exploratory foray into the role and significance of this informal field of battle from the location of its most numerous yet least recognized participants—occupied women.

[I]

GENDER RELATIONS AND THE DEVELOPMENT OF UNION MILITARY POLICY

(Mis)Remembering General Order No. 28

Benjamin Butler, the Woman Order, and Historical Memory

ALECIA P. LONG

Above all else, Benjamin Butler is remembered in Civil War lore, literature, and scholarship for his controversial tenure as the first commanding general of occupied New Orleans, a position he held from early May to late December 1862. Because of his actions in the city, particularly his promulgation of General Order No. 28, better known as the Woman Order, he had become a controversial national and international figure by the end of his time in the city. Despite being dismissed peremptorily in mid-December, Butler was a keen defender of his actions and was extremely energetic in working to shape the historical memory of his command over the city and its inhabitants. Nowhere is this more evident than in the case of General Order No. 28, which Butler repeatedly claimed worked without fail or exception to tame the troublesome she-rebels of New Orleans. Virtually all journalists, biographers, and historians accepted his claims of success for the order at face value in the first century following the Civil War.[1]

In recent decades, however, historians of women and gender have reinvigorated the debate about the Woman Order and have recovered ample evidence demonstrating that Butler's success over the city's women was not as complete or uncontested as he and others had maintained. This essay incorporates some of the evidence marshaled by these recent historians, but it also suggests that, despite abundant evidence to the contrary, many have continued to take Butler at his word about the overarching success of the Woman Order. In fact, most historians, writers, and Civil War buffs have (mis)remembered General Order No. 28 not only because Butler self-consciously sought to shape the historical memory surrounding it but also because his claims supported widespread and enduring assumptions about gender, warfare, and the relative insignificance of occupied women. Beginning in May 1862, the unruly women of New Orleans were one of Butler's most pressing problems, and despite his claims to the contrary—his own dubious claim of mission accomplished for General Order No. 28—these women continued to be a significant problem for him and his men long after he declared an unconditional victory over them.[2]

In hindsight, all or most of Butler's clashes with the civilian population of New Orleans might have been avoided. His initial orders from McClellan regarding New Orleans "suggested that he occupy only the adjacent towns of Algiers and Carrolton, staying out of the city proper if Union sentiment there seemed sufficient to control it." On arrival, however, Butler reported that he found "the city under the dominion of the mob," made a decision to set up his command in the heart of the city, and "indicated to the secretary of war that he intended to get tough."[3] The composition of that mob, and especially the ongoing actions of its female members, would make getting tough a tricky proposition. Expectations about the proper behavior of women combined with the intricacies of occupying a military objective that also happened to be a city full of hungry and often hostile civilians presented Butler with both problems and opportunities.

This was not the first time Butler had decided, more or less unilaterally, to occupy and then tame a highly visible Southern city. Slightly over a year before Butler arrived in New Orleans, an obviously irritated Lieutenant General Winfield Scott recalled him from his unauthorized and, in Scott's opinion, ill-advised and dangerously provocative occupation of Baltimore. Butler returned to the nation's capital forthwith and, on his arrival, gave a brief speech to a group of supporters who had gathered to welcome him. While most of his address focused on the righteousness of the Union cause, Butler made two claims with interesting gender dimensions. First, he noted that if the war effort required it, Massachusetts, his home state, would give "every man in her borders, ay, and woman." Near the end of his remarks Butler expanded and embellished this claim: "If the 25,000 northern soldiers who are here are cut off, in six weeks 50,000 will take their place; and if they die by fever, pestilence, or the sword, a quarter of a million will take their place, till our army of the reserve will be women with their broomsticks to drive every enemy into the gulf." According to a contemporary account, both remarks were greeted by cheers, but the second remark, about women as potential combatants armed with broomsticks, also drew laughter.[4]

Given the events to follow and the profound alterations in conventional gender arrangements that took place during and as a result of the Civil War, especially in the extensive Union occupation of female-dominated Confederate cities, Butler's claims are both significant and ironic. A year and month after he made these remarks, in fact, Butler encountered women who hoped to drive him back into the Gulf or, barring that, to drive him and his troops to distraction through a low-level insurgency of petty insults and rancorous ridicule.

Although historians' explanations for Butler's often controversial and provocative wartime actions vary widely, most would agree with historian Elizabeth Doyle, who wrote in 1955 that Butler's actions, like his later explanations of them, were driven "by his own expressed desire to be remembered." During the war, that meant, as with his incursion into Baltimore, that Butler "instinctively involved himself in controversies which kept him in the public eye," according to historian Gerald Capers. Once his provocations generated news items, he energetically defended his actions to journalists and press outlets, friendly or not. He also generated voluminous correspondence with politicians, military officials, close friends, and even common people with whom he was never personally acquainted.[5]

There is no question that, in the years following the conflict, Butler continued his effort to (re)shape the historical memory of his Civil War exploits to satisfy his desire to be remembered not just widely but also positively. He even invited his first postwar biographer, a then well-known popular writer named James Parton, to live with him and his wife for several months in 1863. Butler gave Parton unfettered access to his letter and order books, as well as to "the official and unofficial correspondence" directed to him, the vast majority of which he kept in his own possession after the ouster from command of New Orleans.[6]

In the preface to Parton's *General Butler in New Orleans*, completed a scant ten months after Butler's dismissal from the city, the author claimed that the general did not "make a single suggestion" but left him free "in every respect" to draw his own conclusions. Yet one is hard pressed to believe that the months Parton was in residence with the Butlers, sometimes spending as much as ten hours a day conversing with them, did not have an impact on his account. In fact, Parton's extremely positive rendering of Butler's time in New Orleans, like Butler's autobiographical account published three decades later, did much to congeal many of the general's claims to success among the broader public. Butler's work on behalf of his own historical legacy beautifully illustrates C. Vann Woodward's observation that "the twilight zone between living memory and written history is one of the favorite breeding places of mythology." In the case of Butler's Woman Order, the mythology of success has permeated the work of popular writers and most historians for nearly a century and a half.[7]

As with the interpretive advances made by historians of women and gender in recent decades, another group of historians have explored how historical memory gets made and what factors help to shape it. In an important observation drawn from this literature David Lowenthal observes that people who write memoirs hope not only to shape historical memory but also to cast "themselves as heroes of a life worth remembering, a drama worth having lived for, . . . the goal of their recollection is justification rather than insight and responsibility."[8] Although many of the Civil War's participants sought to justify themselves and their actions after the fact, few were as successful as Butler at creating a flawed but enduring recapitulation of his actions and especially of his occupation's pièce de résistance, General Order No. 28. Gender matters in the making of this particular memory, as it mattered a great deal in generating Butler's Woman Order in the first place.[9]

An important initial question to consider is why Butler felt compelled to issue an order directed at the women of the city rather than its men, whom he later claimed to have gotten under control almost immediately. Writing in the early 1890s, Butler recalled, "[F]rom the second day after we landed, we had the men . . . so completely under our control that our officers and soldiers could go anywhere in the city without being interfered with." This claim, as is often the case with Butler, is certainly an exaggeration, since there would be numerous arrests, imprisonments, and at least one hanging among the city's Confederate identified men over the next few months. But accuracy aside, Butler claimed that even though the men had proved easily subdued, that "was not so with the women of New Orleans."[10] In order to remedy this issue of control, Butler issued General Order No. 28 on May 15, a mere two weeks after his arrival. It read: "As the officer and soldiers of the United States have been subject to repeated insults from the women (calling themselves ladies) of New Orleans, in return for the most scrupulous noninterference and courtesy on our part, it is ordered that hereafter, when any female shall, by word, gesture, or movement, insult or show contempt for any officer or soldier of the United States, she shall be regarded and held liable to be treated as a woman of the town plying her avocation."[11]

The sexualized implications and the threat of treating ladies as though they were disreputable women, even prostitutes, seemed clear to many observers at the time and accounted for much of the hysteria generated in response to the order, but there were other things that were remarkable about it as well. In a story with a dateline of June 11, less than a month after the order was issued, a reporter for the *New York Times* recognized its extraordinary gender dimensions. The New Orleans correspondent asked: "When was it ever heard before that the Commanding General of a conquering army was obliged to make a special order to protect, not the females of the conquered city, but one to protect the soldiery from the insults of the female population?"[12] On a certain level, the reporter's question provided a preview of how the world would be turned upside down for many Southerners later that year by the Emancipation Proclamation. Only in this case, as the *Times* reporter suggested, many New Orleans women were turning the world upside down by refusing to play their prescribed gender roles. By overtly protesting their occupation, some women in New Orleans were challenging the social order and overturning the expectations of martial glory by refusing to play their proper role in the drama of defeat, deference, and dependence generally presumed by a victorious army, especially over occupied women.

Insult rather than injury became many of these women's weapon of choice. Instead of being greeted as liberators, Butler's men were treated—through word, gesture, and movement—to all manner of verbal and physically symbolic insults. Women would turn their back, cross the street, or leave streetcars rather than share physical space with the Federals. On an unknown number of occasions, even bodily fluids were employed to register their disdain, either by Confederate-sympathizing women or their children spitting on the Federals or, in at least one incident, emptying the contents of a vessel of what Butler called "not very clean water" on the head of no less a prominent personage than Admiral David Farragut and a compatriot.[13]

The abuses certainly seem to have vexed the Federal troops, at least enough so that they generated a flurry of reports to their commander. Like the water (or worse) that rained down on Farragut, Butler noted that "complaints of [poor] treatment from women of all states and conditions and degrees of life came pouring in" on him. After being spit upon, one of his officers even told him, "I can't stand it. This isn't the first time this thing has been attempted against me, but this is the first time it has been accomplished. I want to go home. I came here to fight enemies of the country, not to be insulted and disgusted." Whether or not they could stand it, many soldiers were sincerely surprised by the local women's reaction. Yet gender expectations made it impossible for the soldiers to see these women as full-fledged or legitimate "enemies of the country" they were fighting to defend. General Thomas Williams opined, "Such venom one must see to believe . . . I look at them and think of fallen angels." His observation sagely summarizes the problem of gender expectation versus the reality of the way women "of all states and conditions and degrees of life" were behaving on the ground in the face of occupation.[14]

Butler's men could scarcely believe females were acting in this fashion. Yet after a relatively short period of time, astonishment and irritation gave way to exasperation, complaints, and, finally, official action. A reminder of the short period of time this process took suggests just how powerful the weapons of female insult and rejection could be to men in uniform. Whether it was spitting, emptying chamber pots, or just the ongoing mental wear and tear that the words, gestures, and movements inflicted, it took only a couple of weeks to drive the general to decisive action with explosive potential.

As many writers have noted, the immediate response to the order was both vehement and widespread, reaching even the floor of the British Parliament and the pages of European newspapers within a few weeks. On the local level, the consternation and vacillation of the city's largely ineffectual pre-occupation mayor, John T. Monroe, gave Butler the excuse he had been looking for to remove the mayor from his position and replace him with one of his own officers. According to historian Thomas Helis, using the mayor's "protest over his infamous Woman Order as an excuse, on May 17 [Butler] arrested the mayor, the chief of police, and several of their associates, and imprisoned them at Fort Jackson near the mouth of the Mississippi. He then appointed General [George] Shepley acting mayor, and replaced the police with his own soldiers." According to James Parton, the Woman Order "was the spark which blew up the city government."[15]

While the order had a practical political impact on the ground, it also had symbolic value throughout the Confederacy. P. G. T. Beauregard, a Confederate officer who hailed from New Orleans, opined that the order gave the occupying troops "the right to treat at their pleasure the ladies of the South as common harlots," and he exhorted all Southerners to expel the "infamous invaders of our homes and disturbers of our family ties."[16] Two weeks later, seemingly in answer to Beauregard, the New York Times's New Orleans correspondent wrote, "Throughout the South it has been received with a shout of execration. Be that as it may, it has had the desired effect, and the soldiers ceased to be insulted."[17]

Many writers repeated this claim of success for General Order No. 28. The *Daily Delta*, Butler's officially controlled news outlet in New Orleans, saw fit to print extensive claims of success for the order, once on June 8 and a long, glowing editorial a week later, on June 15. The writers of both pieces agreed that the order had been a "capital stroke of policy" that had put the women back in their place—in short, ensuring that the women behaved as occupied women ought to, with due deference and a lack of overt political or patriotic sentiment.[18]

A year and half later, after most of the hysterical hoopla over the order had receded, Parton reiterated the contemporary journalistic claims of success, asserting succinctly that "[t]he order was published. Its success was immediate and perfect." Yet in the body of the paragraph that followed this claim, even Parton vacillated and admitted that women still managed, through feminine wiles and indirect actions, to register low levels of discontent. Immediately following his claim of perfection he wrote: "Not that the women still did not continue, with the ingenuity of the sex, to manifest their repugnance to the troops. They did so. The piano still greeted the passing office with rebel airs. The fair countenances of the ladies were still averted, and their skirts held gently aside." Yet despite his descriptions of the ways women managed to continue registering their disgust with their occupiers, he concluded the paragraph by reiterating that "the outrageous demonstrations ceased. No more insulting words were uttered; and all the affectations of disgust were such as could be easily and properly borne by officers and men. Gradually even these were discontinued."[19] In short, even though he provided evidence to the contrary, Parton claimed that the order was an unqualified success and that it righted the perplexing imbalance between occupying soldiers and occupied women definitively and in perpetuity in New Orleans.

Butler would repeat, enlarge, elaborate, and embroider this claim of success time and again, especially in his own memoirs written roughly three decades later. In a chapter largely focused on the order he claimed:

> There was no case of aggression after that order was issued, no case of insult by word or look against our officers or soldiers while in New Orleans.
> The order executed itself.
> No arrests were ever made under it or because of it. All the ladies in New Orleans forebore to insult our troops because they didn't want

to be deemed common women, and all the common women forebore to insult our troops because they wanted to be deemed ladies, and of these two classes were all the women secessionists of the city.[20]

Butler claimed victory, patting himself on the back for his sage manipulation of the day's gender politics and for his recognition of women's alleged inability to cope outside the bounds of female respectability. The problem is that his claims are not true. And many other historians, including Catherine Clinton, Drew Faust, George Rable, and Mary Ryan, have written about the cases in which women did, in fact, take actions that flew in the face of the order all throughout and even beyond Butler's tenure as occupying general, which ended in mid-December when he was unceremoniously replaced by Nathanael Banks.[21]

Yet even these pathbreaking historians do not directly contradict or discount Butler's overall claim of success for General Order No. 28. For example, Catherine Clinton, writing in 2006, concluded that most New Orleans women chose to vent "their fury in letters, in diaries, in parlors, and even in prayer. But when New Orleans women unleashed these feelings in the streets, Butler let it be known that they would be given no better treatment than other 'women of the streets,' which shocked them into submission." In short, like Parton, Clinton argues that "following the order, incidents of insult were precipitously reduced."[22] Perhaps this was the case in the short term, but a closer and longer-term look at events on the ground throughout Butler's occupation suggests that the resistance of rebel-identified occupied women was actually more enduring, public, widespread, and troublesome to the occupying forces than historical memory or contemporary scholarship have suggested.

There are a small number of well-known examples that disprove Butler's claim about how perfectly General Order No. 28 worked. First and perhaps most notable would be the case of Eugenia Levy Phillips, whom Butler made the subject of his Special Order No. 150 on June 30, a full month and half after he set down General Order No. 28 and three weeks after the *New York Times* claimed that "soldiers had ceased to be insulted." Levy Phillips's story of arrest and incarceration under harsh conditions at Ship Island for two and half months has been written about extensively, including by Parton. But what is curious is that when Butler penned his own recollections of the event in 1892, he attempted to minimize Eugenia Levy Phillips and her individual agency in his account, thus attempting to reshape the historical memory by employing the fairly common strategy of, in Lowenthal's words, "expung[ing] what seems shameful or harmful by consigning it to ridicule or oblivion."[23]

Butler does refer to Levy Phillips indirectly in the first few paragraphs of his memoir chapter on the Woman Order, but never specifically by name. He recounts that on the third day after the occupation began "a young lad, of not ten years, in the presence of his mother, who is the wife of one of the first lawyers, rushed from her side and spit all over" the uniform of a Massachusetts colonel. Butler, calling Phillip Phillips only "Mr. P.," writes that he called the lawyer to come see him to take up the matter. Of the husband he notes, "I had never heard that he was in any way a violent secessionist, but I had heard that his wife was exceedingly interested on the side of the rebels, and had been ordered out of Washington by the Secretary of War for some treasonable acts." Butler goes on to recount how he spoke with Phillips and left "the correction of the [son's] act" to the father.[24] Yet the text of Butler's order regarding Eugenia Levy Phillips confirms that both the father and mother were present at this encounter and that both apologized to the general. In his later account, however, he does not mention the presence of the mother at all. This is fascinating because Butler admits that the unnamed Levy Phillips had already been punished for treason yet he tells us that, when it came to the matter of correcting her son's behavior, he went to the father—the less political of the two in his view—to resolve the matter, effectively reconstructing the memory of this encounter without Eugenia Levy Phillips in it.[25]

There are a number of issues that are important to reconsider in Butler's shaping of this story. First, it is easy to identify Mr. P. and therefore, by extension, Eugenia Levy Phillips by name. But Butler declines to do so, even though her name had been prominently featured in the press at the time. Thus, Butler turns his struggle with Levy Phillips, a radical rebel female, into a reasonable conversation between two men about the proper behavior of a young boy, in the process consigning Levy Phillips herself and her actions to historical oblivion. Butler preferred, at least in reminiscence, to cast his struggle with her as a struggle between men, even if the facts belied this (re)construction.

He continues this tack by completely failing to acknowledge or remember that she was arrested and imprisoned for actions that certainly fell under the prohibitions enunciated in General Order No. 28, making, in fact, a completely untrue and contradictory claim about the overwhelming success of his Woman Order instead. If the spitting incident involving her son occurred three days after the occupation began, as Butler suggests in his memoir, Levy Phillips was still insulting Butler's forces more than a month later when she allegedly mocked and insulted the funeral cortege of a Union officer passing below the balcony of her home. Interestingly, while Butler's order ostensibly focused on the behavior of women in public, Levy Phillips was arrested for behavior that took place on her own balcony—still a part of her home but public enough to be troublesome and, in Butler's view, intolerable.

It is true that Butler wrote an order specifically for Levy Phillips and, in the process, attempted to deal her out of the terms of General Order No. 28. Special Order No. 150, issued on June 30, included this disclaimer: "It is therefore ordered that she be not regarded and treated as a common woman, of whom no officer or soldier is bound to take notice, but as an uncommonly bad and dangerous woman stirring up stirring up strife and inciting others to riot." This may have been Butler's way of manipulating the facts to strengthen his claim for the unmitigated success of General Order No. 28, but Levy Phillips's actions, especially the charge that she was "on the balcony of her house during the passage of the funeral procession of Lieut. Dekay, laughing and mocking his remains," certainly falls under the letter and the spirit of the behavioral prohibitions enunciated in the Woman Order.[26]

Butler engages in a similar tack of obfuscation and minimization in discussing the case of Anne Larue, which took place nearly two weeks after Levy Phillips was sent to Ship Island. Although Butler claims to cover the Woman Order and its success in chapter 10 of his memoir, he recounts the arrest of Larue one hundred pages later in chapter 12, in the course of discussing the arrest and imprisonment of several males, most of whom were arrested and incarcerated at the same time as Levy Phillips. This seems an obvious tack to separate the cases of Phillips and Larue and, as with Phillips, to consider Larue's case outside the context of his allegedly infallible Woman Order. Butler describes Larue as a "young woman, blond and blue-eyed, wearing flowing silken curls and Confederate colors."[27] And, as he did with Levy Phillips, he attempts to connect her unruly activities with her husband, rather than portraying her as an independent decision maker or political actor in her own right.

The problem is that evidence one of his officers provided at the time, and which he includes in his memoirs three decades later, calls his assertions into doubt. The contemporary officers' report, filed July 11, noted that a "young woman dressed in white and of handsome personal appearance . . . passed by the hotel, wearing a secession badge. She finally insulted one of our soldiers, and was arrested by a policeman, who attempted to take her to the mayor's office." Although shooting and a near riot broke out, Larue was transported to General Shepley's office at city hall. If the officers thought this would end Larue's protestations, they were wrong, for, according to the same report, in the acting mayor's presence "she commenced the utterance of threat and abuse." The next day, she was taken before Butler and continued in her haughty protest. When Butler asked her why she distributed handbills and donned Confederate colors, she replied that "she felt very patriotic that day." In response, Butler sent her to Ship Island, where she remained for three weeks.[28]

Surely Larue's actions were political, even audacious, and by donning Confederate colors and marching through the streets handing out seditious handbills, surely she had by "word, gesture, or movement" challenged or insulted Federal officers and soldiers. But Butler is reluctant to admit this, to connect the dots, or to place Larue's actions squarely within the realm of the political or under the auspices of his allegedly infallible General Order No. 28. Instead, he declared that Larue, "having been found in the public streets, wearing a Confederate flag upon her person, in order to incite a riot, which act has already resulted in a breach of the peace, and a danger to the life of a soldier of the United States, is sent to Ship Island until further orders." Interestingly, his order concluded that she was "to be kept separate and apart from the other women confined there."[29] Just as Butler would separate these women during their incarceration, so would he insist upon separating them and their actions in his memoirs.

During that same hot and frustrating summer, Butler was also engaged in making over the New Orleans school system. Even though General Order No. 28 had been announced in mid-May, it apparently was not enough to discourage the city's public school teachers, most of them female, from continuing their classroom instruction in Confederate patriotism or from leading the children in singing Confederate anthems like the "Bonnie Blue Flag." In response, Butler closed the schools two weeks early and, over the summer of 1862, set out to transform the New Orleans public schools from "Nurseries of Treason" into incubators of Union patriotism. That makeover included purifying the mostly female "faculties by requiring them to take the loyalty oath in June 1862." If teachers refused, they were also refused employment in the revamped schools. Butler attempted a reorganization of "the whole system before schools reopened the next fall," in part by importing books from the North and ending courses in Confederate loyalty. In reiterating these events, historian Gerald Capers notes that "the Federal program met considerable resistance from parents and students alike." What he fails to specify is that in occupied New Orleans most of those "parents" who were resisting were women, many simply deciding to keep their children at home rather than send them to Yankee-run schools. Teachers who refused to swear loyalty either went without work or were hired by private or parochial schools.[30]

There are other instances of women behaving badly—and in the terms described in the Woman Order—even though the information about and the outcome for the women themselves are less conclusive. For instance, on August 17, a *New York Times* correspondent reported that the day after Union soldiers who had been wounded in the Battle of Baton Rouge were returned to New Orleans for treatment, "a well-dressed woman went into the St. James Hospital and commenced abusing our men in the most violent manner. She stated that it did her good to see the suffering before her—it was just punishment on the men for invading the South. When she had got thus far, she was requested to withdraw. Such fanaticism seems wholly incompatible with woman's nature; but it seems that it is not nevertheless."[31]

In the same report the journalist noted that only a few nights earlier Butler had been disturbed while working in his office by some noise outside. "He went to the gallery and, leaning over to catch the face of the orderly on duty, asked 'Who's that?' A woman, superficially a lady, at the instant passing, answered tartly, 'One of your New Orleans she adders.'" According to the reporter, "[t]he General retreated."[32] What is interesting here is that it seems not only that Butler and his men were still being challenged and insulted with impunity by the city's women in late August but that they were in some ways under siege and worn down by the abuse. After all, the reporter tells us, it was Butler who "retreated" back into his office, not the woman in the street below, who, presumably, continued on her way unimpeded and unpunished.

What these examples suggest is that Butler was learning—and others were studying from afar—how difficult occupying cities full of hungry, angry women was going to be and what a thorn in the flesh they could become for their Union occupiers, proclamations of victory over them aside. And in the end, it was not just the occupied women who were getting in Butler's way. There was also, to borrow P. G. T. Beauregard's phrase, the whole issue of "family ties" for the occupying troops. Not only were Confederate-identified women loyal to their men, but many of the Union soldiers wanted their families—new or established—with them as well. For Butler, whose own wife was with him throughout the occupation, this was unacceptable, leading him on September 23 to issue General Order No. 75, which the *New York Times* described with the headline "Women Not Allowed." The order simply specified that no "officer or soldier serving" in Butler's command would "be allowed to bring his family, or any member thereof, without special permission." Based on this order, it would seem that women were bedeviling Butler on all sides, hopelessly blurring the lines between the military and the domestic.[33]

The day after Butler ordered his men to keep their own women out of the city, he also issued an order that explicitly required that the city's occupied women take the loyalty oath by October 1 or prepare to leave the city. If some historians have been reluctant to consider the women of New Orleans in 1862 as political actors or as very real and pressing military problems, by October the general was not, for if any single individual certified the city's occupied women as political and military threats, it was Butler himself. By requiring them to take the oath of loyalty by October 1862—certainly a significant indicator of loyal citizenship—or to leave the city, he recognized them as potential and potentially dangerous combatants, just like the city's men.

In a final example of the still simmering resentments between the occupiers and the women they occupied, in October, when one of Butler's officers sought to shut down a worship service at St. Paul's Church because the minister declined to pray for the health of President Lincoln, it was the women of the church who stayed and defied the Federals. According to a poem written to commemorate the so-called Battle of St. Paul's:

> Up rose the congregation—
> We men were all away
> And our wives and little children
> Alone remained to pray
> But when has the Southern woman
> Before a Yankee quailed?
> And these with tongues undaunted
> The Lincolnites assailed
> In vain he called his soldiers

Their darts around him flew
And the strong men then discovered
What a woman's tongue can do.[34]

Mary Ryan includes this episode, as well as the better-known Battle of the Handkerchiefs, in *Women in Public*. In that incident, which took place nearly three months after Butler was relieved of duty, Confederate-sympathizing women engaged in a standoff with Union troops when they went to the docks to see off a transport of Confederate prisoners of war. Though Banks's troops threatened them, the women refused to back down and continued to wave their handkerchiefs at the departing transport despite threats to their persons if they did not disperse.[35]

Ryan deems women's actions at the Battle of St. Paul's and the Battle of the Handkerchiefs to be part of a "war of symbols" and concludes that while these actions "brought into the open the explosive potential of the ladies' ceremonial role in politics," they "did not break the masculine monopoly on the formal public sphere."[36] But, as the previous examples suggest, the whole notion of a "masculine monopoly on the formal public sphere" was under siege in New Orleans during Butler's term. By continually finding ways to pique, defy, and insult their occupiers, some of the city's women were doing more than simply behaving badly. They were also further rending the ragged boundaries already torn asunder by the complications of military occupation of a largely female civilian population. And even if Ryan is correct in asserting that these women's actions did not break the "masculine monopoly on the formal public sphere," that does not mean that the actions these women took were not political. Nor does the fact that the battle took place on a city's streets mean that the issues inherent in Butler's occupation of New Orleans were not military.

In order to remedy the discomforting gender implications of his tenure in New Orleans, Butler lied, perhaps to himself but certainly to others, about the overwhelming success of General Order No. 28 and either removed or rearranged the other facts to suit his tale. Sadly, most historians have been willing to let him get away with it. Why? Because, even at this late date, the way we define what is properly military and legitimately political sometimes makes it difficult for us to see how women fit into contemporary political and military equations, much less to see that the protesting women of New Orleans in 1862 were both political actors and very real military problems.

Of course some women took the safe course and protected their reputation and gender privilege by changing their behavior, but the numbers of effective political activists and troublesome protesters are almost always small. The significant and often overlooked point is that a few women in New Orleans were willing to take political actions, regardless of the cost. Women like Phillips and Larue claimed their citizenship, named their Confederate loyalty, and, though Butler only reluctantly remembered these instances, paid a very real political price for their actions. General Order No. 28 did not work, certainly not as perfectly as its author claimed, and it seems undeniable that the general took active steps to obscure this fact.[37]

The larger significance of this argument is that if we take women seriously as critical participants, even combatants, in the Civil War, we begin to undercut many of the gendered assumptions that have shaped the audience and alleged seriousness of Civil War studies by identifying battlefields only in traditional, male-oriented ways. If we refuse to (mis)remember these events in ways that minimize the presence and agency of women, we open up many articles of faith—like the success of General Order No. 28—to fresh scrutiny and thorough reevaluation. What if the women in occupied areas were much more political and militarily important than historians have suggested? Even William Tecumseh Sherman, whose occupation of Memphis was simultaneous with Butler's in New Orleans, had begun to recognize and communicate to his superiors how troublesome and intractable cities full of occupied women could be. If we place Sherman alongside Butler in this analytical configuration, we can begin to argue that the tipping point of "hard war" on civilians had come much earlier in the conflict than has generally been acknowledged.[38]

What if the women in occupied areas, becrinolined and bejeweled though many of them were, were the equivalent terrorists of their day—elusive, mercurial, hiding among the population but somehow slippery and uncontrollable, failing to adopt Butler's standards and priorities, failing to flatter him, plotting to overthrow him, the women of the city a deceptive, hissing, slithering pit of determined she-adders, always at the ready to strike? Perhaps if we begin to think from this position, we can we stop puzzling over how many fallen Confederate angels we can fit on the head of a conceptual pin. We can also, as Cynthia Enloe and others have done in contemporary international relations studies, brazenly redefine war and military history to include women full stop.[39] In undertaking this task, the women of New Orleans, Benjamin Butler, and

General Order No. 28 might very well constitute a kind of occupier's ground zero and might be the place where we can begin to forge a new interpretation of the significance of occupied women and of the gender politics and expectations so deeply embedded in their portrayal, in both the past and the present.

Bedrooms as Battlefields

The Role of Gender Politics in Sherman's March

LISA TENDRICH FRANK

Union soldiers, one outraged woman fumed in 1865, were "a hellish crew. . . . No place, no person is sacred from their profanation."[1] Not only had the enemy soldiers destroyed her foodstuffs and valuables, but the Yankees had also violated the sanctity of her domestic sphere and, most important, of her bedroom. This behavior, unacceptable and rare during peacetime, became a sanctioned tactic during Sherman's 1864–65 march through Georgia and the Carolinas. As part of a campaign to destroy the will of the Southern people, General William Tecumseh Sherman and his soldiers regularly brought the war directly to elite women by invading their domestic sphere. Northern soldiers' entering into bedrooms, ransacking wardrobes, tearing up mattresses, and destroying or stealing private possessions infuriated many Southern white women, who had assumed that their feminine sphere was off limits to invaders. Consequently, their resentment often focused on the lost sanctity of female space. Vexation at this breach of wartime etiquette permeated the communities of white Southern women that faced Sherman's soldiers. One North Carolina woman fumed that "there was no place, no chamber, trunk, drawer, desk, garret, closet, or cellar that was private to their unholy eyes."[2] Women could not forgive the enemy soldiers' violations of gendered space and their refusal to abide by the rules of peacetime propriety.

As these women's complaints reveal, gender shaped the interactions and reactions of Confederate women and the Union soldiers that they faced. When General Sherman marched his force of sixty thousand Union soldiers across Georgia and the Carolinas during the American Civil War, he launched a direct assault on Southern femininity and domesticity. This gendered assault on women's sphere, an integral aspect of the campaign, was as essential to Sherman's military aims as was his attack on physical Confederate war resources. Despite officially stated goals that focused on the destruction of war matériel, commanders and soldiers recognized the value of engaging elite Southern women as enemies and demonstrating Union power to them. As a result, Union soldiers repeatedly and purposefully attacked the trappings of femininity and domesticity as they wreaked havoc on Southern homes. Recognizing that they had become the targets, elite white Confederate women often asserted their femininity, as well as their regional identities, to respond to the campaign, playing upon assumptions about their gender and class. Femininity, in these interactions, became both a weapon for women to draw upon and a weakness for soldiers to prey upon.[3] Women appealed to Union soldiers to treat them as ladies, but when necessary they also stepped outside the boundaries of "proper" behavior with the confidence that men, even invading soldiers, would most likely not physically harm them. For their part, Union soldiers deftly used notions about femininity to their advantage. They attacked the material indicators of femininity—bedrooms, journals, letters, china, linens, and fancy dresses—in their effort to demoralize Confederate women and thereby take them out of the war. These violations enraged white Southern women, especially as many of them used the sanctity of the bedroom as well as the presumed inviolability of white ladyhood in attempts to conceal their valuables.

Although Civil War scholars often examine Sherman's March as an event of great military importance and a necessary precursor to the end of the war, they rarely give a thought to the gendered implications of the campaign. Focusing on the military movements and destruction visited upon railroad depots, military supplies, and other physical supports for the Confederacy, countless scholars mistakenly gloss over the constant interactions between Union troops and white Southern women and the gender-specific tactics employed. Military scholars spend significantly more time discussing the lack of resistance by Confederate soldiers and the nature of the march when civilians were not around than they do the confrontations between soldiers and civilians. In addition, they often neuter the home front by using the ungendered term of civilians to describe a region dominated by women. Furthermore, when they mention white Southern women, scholars treat them as afterthoughts of the campaign. The confrontations between soldiers and civilians appear as unintentional, if not inevitable, moments that provide anecdotal color but are not deserving of analysis. Destroyed homes and personal property appear as collateral damage instead of as intentional targets of the military campaign. For example, historian Lee Kennett's *Marching Through Georgia: The Story of Soldiers and Civilians during Sherman's Campaign* dedicates only one chapter to a discussion of the interactions between Northern soldiers and the Southern civilians that are presumably mentioned in the book's subtitle. This chapter, wedged between traditional descriptions of military matters, is entitled "Victims." Not surprisingly, Kennett's Southern women appear as helpless and incidental to the meaning and path of the march.[4]

Even scholars who have placed women at the center of their analysis have not considered their military importance and consequently relegate them to marginal historical significance. Jacqueline Glass Campbell, for example, focuses on "resistance on the Confederate home front" and yet inexplicably overlooks the gendered actions of Union soldiers and the way in which interactions between male soldiers and female civilians were military confrontations. While she recognizes that the behavior of soldiers was constrained by the gender of their opponents, she does not address how gender conventions both created and limited the tactical options for Union soldiers. As a result, she cannot offer a sustained analysis of the gendered nature of warfare for both men and women. In addition, Campbell notes the preponderance of evidence that points to the resiliency of Southern civilian morale, but she fails to demonstrate how white womanhood provided the basis for their continued confidence.[5]

These military and politically based interpretations of Sherman's March do not allow an exploration of how gender shaped the course of a military campaign from the perspectives of both soldiers and civilians. From the planning through the implementation of Sherman's Georgia and Carolinas campaign, and whether examined from the Confederate or Union perspective, gender shaped the behavior of everyone involved in and affected by this military offensive. Union officials designed Sherman's March with gender in mind as they planned an attack on a home front filled with a female enemy. Furthermore, those on the Southern home front understood and reacted to the invasion through the lens of gender. White men and women complained about the "ungentlemanly" enemy even as some of the women responded with what Northern soldiers frequently categorized as unfeminine behavior.[6]

In addition to examining how gender shaped the actions and reactions of white Southern women, this essay demonstrates the gendered nature of the Union's war policy in 1864–65. It contends that Union soldiers specifically targeted elite Southern women and female space not simply as part of the chaos of war but also as part of a concerted effort to wage a gendered form of warfare. Although the Union's attempt to destroy the Southern home front as well as the will of Confederate civilians purportedly focused on the destruction of items of military importance, the campaign was also a domestic battle. Throughout the march Union soldiers purposefully ransacked women' bedrooms, paraded around in dresses, forced women to entertain them with music before smashing their pianos, destroyed female letters and journals, and rummaged through women's lingerie and other "unmentionables." These actions, and the confrontations they created between male Union soldiers and female Confederate civilians, resulted from more than women's numeric dominance on the Confederate home front. They also resulted from the desires of Union soldiers to demonstrate their power over the white South as well as from their use of preconceived ideas about femininity to their tactical advantage. Early in the war, Sherman acknowledged women as enemies, telling his brother, "[T]he entire South, man, *woman*, and child are against us, armed and determined."[7] Consequently, when Ulysses S. Grant asked him to bring the war home to the South, Sherman agreed. He employed an attack on elite Southern women and their domestic sphere as one of many tactics in his campaign. Sherman and his commanders hoped that this campaign, designed to "demonstrate the vulnerability of the South and make its inhabitants feel that war and individual ruin are synonymous terms," would bring the war to a close.[8] In bringing the war directly to Southern civilians, Sherman understood the gendered nature of his campaign and asserted that "this movement is *not* purely military or strategic, but it will illustrate the vulnerability of the South."[9] After all, he wanted Southerners, male and female, to feel the consequences of secession. He assumed that "the utter destruction of its [the South's] roads, houses and people" would demoralize civilians and soldiers and bring an end to the war.[10] Sherman's soldiers assumed that Southern ladies would respond to an attack on their private sphere by quickly abandoning their political loyalties, their soldiers on the field, and their nation. Consequently, to erode Confederate women's support of the Southern war effort, Union soldiers attacked those things that white women held most dear.

As a result of women's numeric dominance on the Confederate home front, Sherman recognized that any attack on it was necessarily one on white Southern women and their worlds.[11] Union soldiers understood that they were marching through a land occupied by elite white Southern women, who had earned reputations as vigilant secessionists. Sherman and many soldiers on his campaign judged that women who had entered the political arena as advocates of disunion and war did not deserve the protection typically due to women of their station. Therefore, plans to end white Southern women's support by literally bringing the war into their homes were an essential component of the campaign. Sherman and his troops recognized the implicit vulnerability of their feminine home-front enemies and hoped to use ideas about femininity to their advantage. In their assault on the home front, Union soldiers assumed that Confederate women could not sustain their regional loyalty in the face of attack. Consequently, to erode women's support of the Confederacy, throughout Sherman's March Union soldiers asserted their masculinity as they directly assaulted the trappings of elite Southern femininity and domesticity. They expected that such an attack on women's personal space and belongings would crush their material and moral support for the Confederacy.

As Sherman and his men approached their homes, elite white women prepared to face the destruction typical of earlier campaigns. Having watched the Union's war policy progress from one that seemed to acknowledge a separation between soldier and civilian to one that treated women as enemies in their own right, white Southern women knew that Yankees waged a gendered war on women.[12] After all, white women across the Confederacy had carefully followed the news of the arrests of Southern women for aiding their nation, the issuance of Benjamin Butler's "Woman Order" in New Orleans, and the stories of depredations in the Shenandoah Valley by Philip Sheridan's Union troops.[13] Furthermore, Sherman's forced evacuation of more than fifteen hundred civilians from Atlanta on September 8, 1864, provoked a vehement outcry from men and women across the Confederacy, who appealed to ideas about gender and the "helplessness" of women.[14] Further angering white Southerners, Sherman, in his response to complaints about the evacuation order, repeatedly justified his actions, often using gendered language. In particular, he stressed that not only would a hostile civilian population impede military activities but the presence of Southern "families" would also unnecessarily burden the Union Army, which would have to feed and shelter Confederate women and children.[15] As he left Atlanta, which burned in his wake, Sherman also promised Grant that he would "make Georgia howl."[16] For many white women, the Yankees had increasingly demonstrated that this war was women's burden.

Initial reports of Sherman's wide swath of destruction further alerted white women in Georgia and the Carolinas to the coming perils. Stories of the Union plunder of food stores, the burning of houses, and destruction of clothing, housewares, personal papers, and furniture made clear the domestic ramifications of the march. Sherman, they realized, would not spare women or households but had instead targeted them to strike at the heart of Southern domesticity and morale.

Despite stories of violations of women's private sphere, many white women remained confident that Union soldiers would not completely disregard gender norms. With this assumption guiding their actions, some women saw their sexuality and nineteenth-century gender conventions as weapons of resistance against the Yankee invaders. Consequently, many elite Confederate women planned to use their femininity to their advantage. They consistently acted in ways that forced Union soldiers to acknowledge or deny their femininity. Prior to the war, the bedroom epitomized the elusive middle-class ideal of separate spheres, as it was the most private and feminized place within the domestic realm.[17] As a result, as Union soldiers approached, elite white women often took their most sacred possessions, although not always those with the highest monetary value, into what they presumed would remain sanctified space—their private chambers. In South Carolina, Sarah Jane Sams heard that "a rumor is rife this morning that the Yankees are but six miles from here . . . [but] reports are so contradictory that they may come upon the town before we are aware of it." She immediately began looking for ways to protect her property. To prepare for the anticipated invasion, "Bet, Ma and myself have been busy all day removing our provisions from the cellar and the pantry into our bedrooms hoping they may be more secure."[18] Sometimes the items were "hidden" in the open with the confidence that enemy soldiers would not disturb bedrooms. Sams assured her husband that their valuables, including her jewelry and his important papers, were out of sight. Still, with everything else stored in the private sanctuary, her room looked "more like a commissary room than a bed room."[19] Ironically, by hiding valuables in their bedrooms Southern women invited persistent Union soldiers to search there.

In other instances, white women found creative hiding places that further demonstrated their confidence in the inviolability of female space. Sams, attempting to safeguard her domestic items, "emptied the cotton out of one of our mattresses and filled it very nicely with all of our cloth, blankets, sheets and gentlemen's clothing, sewed it up like a mattress and put [it] under the rest."

Sams recognized that these precautions might prove useless and Union soldiers might violate her private space. "Whether they discover it will be proved by tomorrow I fear."[20] In any case, most white women continued to expect that the invading armies would follow the conventions of peacetime society and not breach the privacy of a woman's bedroom. Furthermore, if soldiers did violate domestic spaces, women hoped that these men would not linger in these places long enough to uncover their caches. South Carolinian Charlotte St. Julien Ravenel described her attempt to protect her property from the Union invaders. "Pennie and myself sat up until two o['] clock putting a way [sic] things in a mattrys we opened the cotton and put the things between."[21] Despite what she had heard about the Union attack on women, Ravenel still believed some gender boundaries would not be crossed and that Union men would not dare to go into or onto her bed.

As one of Sherman's soldiers reported, however, women's confidence in the protective nature of femininity was frequently misguided, since Union troops rarely hesitated to enter and ransack elite Southern bedrooms. Early in the campaign, journalist and Ohio soldier Thomas T. Taylor described foragers entering and destroying homes in Georgia. After taking all the food, the soldiers smashed the "jars, dishes, furniture &c."[22] The seizure of foodstuffs clearly fell within the stated goals of the march—"to forage liberally."[23] However, Union soldiers continued their raid on this particular house, homing in on domestic and feminine items and spaces. As Thomas reported, the men "then robbed the beds of their bedding, wardrobes of their clothing and cut open mattrasses [sic] even to the one on which the little children slept on their crib." Clearly, mattresses were not the safe haven that Confederate women assumed them to be. This particular group of soldiers did not stop with the insult of invading the women's and children's bedrooms. They then drove from the house a pregnant woman, "her innocent, little children and her aged mother."[24] Although women throughout Georgia and the Carolinas hoped for the best, antebellum gender conventions did little to protect the women of this household or their personal items from Union destruction. In the eyes of invading soldiers, their identities as Confederate traitors superseded their identities as elite Southern ladies.

However, Confederate women remained confident that their bodies were safe from assault. Many white Southern women prepared to hide valuables on their person, hopeful that the crossing of gender boundaries by Union soldiers would not extend to disrespect for women's bodies. These Confederates wholeheartedly believed that Union men would respect the sanctity of Southern womanhood and therefore made plans to take advantage of that respect. They used their personal space as if it were a protected sphere, immune from wartime destruction. Like female spies throughout the Union and Confederacy, white Southern women sewed pockets under large skirts to hide personal possessions and often wore multiple layers of clothing as the enemy approached, assuming that anything on their body would remain untouched. As much as they feared the destruction that Union soldiers would undoubtedly cause, they maintained their belief that gender norms, especially those that governed behavior in regards to a woman's body, would be one thing that Yankees would not break.[25]

For small items, white women routinely turned themselves into safes, confident that they would not be disturbed. For example, from the campus of South Carolina College in Columbia, Emma LeConte confidently remarked in her journal, "I have been hastily making large pockets to wear under my hoop skirt—for they will hardly search our persons."[26] Fellow South Carolinian Sarah Jane Sams, who had already filled her bedroom with what seemed like everything she owned, revealed similar precautions in a letter to her husband. "I woke the children and put on them two suits of underclothing and their dresses and wore the same quantity myself, besides three small bags containing needles, cotton and flax thread, tape and buttons."[27] Although these women understood the destruction Sherman's troops would bring to their state and their homes, they still hoped that ideas about propriety would prevent the enemy soldiers from personally violating them. Even if soldiers dared to enter bedrooms and rummage through their lingerie, many Confederate women confidently maintained their belief that soldiers would refrain from physically touching them.

Even as some women used their bodies to hide items, others feared that their bodies would become targets of enemy aggression. These Confederate women took active precautions against sexual assault, especially as rumors of violations elsewhere arrived before Union troops. As Union soldiers approached, some women slept in their clothes to protect both their property and their virtue.[28] Taking more extreme measures, a white Georgian described to her brother her attempts to avoid harassment by invading Union men. As the enemy approached, one of the slaves "tried to get me not to show myself, for she [said] many were asking her if there [were any] young ladies in the house." She found what she considered a simple solution. "I tried to look as ugly as possible" so that "none were they to see me would take me for any thing but an old married woman."[29] Appearing old and ugly, she assumed, would shield her from the leering eyes of enemy men. Other women took similar precautions. At her family's home near Aiken, South Carolina, Pauline DeCaradeuc heard that the soldiers had "asked the servants if there were any young ladies in the house, how old they were & where they slept." Although frightened by these inquiries, DeCaradeuc felt that she and her friend had some protection because "during all this I had on blue spectacles & my face muffled up. Carrie too." Despite her assumed safety, the hint of a sexual assault made her realize "that burning the house was nothing." For the rest of the night, she remained "almost frantic [and] sat up in a corner, without moving or closing my eyes once the whole night." Although DeCaradeuc "suffered agony [and] trembled *unceasingly* till morning," the experience put the physical destruction around her into perspective. Some things were more valuable than property.[30]

The arrival of enemy soldiers did little to dissipate white Southern women's fears about the invasion or their opinion of the enemy. In Georgia and the Carolinas, the advent of Union troops brought with it widespread destruction of land, commercial property and items, and domestic upheaval. Looting soldiers smashed much of what they found in elite homes, including fine china, pianos, and crystal. In addition, they appropriated many personal treasures of little monetary value to send home to loved ones as souvenirs. In rare cases, soldiers frisked and tore clothing off women who were believed to be hiding valuables. More commonly the enemy troops destroyed the sanctity of domestic space by rummaging through lingerie, tearing up mattresses, shredding wedding gowns, and reading aloud from women's private journals. Confederate women and Union soldiers all reported the seizure of Southern sheet music, jewelry, personal correspondence, and diaries. These breaches of wartime etiquette, more than the widespread destruction, drew the ire of elite women.

Confederate women recognized that war brought inevitable hardships, but they drew sharp distinctions between these depredations and the violation of their homes. As a result, their hostility became particularly pointed when Union soldiers physically attacked Southern homes. When looking back on Sherman's March, Union soldier Robert Hale Strong observed that "some [women] were rabid rebels and took no pains to conceal it, but all were polite to us except when we were searching their houses."[31] The reaction to the invasion of homes demonstrated women's view of the invasion of domestic space as both unprovoked and unforgivable.[32] North Carolinian Eliza Tillinghast summed her reactions up by noting that "a visit from the Yankee Army is not calculated to make us love the hated race any more" because "to have our private apartments at the mercy of rabble soldiery is not particularly pleasant. Every box, drawer, trunk, closet, . . . and cranny in this house was turned inside out and thoroughly searc[h]ed by Sherman's men."[33] Other women came to similar assessments. This breach of civility made Union soldiers seem hardly human to the Confederate women who confronted them. The impropriety and seeming inhumanity of the ungentlemanly invading soldiers, portrayed by many white women as vicious animals, "demons," "devils," "fiends incarnate," "Vandals," and "Goths," confirmed Confederate women's belief that the two regions were irreconcilable and magnified their desire for vengeance.[34]

For their part, Union soldiers also saw Confederate women as a different set of people. Elite white Southern women, the soldiers reasoned, deserved harsh treatment because of their culpability for the war. These men could separate ideas of femininity from the white Southern women in their path, women whose behavior in support of the Confederacy had clearly shown them as Southerners, not ladies. Furthermore, these invading men were more than willing to demonstrate their masculine power and superiority over the enemy civilians.[35] Northern soldiers wanted to make Confederate women pay for their role in the Southern war effort. In Columbia, South Carolina, Union Lieutenant Colonel Jeremiah W. Jenkins, provost marshal of the invaded city, tellingly declared, "[T]he women of the South kept the war alive—and it is only by making them suffer that we can subdue the men."[36] Jenkins saw attacking Southern domesticity as a way to punish both contemptuous civilians and soldiers. Any attack on Southern women, he realized, was also an assault on Southern manhood and honor.[37] A Union Army chaplain with Sherman similarly justified the assault on women. "So far as the *women* are concerned, we might as well spare our pity, for they are the worst secessionists, and why should *they* not suffer?" he asked. "Would you now spare them a proper amount of suffering? We say no. Let them understand that secession means something more than a holiday parade."[38] The chaplain's statement reveals an animosity toward Southern women not only as secessionists but also as frivolous girls who, he assumed, saw secession and war as nothing more than spectacle. Union troops saw a need to punish misbehaving Southerners, despite their gender or age, for their roles in the Civil War. As a result, soldiers even extended their hostility to white Southern children. Although during peacetime men served as fatherly protectors of all youngsters, during the Civil War they considered children enemies. As he took blankets away from children in Columbia, one Union soldier said, "[L]et the d——d little rebels suffer as we have had to do for the past four years."[39]

Although frustrated by the destruction of their farms, foodstuffs, and crops, Confederate women were frequently more outraged by the enemy's violations of domestic space. For example, South Carolinian Pauline DeCaradeuc particularly resented the soldiers' defacing of the domestic trappings of the household. Not only had the men taken "every blanket & pillow case & towel . . . they even made the servants get our chemises & tear them up into pocket handkerchiefs." The destruction of her lingerie, items never shown to strange men in peacetime, symbolized the violation of women's private sphere. However, the soldiers did not stop with this insult. When raids resumed the next day, the soldiers "said this house was the root of the rebellion & burn it they would." Although stopping short of torching the house, the Northern men continued to threaten its inhabitants, proclaiming "that they had to arrest and shoot every influential citizen in S.C., every mover of secession." Indeed, the elite women of South Carolina received especially harsh treatment at the hands of Union troops, who justified their behavior on the basis that the Palmetto State had been the first to secede and had led other Southern states in the same direction. For DeCaradeuc and her family, this desire for vengeance translated into continuous raids from enemy soldiers. Each day the "Yankees came here in a body & dispersed over the house & place, carrying off everything they could."[40]

In numerous scenes across the South, elite white women demonstrated that a violation of their feminine sphere served to strengthen their support of Confederate independence. Perhaps because "every trunk, Bureau, Box, room, [and] closet has been opened or broken open" and "the whole house [was] turned topsey-turvey," Georgia matron Mary Sharpe Jones refused to budge. She and the white women of her household remained composed and unruffled as they faced the vandals. "God alone has enabled us to speak with the enemy in the Gates, and calmly without a tear to see my house broken open, entered with false keys, threatened to be burned to ashes, refused food & ordered to be starved to death, told . . . that I should be 'humbled in the very dust I walked upon,' a pistol and carbine presented to my breast, cursed & reviled as a Rebel, a hypocrite, a devil."[41] After initially restraining herself to a quiet opposition to the Union soldiers in her home, Jones eventually displayed her patriotism. The invaders, she exulted, "always addressed me as an uncompromising rebel," and she proudly concurred. "I never failed to let them know that before High Heaven, I believed our cause was just & right."[42]

Antebellum gender conventions, which allowed white Southern women to confidently assume that their bodies and bedrooms were inviolable, also led them to understand an invasion of their home as an unforgivable violation. Consequently, they often used the rhetoric of rape when describing the horrors that they expected to, and did, face upon Sherman's arrival in their towns.[43] As did many other elite women, Columbian Emma LeConte understood the enemy's actions in sexualized terms. In her diary, she wrote that "[Union troops] are preparing to hurl destruction upon the State they hate most of all." The assault that she feared would do more than destroy the means to wage war. "Sherman the brute avows his intention of converting South Carolina into a wilderness. Not one house he says shall be left standing and his licentious troops whites and negroes shall be turned loose to *ravage* and *violate*."[44] Her fears about rape may have been unfounded, as very few white women were raped during the march. Still, the behavior of Union men led others to understand the invasion in terms of a sexual assault. Rumors about events prompted impassioned responses from Southern women around the Confederacy. From Mississippi, Matilda Champion acknowledged the inappropriate words and behavior of the approaching Union soldiers while asserting the failure of such tactics. "I am not astonished to hear of Gen. Sherman saying he could buy the chastity of any Southern woman with a few pounds of coffee. He would find himself woefully mistaken if he were to try that."[45] The rumors of Sherman's references to Southern ladies' virtue no doubt fueled the fears and anger of Confederate women.

Sherman, like many of his soldiers, judged Southern women's patriotism as unfeminine. According to Northerners, Confederate women's confrontational defense of their nation betrayed their supposed identity as ladies. Ellen Devereux Hinsdale related a story of one woman's confrontation with Sherman. According to the story, "he cursed the women called us d——d rebels, & the cause of the trouble in the country." The outrage continued as she relayed that Sherman threatened "that the next time he comes here he will treat us as the Indians would."[46] Sherman's declaration that Southern women and Indians deserved to be treated with the same rules of war defined the growing distance between the Confederacy and the Union. After all, if the Union equated Confederate women with savages, the only solution was to conquer and control the "savage" population by whatever means possible.

When invading Union troops marched out of Southern towns and homesteads, they did not leave behind a demoralized civilian population. Confederate women did not behave as Sherman and others had predicted. Early in the campaign, and even as male politicians peacefully surrendered the city, Sherman had discovered that in Savannah "the girls remain, bright and haughty and proud as ever. There seems no end but utter annihilation that will satisfy their hate of the 'sneaking Yankee' and 'ruthless invader.'" He expressed his shock that "although I have come right through the heart of Georgia they talk as defiantly as ever."[47] Sherman had assumed that elite women's persistent loyalty to the Confederacy would wane and that the continuation of his destructive campaign would undoubtedly subdue Southern women. Sherman had confidently asserted, again in gendered language, that his campaign would "cure her of her pride and boasting," but to his surprise the military invasion did little to dampen the patriotism of Confederate women.[48] Instead, it strengthened the resolve of white Southern women, who saw the march as confirmation that the North and South had irreconcilable cultural differences and gender ideals.

Gendered Union tactics along Sherman's March served to increase many white women's dedication to the Confederacy. After Union soldiers ransacked her Georgia house, burned her outhouses, and stole most of her valuables and food, a woman known only as Loula pronounced, "I thought my hatred was deep enough before, but now I am a hotter rebel than ever, and *never will* be resigned to going back into the Union with such a corrupt people." Her basis for labeling Northerners "a corrupt people" was made clear in her May 1865 letter. In it, she decried Union tactics, especially those that targeted her domesticity. "They are so low down, and had no respect whatever for a lady's private room, tore up the whole house and stole whatever they wanted." After the enemy repeatedly "[pried] into every sacred thing in the house," she vowed to never forgive. "If I live a thousand years I shall never forget the enemies of our country." She would never "[regard] them as brothers & friends, I think it a contamination to be compelled to breathe the same air, much less tolerate their society among us."[49] Union actions and disregard for gender ideals would translate into a long and bitter hatred in many of the women who faced the troops along Sherman's campaign.

Like other white women in Sherman's path, Emma LeConte particularly resented the invasion of her domestic sphere and found that it increased her animosity toward the enemy and her determination to continue the fight. LeConte recorded her shift in attitudes, noting, "[B]efore they came here, I thought I hated [the Yankees] as much as was possible—now I know there are no limits to the feeling of hatred."[50] Fellow South Carolinian Grace Brown Elmore agreed: "[W]icked as we knew the Yankee to be, we never could realize the extent of their malice until their occupying of Columbia."[51] The incidents surrounding the destruction of private homes in Columbia provoked LeConte to conclude, "[T]he more we suffer, the more we should be willing to undergo rather than submit. Somehow I can not feel we can be conquered." Echoing the sentiments of other Confederate women, LeConte continued: "[W]e have lost everything," but "if everything . . . could be given back a hundred fold I would not be willing to go back to them." Instead she "would rather endure any poverty than live under Yankee rule. . . . Anything but live as one nation with Yankees—that word in my mind is a synonym with *all* that is *mean* despicable and abhorrent."[52] Grace Brown Elmore's experience in Columbia resulted in a similar hostility toward the Yankees. "The very devils from hell could not rouse greater feelings of disgust and abhorrence than those cowardly wretches did in us."[53] The invasion demonstrated to these elite women that Northerners were completely different from Southerners—a separate race and culture. The troops' invasion of the domestic sphere and attack on white womanhood proved the lack of common values.

The possibility of peace with the Union horrified many Confederate women, especially those that had dealt with the gendered tactics of Sherman's March. North Carolinian Eliza Tillinghast assured her brother that "if [he] knew what we have suffered . . . [he] would not wonder" at her bitterness toward the enemy. As she portrayed it, "[W]e have lost every thing but our honor." Consequently, "there is a wall of bones, and a River of blood and it will flow forever between the foe and us, and until they cut a canal to the waters of Oblivion and deluge our land with Forgetfulness we can never consider a yankee any thing but an oppressor and an enemy[.] While I have no personal feeling towards any one of them I hate the nation from the bottom of my soul, Even as I hate Satan, and all things low, mean and hateful."[54] She blamed the Union as a whole for violating her home and instituting an assault on Southern domesticity. She could not forgive Union policies that allowed for the desecration of Southern homes and private sanctuaries.[55]

In part, Confederate women's inability to come to grips with surrender resulted from their disdain for an enemy that had invaded the domestic sphere and employed other similarly improper gendered methods. "How humiliating it is to think of our being given up to such a people," Georgian Loula Kendall Rogers lamented. "There is no word in the English language strong enough to express our hatred and contempt for an enemy so degraded—if they were *gentlemen* we could bear it better."[56] The use of the gendered term "gentlemen" demonstrated Rogers's conviction that the campaign had been unjust and pursued by an uncivilized enemy. Furthermore, the wrongs done to Southern women by the enemy soldiers inspired many to hope for retaliation weeks after Sherman's March had ended and Confederate generals had surrendered. Rogers stressed that she could not "help to save my life from wishing that the North may feel all the horrors of war as we have done." She hoped for a vengeance in order that Northerners would similarly have "their homes desolated, their private property stolen and every depredation they have committed here be measured out to them in *their own coin*." Despite her desire for revenge, Rogers realized that she could "*never wish* that our *Southern sons* should be guilty of such wickedness." Instead, she "[hoped] and [prayed] that *our* brothers, husbands and sons may never invade the holy sanctuaries of a private family, insult poor helpless women, and so degrade themselves by every revolting crime that could come under the head of sin, as did the barbarous soldiers of the United States."[57] Rogers, like other Confederate women in Georgia and the Carolinas, maintained her belief in the inviolability of the domestic sphere. Although Confederate women hoped for retribution, they could not sanction a retaliatory assault on the Northern domestic sphere.

Confederate women understood Sherman's March in a way that many scholars have not. White Southern women realized that during the war the enemy had increasingly corrupted and, they thought, misused gender ideals. The bedroom, which should have been a refuge, had turned into a battleground. Sherman's soldiers asserted their masculine power as they violated the sanctity of private chambers, destroyed women's clothes and lingerie, ripped apart mattresses, and otherwise desecrated the feminine sphere. These actions, in turn, forced white Southern ladies to assert their regional loyalties and engage the enemy in ways that Northerners took as further proof of Southern women's "unfeminine" nature. When Union soldiers left their bedrooms, homes, and communities in shambles, Confederate women held on to their regional identities, perhaps even more stalwartly and confidently than they had before. They understood the invasion of their domestic sphere as an unforgivable violation and used it to further their dedication to the Confederacy. As a result, most elite white women were not subdued by Sherman's gendered form of warfare. These women understood the Union campaign for what it was: one as much focused on the ruin of feminine space as it was on the destruction of railroads, military posts, and foodstuffs. Confederate women recognized Sherman's March as a struggle over the wartime boundaries of femininity and domesticity. This struggle over Confederate bedrooms shaped the loyalty of many Southern white women for years to come, as they could not forgive the Union soldiers' violation of feminine spaces and disregard for gender boundaries.

"Physical Abuse . . . and Rough Handling"

Race, Gender, and Sexual Justice in the Occupied South

E. SUSAN BARBER AND CHARLES F. RITTER

On March 3, 1863, Congress passed Senate Bill 511, euphemistically titled the "Enrollment Act." This was the first conscription legislation passed by the U.S. Congress, and its impact was felt in every corner of the nation. Buried deep in the act was Section 30, a provision that gave U.S. Army courts-martial and military commissions jurisdiction over common-law felonies such as rape, murder, larceny, and arson when committed by U.S. military personnel. Section 30 had a powerful implication for occupied women because it brought the rule of law to conflict zones. It permitted them to use military courts to seek justice for the plunder, pillage, and depredations committed by Union soldiers.

In scores of letters and diaries, women throughout the occupied South related accounts of Union soldiers who confiscated foodstuffs, seized horses and weapons, destroyed fences and outbuildings, and terrorized female households. Although Southern women feared plunder and pillage by Union soldiers, they may have dreaded ravishment and its consequences most of all. Section 30 of the Enrollment Act provided occupied women with the ability to make accusations of sexual crimes committed by Union servicemen with some expectation that their charges would be heard. Although not perfect, the system functioned to bring to justice soldiers who committed sexual crimes. In so doing, the Union Army's military justice system broke new ground by rendering a measure of sexual justice to occupied women.

The story of sexual justice in the occupied South rests on the testimony of women and men who have eluded the historian's glance. Most left no diaries or

The authors wish to thank the Harry Frank Guggenheim Foundation and the College of Notre Dame of Maryland for their generous support that made the research for this essay possible.

letters. Their legacy to us is in their vivid, often gripping, and always compelling testimony. They are women like Mary Melissa Kirksey of Wauhatchie Station, Tennessee, whose story is an example of the sexual violence occupied women faced.

On May 18, 1864, Charles Hunter, a private in Company I of the Seventh Kentucky Cavalry, entered the home of Mary Melissa Kirksey, a thirty-five-year-old white widow living in Hamilton County, Tennessee, and brutally raped her. In her testimony before the court-martial that heard Hunter's case, Kirksey testified that she pleaded with Hunter to leave her alone and that she "kicked and hollered as loud as she could," whereupon Hunter bound and gagged her with a leather strap, threw her on the bed, and sexually assaulted her. Two days later Hunter returned and, according to Kirksey, raped her a second time.[1]

Mary Kirksey's case was not unique. During the American Civil War, several hundred women in occupied Southern and border states brought charges of rape or attempted rape against Union soldiers or civilians attached to the U.S. Army. However, most early histories of the Civil War, if they mention sexual assaults at all, either dismissed them as isolated events or claimed that they were too difficult to research because there was little, if any, documentary evidence aside from anecdotal references found in women's letters and diaries.[2] Recent social historians of the Civil War South have based their conclusions on these earlier assumptions. George Rable, for example, has noted that although "rapes did occur" there has been a paucity of research devoted to the subject. Victoria Bynum concurs, noting that, although sexual assaults occurred, "rape charges were unlikely to reach a courtroom" because of "deeply embedded notions of shame and honor" that "encouraged private vengeance rather than public justice." Indeed, Ervin L. Jordan Jr. has called rape "[t]he silent subject of the Civil War . . . alluded to in letters, memoirs, and reported in a cloud of euphemisms."[3]

A few historians have recently suggested that black women's bodies, particularly but not exclusively in the Confederate South, constituted another Civil War battlefield on which soldiers used rape, attempted rape, and lesser sexual assaults as weapons. Drew Faust, for example, maintains that, although "[w]hite females, particularly those of the elite, were rarely victims of rape by invading soldiers," black women "served as the unfortunate sexual spoils when Union soldiers asserted their traditional right of military conquest."[4] Mark Grimsley punctuates Faust's point in a 2002 essay when he writes, "Few white Southern women suffered rape or sexual abuse" at the hands of Union soldiers.[5] Likewise, in his study of the Civil War in Missouri, Michael Fellman maintains that "there are only infrequent reports of rape of white women, and all of those second hand."[6] While historians such as Martha Hodes, Laura Edwards, Catherine Clinton, Diane Sommerville, and Hannah Rosen have uncovered evidence of sexual assault in the colonial, antebellum, and postbellum United States, no historian has undertaken a comprehensive study of the subject for the Civil War.[7]

This essay argues, however, that the American Civil War was not a "no rape" or "low-rape" war. It asserts that documented Civil War sexual crimes occurred against white and black women and girls of all social classes, and it reveals for the first time that Union military courts prosecuted approximately 450 of those crimes and in so doing broke new ground by providing sexual justice to the war's female victims. By not limiting its purview to accusations made by white women only, the military justice system made a stunning departure from Southern legal conventions: Union courts-martial and military commissions held trials on behalf of both black and white women and based convictions of white soldiers on testimony of black witnesses. Thus, although invasion and military occupation left Southern women more vulnerable to sexual assault, paradoxically, the Union military justice system provided them with a venue to seek redress for sexual crimes. Although sexual assault cases constitute a small percentage of all the crimes heard by military courts, they were among the most frequently prosecuted civilian crimes tried by the military.[8] The testimony from these trials, located in the records of the Judge Advocate General's Office of the Union Army, illuminates the dynamics of sexual justice in occupied territory and sheds light on this little-known aspect of the American Civil War.

Union provost marshals and judge advocates, who were charged with administering justice, took accusations of sexual misconduct seriously; commanders and judges moved with speed to try accused soldiers and punish the convicted, thus maintaining the rule of law in the midst of war's chaos. Motives for doing so appear to be twofold: a determination to ensure discipline in the ranks, and a desire to maintain both internal and external order.[9] In the process of accomplishing these two military objectives, military courts—although unintentionally at first—redressed sexual offenses committed against women like Mary Kirksey.

Kirksey lived in Lookout Valley, just outside Chattanooga, Tennessee, which had been occupied by Union troops after the Battle of Wauhatchie Station on October 29, 1863. Thus, by the spring of 1864, she had grown accustomed to the presence of Union soldiers in her neighborhood and had, at times, provided them succor. Her house had been used as a hospital and as the headquarters for the Twenty-eighth Pennsylvania Regiment. For a short time, two Union officers who were recovering from amputations lodged with Kirksey and her young son. The Philadelphia sister of one of the injured men stayed with Kirksey, too. Furthermore, Kirksey earned her living by washing soldiers' clothes and selling them eggs and milk. So on the morning of May 18, 1864, she probably had no reason to fear Charles Hunter. Hunter's unit, the Seventh Kentucky Cavalry, had been stationed since May 3, 1864, at Wauhatchie Station, seven miles from Chattanooga and a mile from Kirksey's house. On the day of Hunter's first assault, five Union soldiers visited Kirksey's house, several coming more than once that day to drop off and pick up their laundry.

Frequent visits by Union soldiers did not necessarily bode well for Southern women who later brought sexual assault charges. In his defense, Hunter claimed that the soldiers' frequent visits led him to believe that Kirksey was a prostitute. Testifying for the prosecution, Private David Crutchfield partially confirmed Hunter's assumption when he related under oath that he had originally presumed Kirksey was a woman of "base character" but that he had quickly concluded, after a brief visit to Kirksey's house, that she was "an upright honest lady."[10] Hunter evidently did not arrive at the same conclusion.

Following Hunter's first assault, a distraught Kirksey confided the intimate details of her ordeal to her neighbor, Mrs. Mary Frist. She also reported to several soldiers and officers that another soldier had "treated [her] very badly," although she withheld from the men the specific sexual nature of Hunter's crime. The soldiers provided Kirksey with information about the procedure for reporting an offense to the provost marshal, but, for reasons she never revealed, she deferred making a report. However, after Hunter's second assault a few days later, which was accompanied by his brandishing a knife and threatening to "cut [her] liver out," a distraught Kirksey appeared before the provost marshal to lodge a formal accusation. Hunter was taken into custody and a court-martial, which had already been convened to hear other cases, swung into action, scheduling a trial date and notifying witnesses—all within a matter of a few days after Kirksey filed her complaint.[11]

The court-martial of Private Hunter was one of some eighty-one thousand military trials held during the Civil War. Such trials were the cornerstone of the Union system of military justice, a system that punished infractions of the

Articles of War and, after March 1863, common-law felonies. The army's system of justice dated from the American Revolution and was derived from British military law. The U.S. Articles of War, which governed military behavior, were first drafted in 1775 and revised in 1776. They were revised again in 1806, and it was those articles that were in effect when the Civil War began.[12]

Any general officer commanding a Union Army, or field officer commanding a department or brigade, could convene a general court-martial to try infractions of the Articles of War.[13] Typically the courts were convened within a month, and sometimes a few days, of an accusation, if they were not already sitting. Trials proceeded quickly, usually in one or two days, although complex cases could go on for months. The courts consisted of five to thirteen officers and a judge advocate who was both a member of the court and the prosecuting attorney. Trials proceeded with direct testimony and cross-examination, both conducted by the judge advocate.[14] He also advised the accused if the defendant did not have counsel, which, given the speed at which these cases were brought to trial and the fact that most defendants were privates, describes the situation of most of the cases.[15] Once established by an appropriate commanding officer and staffed with officers, the court heard cases that the provost marshal and a commissioned officer prepared for it.[16]

Although the president of the court was "the organ" who "speaks and acts for the court,"[17] it was the judge advocate who conducted the trial. The Civil War judge advocates were expected to have some acquaintance with military life, law, and custom, as well as some experience with criminal law and courtroom proceedings, although it appears that few had any legal training.[18] Although Congress authorized the president to appoint a judge advocate for each army in the field,[19] commanders who called courts-martial into existence appointed others.[20] The judge advocates ran the trials: they summoned the witnesses, swore in the judges of the court (the court president then swore in the judge advocate), prosecuted the case for the United States, and even assisted the defendant in preparing and presenting his case.[21] The judge advocate also assured that the court was properly constituted, prepared a rough transcript of the day's proceedings, which was read at the next court session, and was responsible for sending an authenticated copy of the trial proceedings to the authorizing commander for review.[22]

Decisions and sentences of the court-martial were not self-executing. It remained for the commander who convened the court to review the proceedings and to confirm, deny, or mitigate them.[23] In cases of the death penalty or a lengthy penitentiary prison term, the review proceeded up the chain of command to the secretary of war, and ultimately to the president.[24] The judge advocate general, Joseph Holt, reviewed cases for the secretary and the president and offered his judgment of the proceedings, the sentences, and any mitigation. As a gatekeeper of justice, he was tough minded but fair, and he was not shy about expressing his views regarding the justice of sentences and mitigations. For instance, hospital steward Eugene Hannel was convicted of raping an African American washerwoman in a hospital camp in New Bern, North Carolina. General John Palmer mitigated the court's sentence of two years at hard labor to three months in the brig. Upon review, Holt advised Secretary of War Edwin Stanton that "the testimony of the woman who was ravished fully justifies the sentence pronounced by the Court. The punishment as mitigated by Genl. Palmer is believed to fall far short of what the prisoner richly deserves to suffer."[25]

The military justice system functioned efficiently for trying infractions of the Articles of War, but it proved to be less effective at dealing with the increased number of civilian crimes that Civil War soldiers committed because the Articles of War did not include a provision for prosecuting common-law felonies in courts-martial. Prior to the Civil War, military commanders dealt with this issue in one of several ways. Soldiers who ran afoul of civilian criminal law were prosecuted occasionally by civilian authorities. More often than not, military authorities considered the infractions a breach of military discipline and prosecuted soldiers in a general court-martial under the "general article," at that time Article of War 99. The general article allowed commanders to prosecute soldiers for conduct unbecoming an officer and a gentleman or conduct prejudicial to good order and military discipline.[26] Commanders who were reluctant to use the general article to prosecute common-law crimes[27] could employ a third option, a military commission.[28]

The use of military commissions dates from February 19, 1847, when General Winfield Scott issued General Order No. 20 from his headquarters in Tampico, Mexico. General Order No. 20 authorized the prosecution of "Mexicans and other civilians" not subject to the U.S. Articles of War as well as U. S. military personnel who committed offenses not mentioned in the Articles of War.[29] The crimes that Scott enumerated in General Order No. 20 were civilian felonies such as rape and murder.[30] On January 1, 1862, Major General Henry Halleck issued General Order No. 1 from his headquarters in the Department of Missouri, authorizing the use of military commissions and mandating that they follow the procedures of general courts-martial.[31] Other commanders followed suit.[32]

U. S. judge advocate J. F. Lee was not so sure of the military commissions' legality, however. In June 1862 Lee noted that a general court-martial had no jurisdiction over a soldier charged with murder "or any capital crime not enumerated in the Articles of War." He observed that in such cases commanders had resorted in the past to military commissions, but those, he said, when employed on U.S. territory, "are tribunals unknown to our laws."[33]

Joseph Holt, who replaced Lee as judge advocate general of the army on September 3, 1862, had no such qualms about using military commissions on domestic soil.[34] He was fully in accord with Lincoln's policy of using commissions to combat disloyal civilian behavior,[35] but he also saw their usefulness for prosecuting military personnel who committed civilian felonies.[36] Yet despite legislative legitimization of military commissions,[37] there was still uncertainty about whether civilian felonies were military crimes.[38] To clarify that issue, Holt sent to Henry Wilson, chairman of the Senate Committee on Military Affairs, a proposed "Act concerning Military Courts" to address "some of the defects in the existing laws governing the military service." Among those proposals was the prototype for what became Section 30 of Senate Bill 511. Holt recommended that civilian felonies such as rape and murder "be punishable by sentence of a General Court Martial when committed by persons who are in the military service of the United States."[39] Surprisingly, Holt did not specify that the offenses could be tried by military commission as well as courts-martial. Wilson attended to that little oversight; the final act contained the provision for trying infractions of civilian felonies by "courts-martial or military commissions, when committed by persons who are in the military service of the United States."[40]

Holt understood Section 30 as turning civilian felonies such as rape and murder into "military crimes." He said "the highest interests of the military service, as well as the public at large, demand prompt and summary punishment of these offenses." That is why Congress transferred "the jurisdiction from the civil to the military courts," he said, and that jurisdiction "is exclusive" to the courts-martial and military commissions. Hence, civilian felonies became "triable by military courts when committed, anywhere in the United States in time of war, insurrection, or rebellion by persons in the military service of the United States, and subject to the articles of war."[41] It was in this context that sexual justice came to women in the occupied South.

Although Section 30 of the Enrollment Act militarized civilian crimes such as rape and attempted rape as a wartime measure, there was still no federal law concerning rape. Thus, courts-martial relied upon the definition of rape in English common law, where it was understood as a heterosexual crime requiring genital contact that resulted in sexual penetration.[42] Blackstone defined rape as "carnal knowledge of a woman forcibly and against her will,"[43] a definition that many states adopted.[44] The charge of attempted rape encompassed a broader array of behaviors that included fondling, kissing, and what were often referred to as "lewd" or "indecent suggestions."

When Congress militarized rape and attempted rape in Senate Bill 511, it also provided that military tribunals be guided by state law regarding rape. Southern state laws concerning rape and attempted rape, however, varied widely in their clarity and precision. In Louisiana, for example, there was no statutory definition either of rape or attempted rape in the 1856 code. The law merely provided the death penalty for those who committed rape. Louisiana's Black Code provided that a slave or free black person who raped a white woman—but presumably not a black woman—would also be subject to the death penalty.[45] Georgia, in contrast, defined rape as "the carnal knowledge of a female, forcibly and against her will," criminalized assault with intent to rape, and defined assault. The penalty for rape was "imprisonment at labor" for two to twenty years, and for an attempted rape, imprisonment for one to five years.[46] Beyond being guided by state rape laws, however, Union courts-martial routinely ignored racial prohibitions embedded in these laws against admitting testimony of black witnesses against white assailants. In a stunning and unprecedented departure from Southern law and custom, they permitted black females and males to bring charges and testify against white defendants.[47] Indeed, court-martial trials provided African American women with a personal agency they had not previously known.

Yet while Union courts-martial provided receptive venues for women to air their charges, female plaintiffs often had to establish their credibility regarding their reputation—as Kirksey did—as well as their age and their ability to testify. Female plaintiffs had to prove that they had neither encouraged nor acquiesced to the assault.[48] The burden of this proof in mid-nineteenth-century sexual assault cases was high. It was not uncommon for courts to require plaintiffs to provide physical evidence—bruises, scratches, torn and bloody clothing—to document that they had resisted with all their might. Almost routinely, poor white women and women of color could expect to have their reputation and integrity questioned: any blemish on a woman's reputation could lead to an acquittal. For example, Martha Hall and her sisters, the daughters of William Hall, a poor white Tennessee farmer who moved his family to Camp Nelson, Kentucky, where the girls worked as laundresses and cooks for the Union Army, were accused of being prostitutes. Defending Captain Samuel Fitch against charges of invading the Hall home and threatening to "fuck some of you before I leave," defense attorney J. B. Houston argued that although he knew the house was not a house of ill fame, it was "undeniable that it had that reputation and was so esteemed by the accused. . . . This is sufficient," Houston concluded, "for this defense." The judge advocate provided his own parade of character witnesses who successfully refuted these accusations against the Hall women. In this case, the court convicted this defendant and his accomplice, Captain Jacob Schuck, and dismissed them from the service.[49] Even girls as young as ten-year-old Alice McDonnagh and twelve-year-old Nancy Short could expect to have their purity called into question when soldiers stood accused of rape or sexual assault.[50] Given this burden, it is surprising that any women came forward at all, and probably most did not.[51] But this did not deter some women, many of whom had little or no education, from bringing complaints before the court. This suggests that, despite the exigencies of war and the high standards of accountability to which women were held, some women expected to receive, at the very least, a hearing of their complaints.

In addition to having their reputation challenged, young plaintiffs might also be required to provide proof of their age because—if the plaintiff was under the age of consent—the defendant could not claim that she acquiesced in the assault. Further, the law provided that these defendants, if convicted, receive the harshest sentences, although these penalties were occasionally mitigated on review. Age of consent varied from state to state, but in the mid-nineteenth-century South it was usually surprisingly low. Louisiana's, Mississippi's, and Kentucky's age of consent, for example, was ten; Virginia's was twelve.[52] This requirement, of course, was more easily met by white girls than by African American girls, whose accurate age was often unknown. Amelia Brown's parents, for example, submitted an 1856 bill of sale for Amelia and her mother as proof of their daughter's youth.[53]

Some historians of the Civil War have observed that rapes were most often perpetrated on poor white women or female slaves, but in fact no woman was safe from wartime sexual predation.[54] The female victims came from all economic and social strata of Southern society. For instance, twenty-four-year-old Margaret Brooks was the wife of an affluent white Tennessee planter when she was accosted in her carriage and raped by three Union soldiers on her way back from Memphis with a wagonload of supplies.[55] Grace Barnes worked as a camp laundress. A free black woman living near Pongo Bridge, Virginia, Barnes was dragged into a wooded area and gang-raped by seven enlisted men as she carried clean laundry to the camp of the Twentieth New York Cavalry.[56] Similarly, the plaintiffs' ages ranged from ten to eighty-two years old. Thirteen-year-old Eliza Woodson, a white teenager, was raped at her aunt's farm in Richmond, Virginia.[57] Ann Booze, a sixty-three-year-old black grandmother, was raped in her Port Hudson, Louisiana, home on April 21, 1865, by Charles Wenz, a white officer of the Fourth Regiment, New York Colored Cavalry.[58] And, of course, rape and sexual assault respected no physical condition. Susan, a twenty-four-year-old slave was raped on a plantation in Salisbury, North Carolina, in her ninth month of pregnancy,[59] while Harriet Smith was sexually assaulted on her deathbed.[60]

These women and others who brought assault charges to Union officials seemingly did so with the expectation that their accusations would be heard. It is not completely clear how occupied women learned about the process for making an accusation to a provost marshal or to a company commander, although it seems that Mary Kirksey's ignorance about this process was an anomaly. When asked by the court why she had waited until Hunter's third visit to lodge a complaint, Kirksey replied that she "did not know Military rules . . . did not know what protection I was entitled to." Not surprisingly, she also testified that she "did not like to tell what had been done." Other women, however, appear to have had a better understanding of the avenue to achieve sexual justice under wartime occupation. Many made an immediate charge, either in person or through a surrogate, to a commanding officer or provost marshal within a day or two of the assault. Kate Bayliss, for example, went to the camp of the Sixteenth U.S. Colored Troops (USCT) on the morning of December 27, 1863, and identified Richard Michelson as the soldier who attempted to rape her at her home the evening before.[61] Laura Ennis, a married woman of color, picked her assailant, Charles Cook, out of a lineup at the headquarters of the Twentieth New York Cavalry, despite Clark's threats to do her bodily harm and his attempts to bribe her with coffee and sugar to prevent her from reporting the assault.[62] Some would-be assaulters got more than they bargained for. After Sarah Beauford, a married free woman of color, foiled Private John Lewis's attempted assault, she followed him back to the camp of the 16th USCT, threatening to report him. Lewis tried to stop her by shooting at her, but Beauford persisted until she tired. She then returned home but reported Lewis to Lieutenant John Scott, commander of Company C, the next day.[63]

In order to satisfy nineteenth-century legal standards of proving resistance to the attack, some woman and girls sought immediate medical attention, which often became the basis of testimony at the trial. Margaret Brooks, for example, was examined by Dr. F. T. Payne on Sunday, March 13, 1863, the morning after she was gang-raped by three white soldiers in a carriage that was stuck in the middle of Nonconnah Creek, just outside Memphis. At trial, Dr. Payne testified that Brooks's "face and eyes were swollen and her eyes suffused with tears. The surface of [her] neck had the appearance of being chapped with slight abrasions under the eye." When asked for his professional opinion as to the cause of her condition, Payne replied that it was due to "physical abuse . . . and rough handling." Shortly after being examined by Dr. Payne, Brooks reported the attack at the headquarters of the Second New Jersey Cavalry at White Station, eight miles from Memphis, and identified her assailants in the office of a detective who was probably a civilian employed by the military. Eight days later, two of the three men were on trial for their lives. All three assailants were eventually executed for the crime.[64] Similarly, ten-year-old America Pearman told her father about a Union soldier who raped her after he lured the youngster into his tent with the promise of jackets for her two older brothers. The next morning, Pearman's father, Henry, a free black, brought his daughter to camp, where she identified Thomas Mitchell as her rapist. Company commander First Lieutenant Henry St. Grenol ordered Pearman examined by the camp doctor, Robert Loughrain, who discovered evidence of the sexual assault as well as proof that Pearman had been a virgin before the attack.

Women who did file a complaint of being raped or sexually assaulted and whose cases were heard entered the alien world of the courtroom. Although some women occasionally appeared in court to settle estates, dispute claims by creditors, or answer misdemeanor and felony accusations, many women lived their entire lives without testifying in a court of law. For Southern women bringing claims against Union soldiers, this search for sexual justice was made even more complex by the fact that the men they faced wore Union blue. The court represented the enemy and the source of their travail. Regardless of their class, the courtroom, for white women, was both alien and familiar in that all the members of the court, although male, were white. For black women, although the men were Union soldiers who might have been considered their "liberators," the members of the court were all white, which left black women attempting to obtain sexual justice across a racial divide, something that was not possible in the antebellum South. Furthermore, blacks were invited to speak candidly, with no dissembling, which is not something they were accustomed to do with whites. In all these cases, it is impossible to touch the emotion that was contained in those courtrooms, as the transcripts rarely make mention of women breaking down on the witness stand or exhibiting anger toward the accused. It is also unclear how they might have been prepared to give their testimony—whether they were coached in any way. Yet in areas where civil law had been suspended, Union courts-martial represented the only avenue for seeking legal redress, including sexual justice.[65]

Most Union soldiers who were accused of sexual assault were privates, although officers who ranged in rank from sergeants to majors also sometimes faced their accusers in a military court. Most privates did not have benefit of legal counsel either because it was too expensive or because they did not know someone in the ranks who could or would defend them. Higher-ranking officers more frequently were represented by defense attorneys who cross-examined witnesses and pleaded the assailant's case. Officers also sometimes used the privilege of their rank to postpone trial dates. Since courts-martial frequently occurred while armies were on the march, these postponements often frustrated the victim's ability to obtain sexual justice because of the difficulty of locating and transporting witnesses to the trial site. More than 80 percent of the accused men were white; most were also young, many between the age of twenty and forty. The marital status of most is unknown.

Contemporary warfare in Rwanda, Bosnia, and the Sudan has pointed to the rape of women and girls as a military tactic aimed at demoralizing the enemy. However, with the exception of Benjamin Butler's infamous 1862 General Order No. 28, which some high-ranking Louisiana politicians interpreted as a direct invitation to rapine,[66] there is no existing evidence that Union commanders ever intended to use rape as an instrument of war or that they encouraged men to sexually assault Southern women as a tactic of war. On the contrary, there is compelling evidence to suggest that these Civil War military rapes that took place in occupied territory were opportunistic crimes that occurred most frequently in the areas surrounding picket lines, where soldiers bored with the tedium of picket duty wandered into nearby neighborhoods and communities to commit crimes, sometimes on lone women whom soldiers had observed going about their daily household chores. More than 70 percent of the rapes that occurred in occupied territory took place within the homes or fields belonging to the victim or her family, sometimes in the presence of family members, including husbands, parents, and children. Women like laundress Grace Barnes who crossed picket lines to bring clean laundry or food into the camps often incurred an increased risk of being attacked. The day after her attack, Barnes was accosted in camp by one of her rapists, James Halon, who taunted her, asking if she wanted to "diddle" again.[67] Marcy Whippey was assaulted by the soldier assigned to protect her when she visited her wounded son at a military hospital near Potomac Creek.[68] Indeed, the government acted officially to curb sexual depredations.

After Congress militarized civilian felonies in March 1863, the Adjutant General's Office in the War Department issued General Order No. 100 in April 1863. General Order No. 100, Francis Lieber's famous "Instructions for the Government of Armies of the United States in the Field," was the product of an effort by Lieber and General Henry Halleck "to produce a set of regulations to make the Union Army a more efficient fighting machine."[69] Regarding women, the code provided that "[a]ll wanton violence committed against persons in the invaded country, all destruction of property not commanded by the authorized officer, all robbery, all pillage or sacking, even after taking a place by main force, all rape, wounding, maiming, or killing of such inhabitants, are prohibited under the penalty of death, or such other severe punishment as may seem adequate for the gravity of the offense."[70]

In the field, however, commanders often gave their troops wide latitude to plunder and pillage Southern larders for poultry, hogs, corn, and other foodstuffs. These plundering expeditions often extended to home invasions that included the destruction of private property and the theft of clothing, money, jewelry, and other household goods. Thus, in the minds of enlisted men, the rape of Southern women may have been construed as one of the other spoils of war to which they were entitled.[71] In at least a few cases, sexual assaults appear to have been politically charged attacks on defiant Confederate women who wore their patriotism as a badge of honor. For example, when Lewis Sorg, Lewis Troest, and Jerry Spades plundered the widow Swindler's house in July 1862, they repeatedly cursed Swindler and called her a "damned secessionist bitch." Ironically, they then turned their anger on Swindler's slave, Polly Walker, in a violent sexual attack. Walker's rape seems to have been precipitated when the men noticed two tiny Confederate flags on a clock above Swindler's mantelpiece.[72]

White and black women and girls who brought sexual assault charges against Union soldiers set in motion a legal process that provides intriguing insights into the ways in which issues of race, class, and age were played out in the proceedings and may have influenced the outcomes. As these courts rendered their verdicts, they sometimes confirmed and occasionally challenged existing stereotypes about black and white sexuality and the appropriateness and reliability of testimony by slaves and free people of color.

Persons of color routinely had their competency to testify challenged. For example, the attorneys representing Private James Lee claimed that Martha Tabor, a mulatto, was incompetent to offer evidence "because she is a free person of color, within the fourth degree," meaning that she "has one sixteenth negro blood. To this extent the Negro race is excluded," they argued. "Such," they said, "is the rule of evidence in North Carolina, and has been for many years before the rebellion of 1861."[73] Typically, the court-martial panel rejected Lee's objection. Indeed, although defendants often challenged their competency, the military courts usually accepted the testimony of African Americans without hesitation.[74] This permitted African American women to define their sexuality on their own terms, rather than have it defined according to white misconceptions of African American females as exceptionally lustful or promiscuous. Thus, many white soldiers, including officers, were tried and found guilty on the testimony of slaves or free people of color, usually in cases involving black victims. For example, Private William Hilton, of the Sixteenth Indiana Infantry, was convicted on the testimony of Felix Jackson and Nancy Simpson, two slaves on the Louisiana plantation where the crime occurred.[75] In March 1865, Dudley O. Bravard, a second lieutenant in Company K of the Fifty-fourth Kentucky Volunteer Infantry, was sentenced to dismissal from military service and five years of hard labor at the Kentucky State Penitentiary for the rape of eleven-year-old Biddy Lewis on the testimony of her parents, Beverly and Sarah Lewis. The Lewises were all people of color living in Greensburg, Kentucky.[76] And in June 1865, Adolph Bork, a private in Company H of the 183rd Ohio Volunteers, was sentenced to be shot with musketry for the rape of Susan, a twenty-four-year-old pregnant woman of color living on a plantation near Salisbury, North Carolina.[77]

Sexual justice trials involved assaults that cut across all racial lines. Yet while it seems evident that military courts strove to render fair and impartial justice, it is also clear that they were seldom able to rise above racial stereotyping that labeled black men as sexual predators and black women and girls as more appropriate sexual prey. An analysis of twenty-six cases from Virginia demonstrates that, although swift, military justice was not necessarily color-blind. Of the twenty-six assailants in the Virginia group, twenty were white and six were African American. Five of the six African American assailants (83 percent) were executed. In comparison, only four white soldiers (20 percent) in the Virginia cohort were executed. All the white and black executed soldiers were found guilty of assaulting white women and girls. Defendants of either race who were convicted of assaulting African American women and girls received lighter sentences, including a reduction in rank, the forfeiture of pay, or prison terms that ranged from two to ten years. In addition, these sentences tended more frequently to be mitigated, which leads to the conclusion that the Union officers who sat on courts-martial viewed the sexual assault of black women and girls as a less serious offense than attacks made on white Southern womanhood. One example from Virginia illustrates this point.

On May 17, 1864, Jenny Green, a young African American contraband in City Point, Virginia, was sexually assaulted by Andrew J. Smith, a white officer in the Eleventh Pennsylvania Cavalry. In the court-martial trial, Green testified that Smith, a twenty-six-year-old former lawyer, dragged her into an empty room, threw her on the floor, threatened to kill her, and then "did the same thing that married people do."[78] Green's testimony was corroborated by William Hunter, the black chaplain of the Fourth USCT, and by Nellie Wyatt, who, like Green, lived in the contraband camp where the two young women cooked and washed for Union troops. Smith was found guilty of rape and conduct unbecoming an officer and a gentleman and was sentenced to dismissal from the service and confinement in a penitentiary for ten years at hard labor. But the court-martial panel that tried Smith's case enclosed a plea for clemency with the trial transcript they forwarded for review. "We the undersigned members of the General Court Martial," they wrote, "taking into consideration the previous good character of the accused[,] his family relation (it appearing outside the record that he has a wife and child dependant upon him for support) and all the circumstances of the case; cannot refrain from the expression of a desire . . . to recommend Lieut Smith to the mercy of the Reviewing Office, and respectfully suggest the term of imprisonment proscribed by the Code of Virginia, as embodied in our sentence, be commuted in whole or in part."[79] Although reviewing officers, the judge advocate general, and the secretary of war opposed clemency, President Lincoln, in an uncharacteristic move, requested that attorney William Johnston review the proceedings. In his report to Lincoln, Johnston redefined Jenny Green's identity from witness Nellie Wyatt's description of her as "nothing at all but a child" to a "young woman [who was] caught abruptly in an act of shame, and pretended to be ravished. . . . Courts Martial," Johnston wrote, "do not sit to try offenses against good morals so much as offenses against our country. At this moment the highest morality is devotion to our country and the deepest curse is treason. Had Lieut. Smith by words or actions given aid and comfort to the enemy, had he lacked zeal or devotion to his duties as an officer and a soldier . . . I should have rejoiced to see him punished. [But based on] . . . the good character of the young man; the valuable services he has rendered, and the vague, contradictory, and unsatisfactory character of the evidence against him; the recommendation of the officers who tried him ought to be followed."[80]

Commanding officers were sometimes aware of this racial injustice. Benjamin Butler, for example, was irate about the request for clemency for Andrew Smith. "But a day or two since," Butler fumed, "a Negro man was hung in the presence of the army for the attempted violation of the person of a white woman. Equal and exact justice would have taken *this* officers life [also], but imprisonment in the penitentiary for a long term of years, his loss of rank and position, if that imprisonment is without hope or possibility of pardon as it should be, would be *almost* an equal example."[81] Despite Butler's strong words, Smith received a presidential pardon for the unexecuted portion of his sentence, which was 9½ years.

The Smith-Green case points to the limitations of military sexual justice and the ways in which the privileges of race and class affected the outcome. In this case, sexual justice was denied. Yet in many other cases it succeeded. Thus, through these trial transcripts women and girls living in occupied territory emerge from the shadows of the past to speak of horrible events committed in a time of war. They deepen our understanding of what it meant to live under the chaos of wartime occupation. Amid the war's chaos, Union courts-martial attempted to mete out some measure of sexual justice to white and black Southern women and girls. Sometimes the courts succeeded; sometimes—as in Jenny Green's case—they did not. What matters most is that they managed to achieve some measure of sexual justice at all.

[II]

OCCUPIED WOMEN AND
THE WAR AT HOME

Gettysburg Out of Bounds

Women and Soldiers in the Embattled Borough, 1863

MARGARET CREIGHTON

Every year new books about the Battle of Gettysburg emerge like a predictable crop. They top the tables at the big bookstores; they crowd the Civil War shelves; they are signed, talked about, reviewed, and revered. Their authors have worked hard and long to find some nuance, some slight new angle, some vestige of evidence that has never before been publicly discussed. But despite the huge numbers of these offerings and all the optimism that this or that book about America's most well-known battle will be different, these volumes are more alike than not. They share the same set of characters—their heroes are the soldiers of two mighty armies. Their timeline is the same too—they set the story in a three-day battle at the beginning of July 1863. And their setting is the same one—their battlefield is centered along extended promontories, Seminary Ridge to the southwest and Cemetery Ridge to the south.

Yet there are new stories to tell about Gettysburg. One that substantially challenges prevailing accounts takes the vantage point of Pennsylvania women. African American women, for instance, understood the Gettysburg campaign as an experience of kidnapping, human hunting, near escape, and flight. Confederate efforts to round up people of color, whether freeborn or formerly enslaved, overshadowed every other dimension of the invasion for these individuals.[1]

White women who lived near the borough, whose involvement is described here, also had a unique understanding of Gettysburg. Their battle had a distinct space and social dynamics. It has not only a wider cast of characters than does the familiar Gettysburg but also a longer chronology and a bigger field of engagement. It took place not only on the hills and rocky slopes that have traditionally defined the battlefield but also in brick houses in the Confederate-occupied town and on farms for miles and miles around. And it featured not only soldiers who came to south central Pennsylvania to strike each other down but also soldiers who sought women's assistance and company. This essay, which is based on the memoirs, diaries, letters, and newspaper reports of forty white civilian women, makes a case for this more inclusive battle. It reveals the energetic involvement of Gettysburg's female residents and demonstrates how readily civilian women used and abused prevailing gender norms as a means of providing military assistance and ensuring self-protection. Local women also employed domesticity as a powerful tool of negotiation, and frailty as a shield for safety, and then dropped those attributes to become unarmed partisans in a world of active warfare.

The story of women at Gettysburg is necessarily a tale of soldiers, too, and female accounts unveil a new sort of Gettysburg soldier. While popular memory places Union and Confederate troops on literal "fields" of battle, in reality some men spent time in domestic settings. As military front merged into home front in Pennsylvania, Union soldiers sought out local residences for protection, and Confederate soldiers looked to women for assistance and company. Both of these sets of men dropped their steely reserve to indulge in social sentimentality. There were, of course, limits to these battlefield relationships. Gettysburg women and the Southern men who occupied their town could drop goodwill and social niceties at a moment's notice. Using unwomanly behavior and ungentlemanly conduct, they became serious and even deadly adversaries.

Women's accounts thus reveal multiple sides to the Gettysburg story, and they challenge the popular and long-standing cultural oppositions of wartime: battlefield and home front, female fearfulness and male courage, and women's sentimentality and soldiers' stoicism. Their narratives also compel us to consider how and why women's perspectives on this momentous event were obscured for such a long time. A review of press accounts of battle reunions shows us that veterans of the battle actually did acknowledge the work of women in 1863, although their public memories edited out the active military work of women (as well as the domestic experience of soldiers). Then, throughout the twentieth century, Gettysburg women largely disappeared. As this essay will argue, this fact points not only to shifting gender ideals in American society as a whole but to America's changing understanding about the conduct of war, as well.

Any understanding of how women participated in Gettysburg rests on an insight into how the military and social dynamics of the battle took shape. The circumstances that brought soldiers and female civilians together in July 1863 reflected both the rigidity of gender codes of wartime and their mutability. When Confederate and Union soldiers converged on a town of twenty-four hundred, they found much of the place inhabited by local women, their children, and their elderly parents. Many resident men had enlisted in the Union Army months or even years earlier and were far away in the South. Remaining husbands and sons had taken family livestock and had moved them north or to nearby hills and woods, away from the marauding enemy. Still others, like post office officials and telegraph operators who feared capture, had also decamped. These men had all left home assuming that "home" was safe.

Military commanders, though, had slightly different notions of wartime divisions. Confederate invaders first merged soldier and civilian worlds when they stormed into town on June 26, 1863, and occupied the borough for a night. The enemy armies converged on Gettysburg on July 1, and, with a viselike grip on the town, began fighting in earnest. Union generals initially posted troops north of town and chose a defensive position south of town, and when Confederate attackers overwhelmed them, the battle moved through residential areas and up onto Cemetery Hill. Union officers, eager to take advantage of good fighting ground, had urged townspeople to relocate when the bullets and shells began to fly, but the shooting soon implicated most of the town.[2]

Confederate infantrymen occupied the borough of Gettysburg for the better part of three days (July 1–3), and Union soldiers held areas on the borough's southern margins. Some residents had batteries in their backyards and witnessed soldiers charge and retreat through their streets, their yards, and even their front halls. Many civilians lived in houses "under fire of both armies," with more than one family coping with Union soldiers at their front porches and Confederate soldiers at their rear. The intersection of soldier and civilian domains shocked people. "Why do you come to town to have a fight? There are some old fields out there," queried one resident. A soldier expressed similar surprise: "It was the first time," he recollected later, "that I had seen warfare carried on in this way."[3]

As Union soldiers fought and fled through the maze of Gettysburg on July 1, they quickly turned to residents for help in hiding them. Breaching civilian boundaries with their guns and horses, they looked to residential spaces for protection from capture. General Alexander Schimmelfennig, the Union Army's most celebrated refugee, hid for almost three days in a woman's woodshed, but other soldiers, too, sought to avoid the enemy by hiding in barns, stables, cellars, attics, and even fireplaces and closets. One woman described the chaos in her house as enemies battled around her and Union troops joined them: "When the rebels came into town," she noted, "they came into our house and took what they wanted, scattering the rest on the floor. The noise was so great in the entry, back-room and kitchen that we were afraid the floor would break down, and to make it worse a number of the gallant 11th Corps came crowding into the cellar & nearly suffocated us."[4]

In the Gettysburg that became both a battleground and a home front, women readily accepted convention and boldly thwarted it. On the one hand they represented access to a safe sphere, and they offered to grant that access. Those men unlucky enough to be captured appealed to women to be the secure conduits of family information. A number of soldiers begged residents to take down addresses and names of "a far away mother or friend." One family looking out of cellar windows spoke to soldiers who had been taken prisoners, who "wished we would write to their home people."[5] On the other hand, women used their protected status as military shields, even bringing their persons into use. Soldiers who had entered houses frequently asked women to safeguard their possessions. They handed over knapsacks and weapons and "various treasures." Women offered these men what they considered the safest hiding places: their bodices and dresses. One resident suggested that she protect the sword of a Union colonel "in the folds of my dress." Another woman was asked by a Union officer to hide his diary from Confederate soldiers, but she did not know at first "where to put it." Then she got an idea. "I opened my dress." The officer was satisfied. "That's the place," he said. "They will not get it there."[6]

Women drew on their supposed untouchability not only to guard private possessions but to enter active fighting. The young woman who hid a sword in her dress stepped between enemy officers with drawn weapons and urged them to cool down. And even as the shield of sex broke down, women persisted. A sixteen-year-old girl was unable to stomach the sight of Union soldiers being shot by Confederate pickets at a Gettysburg intersection. She stationed herself where Union men could see her and shouted out a warning: "Look Out! Pickets below! They'll fire on you!" The men she alarmed made their way through with "flying dashes." And enemy riflemen, realizing her effectiveness, "turned their guns on her." Bullets zinged the door where she stood, but for half an hour she sent out her cries until Union pickets took over her work.[7]

Women and soldiers carried with them in this heated fracas an acute sense of propriety and debated whether it could be breached. On July 1, with the battle in its early fury, a soldier with "straps on his shoulders" came to the Evergreen Cemetery gatehouse, where pregnant Elizabeth Thorn lived with her children and aged parents. He asked Thorn if there was a man available to point out the lay of the land to him. Unwilling to offer up her young children or her elderly father, she volunteered herself. The officer said there must be a man somewhere, for there was "too much danger for a woman." Thorn convinced him that she was not afraid and told him that there was no choice—either she went and exposed herself to artillery fire, or a slip of a boy or an old man would have to go. The officer accepted, and she took on the job.[8]

Female residents of Gettysburg, stepping outside into the battle's whirlwind, readily suspended gender rules to answer soldiers' calls for help or to offer military assistance where they saw fit. They also traversed the battlefield, not only their backyards and streets but the more traditional fields, to secure help for their families and to care for wounded men. Women's accounts are replete with stories of close encounters with shells, descriptions of clothing perforated by bullets, and rebukes by soldiers who were alarmed by their risk taking.

Women also encountered Gettysburg's soldiers closer to home. In this mixed-up affair, soldiers were drawn to domestic spheres as easily as women moved beyond them. Standard Gettysburg battle accounts, of course, feature men locked in fierce armed duels. And they tell the truth: men were predominantly engaged in charging, retreating, firing at each other, or recovering from the same. But that is not all they were doing. Soldiers in the occupied borough and positioned near farmhouses were strongly attracted to women's residences and sought entry and company where they could. There, they dropped their martial personae and tapped deep wells of sentiment and emotion. "Oh, the poor children," cried one officer, as he picked up a four-year-old girl at a farmhouse and kissed her. Another soldier, worried less about how to protect local children than how they might comfort him, sat on a doorstep in town and asked a young girl to come and talk with him. As the girl later recalled, "[H]e then told me he had a little Girl at home, and that on the coming day there would be a great battle fought, and he might never see his little Girl again. He asked me if I would kiss him for her sake, so I said I would go ask my Mother and she said, Yes under the circumstances I could do so, which I did. He then gave me a beautiful silk handkerchief."[9]

Confederate soldiers also sought a measure of social surrogacy. One seventeen-year-old Southerner stopped by a house to ask for milk and then later returned to ask if the woman at the house "would converse with him." As the woman recalled, "[H]e showed me a small picture and said it was his mother and sister, pretty and refined looking people I thought. He said he had been a student at Williams' and Mary's College [sic], leaving to go into the army as many of the young men had done. He never alluded to the cause—nor did I, except to ask him how he felt in battle." A Confederate surgeon came into another yard and, "lifting his hat," asked if he "might sit on the porch and rest a while." A nine-year-old girl was "standing near him and he took her hand and asked mother if he might hold her on his knee. He said she reminded him so much of his sister's little girl." And a mortally injured Confederate drummer boy needed comfort as well. A young woman who lived near one of the Round Tops "was sent for to go out to the barn, because some little drummer boy was dying and crying for his mother." The woman went. It was not the only Southern soldier she held. A cousin reported that she took care of "more than one dying boy . . . as he breathed his last, thinking his own mother was there."[10]

Women at Gettysburg elicited the familial side of soldiers, and they also brought forth men's domestic skills. Union soldiers who were hidden or injured, or who came into women's homes to provide medical care to their fellow soldiers, sometimes made themselves useful parts of the family, if only briefly. Fannie Buehler, a townswoman with Union Eleventh Corps soldiers living in her house, took advantage of their presence. According to Fannie, one of the men, a German, was "of genial disposition, very fatherly in his ways and fond of children." He helped take care of Fannie's two-year-old son. The other soldier, an Irishman, "proved himself to be 'the right man in the right place.' He could, and did make the kitchen fire, brought the coal and wood, kept plenty of water boiling on the stove for any emergency, pared the vegetables, washed the dishes, said funny things, and kept us all in good humor."[11]

Local women were also not shy about asking enemy men to assist them in household tasks. One set of soldiers helped round up family chickens. Another two men agreed to help a woman cut grass for livestock. "The shells were falling all around at the time," said a witness. "Laughing they said yes they would try although they never [had] in their lives. They got the scythe and cut some grass." Harriet Bayly's family took this surrogacy one step further. When a young Confederate deserter begged to be taken in and protected at the farm, he posed as one of the Bayly boys. "Among the first things insisted upon by father when he found that a deserter was concealed in the house," reported Harriet's son William, "was to direct him to come out and take his chances with the family, which he did, passing as one of the boys of the household." The young soldier was put to work with the rest of the family picking cherries, and his disguise was so effective he broke off branches and threw them down to his former comrades as they walked beneath the fruit trees."[12]

Civilians and soldiers found "family" in this domestic battle of Gettysburg, and they found romance as well. It did not take a large leap for Confederate soldiers and occupied white women, however loyal, to consider flirtation. In a house east of the borough, on July 2, two young Southern soldiers knocked on the door for some milk, and they found sociable company as well. They "had fun with the girls," described an older witness, and "asked them if all Pennsylvania girls were so fat and said they were coming back here for wives." In a different occupied house, a young girl bubbled with excitement over the "visit" of "handsome" Confederate officers. Ignoring the battle's sober realities, she could barely contain her enthusiasm: "Our house & yard was filled with wounded that night & Gen. Ewell & staff took tea with us!!" she exuded. "They were all very polite and kind, I sat at the head of the table & gave them their coffee so I had a fine opportunity to see them all. With a few I was completely captivated."[13]

Loyalty did not yield completely to sexual appeal, however. On July 2, a "number of Rebels" entered a Gettysburg yard and found a young girl named Julia at the house. They begged her to sing for them. Julia, being "very patriotic," agreed to do so, but only Union songs, so that the Union soldiers might hear her "and be cheered." The Confederate soldiers returned the favor and entertained her with Southern songs—an enemies' duet. Another Gettysburg girl, nineteen years old, also mixed loyalty with pleasure with an enemy soldier who was "winning in his manners." They got to talking, and she mentioned she and her friends might like to sing some patriotic songs. He, of course, preferred "the Bonny Blue Flag," explaining that it was "a song of the South." The girls said it was unfamiliar, so he tried to teach it to them. But they were refractory, even "very dumb," and for some reason could not learn it.[14]

These encounters point once again to Gettysburg's many-sided battle and to the readiness with which enemy women and men dropped animosity. They suggest as well how some social codes were stronger than others. Even though these girls were willing to flirt with "enemies," they did try to stay true to social class. Girls of some education and property were most entranced by Confederate soldiers, particularly officers, who seemed tutored and well bred—who had "manners." Romance, such as it was, did not easily extend to enlisted men. Confederate troops from Louisiana, who had a national reputation for rowdyism (many were immigrants), were especially suspect. The girl who struggled to learn the "Bonny Blue Flag" was typically prejudiced against the Louisiana troops. As she grew more intimate and bold with her music "tutor," she confessed that, present company obviously excepted, she didn't really like some of the Confederate troops—most particularly the "Louisiana Tigers." Imagine her surprise, then, when "her" soldier opened his shirt to reveal the Tiger's badge.[15]

Union soldiers could also be deemed romantically unappealing. German American soldiers from the Union's Eleventh Corps, some of whom took refuge or assisted the wounded in civilian houses, did not see not much flirting. The very act of hiding, of course, carried an unmanly taint, but it was clear that the men's foreignness dampened romance as well. Julie, the young girl who had engaged enemy soldiers in a singing contest, captivated a German American soldier, known as George. George, who had hidden in Julie's barn, was "in love" with her, reported a member of the family. Everybody found him lovable, too, but silly. In heavily accented English, George allegedly pledged his loyalty: "Now, Yulie, you say Chorge no more drink, and Chorge no more drink." Soldier George was perhaps his own worst enemy. "He would also repeat the saying that was common among the Germans of the Eleventh Corps," said the sister, "I fights mit Sigel, but I runs mit Howard." Other women in town echoed the man's sentiment, commenting on the rapidity of the retreat on July 1. Not everybody had a part to play in Gettysburg's flirtations.[16]

This social battle of Gettysburg, with its "romantic" occupation and surrogate relationships, was also limited to white people. No young African American women dared engage in banter and flirtation. Fearing kidnapping, they had done their best to be out of town or out of sight. This intercourse, and all the ways it relieved the battle's brutality, was exclusive. And this limited détente was a foretaste, in a sense, of the future. Years later, many white Confederate and Union veterans forgot some of the animosity of the Civil War, forgot the contentious and repugnant history of slavery, and forgave each other in what one historian has termed a "Romance of Reunion."[17] In the occupied houses of Gettysburg, the groundwork for sympathetic sexual attraction and mutual respect was already laid out.

Despite all the moments of amity that arose between local women and soldiers, Gettysburg residents knew that the soldiers encamped on their streets and surrounding their farmhouses were heavily armed and had been hardened by months of army life. They watched as houses were looted, repeatedly, and they did not know to what degree occupation might lead to intrusion. White women of means, though, were able to wield domestic power and negotiate for protection. Their access to food in storage and their ability to cook was a medium of exchange, and they used it, readily, to establish a contract of sorts. They traded hot food for forbearance—or at least the expectation of forbearance—from looting or intrusion. Several women also cooked in order to safeguard their valuable horses.[18]

Besides limiting depredation, offering cooked food also earned local women the right to speak freely with enemy soldiers. Over meals, women and soldiers discussed the battle at hand and the war in general. They conferred about the relative positions of the army, the merits of certain fighting units, the likelihood of a next engagement. The soldiers were optimistic about who might prevail— they would, of course; their hosts were similarly confident about who might defeat them. They agreed, cordially, to disagree. When Confederate General Richard S. Ewell visited one house and shared refreshments with the family, the women who served them "very freely gave them our opinion on the war." The visiting enemy officers "were not at all offended but said if our men had half the spirit [we did] they would fight better."[19]

Out on her farm in occupied territory, farmwoman Harriet Bayly doled out bread and soup to Confederates and coolly engaged in controversial talk. "They talked their slavery and their secession notions," recalled Bayly, "and they found out before long that I was an abolitionist; for if they felt no shame in buying and selling and owning human beings why should I be ashamed of not doing it? So I stuck to my colors." A day earlier, when she had been discovered traversing a field of battle, Confederate invaders had briefly taken her prisoner; now, while she did domestic work and served food, her political ardor was as easily swallowed as her soup.[20]

Poorer white women were multiply handicapped in these gendered negotiations. Not only did they lack the abundance of stored meats or barrels of flour that would have helped protect or empower them during the battle, but many of them simply were badly located. A number of immigrant women lived on the relatively poor soil of Cemetery Ridge, right in the heart of combat. If their houses and fields weren't damaged or destroyed by the fighting, they spent much of their energy trying to protect their possessions or taking flight from the shooting. They had little opportunity to barter domestic goods for military courtesy or for a voice in the military action.

To some degree, though, all women who remained in Gettysburg, regardless of their resources, faced a level of hostility from Confederate occupiers. Every courteous encounter or negotiated exchange that took place during the battle of Gettysburg, in fact, was matched by something nastier. As hard as they might try, civilians and the soldiers in their midst frequently could not imagine the bloody battle away. Furthermore, women could be determined partisans, and Southern men often had more on their mind than chivalry and family. Sometimes women and men faced off quite evenly: the fear of military weapons matched fear of domestic weapons.

"I think the people of this place are very kind," one woman overheard a soldier say when he first arrived in town, "considering we came here to kill off their husbands and sons."[21] The problem was that Confederate soldiers targeted more than husbands and sons. They were sometimes quite willing to direct enmity toward local women. Instead of asking favors and working bargains, they walked into houses and used force or the threat of force to make women obey and serve them, or, if not obey, to keep quiet. Many of them demanded domestic work without promising anything in return, and in many households, that is what they got. But angry soldiers also met angry women. Gettysburg's female residents used not only subterfuge to counter the invaders but also twisted codes of chivalry to their advantage. And sometimes they simply refused to comply with the occupiers' demands. Sometimes this worked and sometimes it did not.

Without any pretense of chivalry and without bothering with social bargains, invading soldiers broke into houses with axes, ripped down doors, and carried off anything and everything. Gettysburg civilians found Confederate men in cupboards looting family food and discovered them searching through their bedrooms. They watched them rip away limbs from their fruit trees, saw them butcher their animals, or if they did not see them in action, they found what was left—bloody skins or hooves. They saw them search people, too. A group of enemy soldiers pulled one blind man out of bed, unwound his bandages, and looked him over for money.[22]

Occupying soldiers took what they needed, and to some extent they did what they wanted, out of spite and revenge. More than a year before Sherman's March, Confederate troops already carried with them sour memories of Federal depredations in their home territory. In one house outside town they carried family pictures up to the woods, fed army horses out of dough trays, and mixed flour in bureau drawers. Then they got a jar of black cherries—it looked like blood—poured the mess down the stairs, and poured chaff over that. On the wall they smeared the words, "Done in retaliation for what was done in the South." They took silk dresses out of another house, dragged them through mud, stomped on them, and hung them on a fence. They "tore and broke everything to pieces." In a different establishment, Confederate soldiers worked with flour. They mixed it with water, added feathers from a bed, and threw their destructive concoction over walls and furniture.[23]

Confederate troops vented their anger on people as well as on personal property. They threatened repeatedly to shell the town, and their cockiness lent credence to their threats. Out at Harriet Bayly's farm, on July 2, Robert E. Lee's soldiers radiated confidence when they came asking for bread and apple butter. "I told you so," they said to the family. "Didn't I tell you that we would whip the Yanks." In town, Confederate occupiers were similarly boastful. One woman heard that the Union had the "best position," but "cannot hold it much longer." The rebels, she said, "do so much bragging that we do not know how much to believe."[24] The problem was that no one could really be sure where war's brutality would stop. How did a major victory or defeat affect a man's comportment? Did success mean that a Confederate soldier got uglier or that he became more circumspect? One woman asserted that by July 3 Confederate soldiers surrounding her house were "becoming quite impudent" and feared that if they had gained a victory "we would have suffered very much."[25]

With their weapons and their numbers, Southern soldiers could keep women guessing and on edge. There were some things, like personal physical violence, that they may not have directed at white borough women—General Lee with his ideas about limited war may have helped see to that—but that did not mean that women did not fear physical and sexual assault or that they did not hear about it elsewhere. Just west of Carlisle, Pennsylvania, according to a Lancaster newspaper on July 2, a "Miss Worst" was raped by Confederate soldiers.[26]

Confederate men may not have actively or obviously molested these particular borough women, but their armed presence was enough to force women's accommodation to certain requests. The invaders demanded cooked food, and women complied. Under the stern eye of the enemy, women baked bread, made cake, brought out pies, cooked chickens, and broiled fish. One soldier who appeared at a front door claimed that "General Lee had said that they should ask for food and if they would not give it they should demand it and that was what he was going to do." He was fed some bread and ham. He ate some of it and then insulted the woman who had made the meal. The bread, he complained, was not fit to eat. "Madam," he said, "I can go into any cabin in Virginia, poor and desolate as it is, from Winchester to Richmond, with not a fence standing, and get a better dinner than this."[27]

Confederate soldiers not only tried to make local women cook for them; they also tried to put a lid on occupied female opinion. There had been Southern talk before the Civil War about Northern women who were bold and outspoken and who did not know the bounds of feminine behavior. Southern media had accused Northern abolition movements (and passive Northern men) of producing and allowing the proliferation of vocal "Amazons." When Confederate men came to Gettysburg, they could tap into this conversation in at least two ways. They could defeat Yankees on the battlefield, of course, and unveil the weakness of Northern men that way. But they could also make Yankee women serve and obey and know their proper place.[28]

Confederate soldiers sometimes had no difficulty silencing Gettysburg women. The mother of one twenty-year-old woman was horrified when her daughter seemed unable or unwilling to temper her outspokenness. The occupation of her home had made the girl "very angry." When one enemy soldier asked her if she had "any friends in the Army," she replied, "Yes a Bro. In the Artillery no doubt fighting against you." The enemy soldier responded, "How I would like to capture him." And she let him have it. "It would take braver blood than you have to capture a brother of mine." Her mother was aghast. "Hush," she said, "They might kill you."[29]

But other women refused to hush and entered into a war of words with enemy men. When Confederate soldiers began to take one woman's well water, she went over to the pump and told them, "Boys I would not waste the water, we do not know how long this may last and all of us need it." One of the men looked at her. "If you say much old lady we will take your well up." Another borough resident endured a similar rebuke when she attempted to save a barrel of molasses. "Don't knock that barrel over, it is mine," she told enemy soldiers. That was enough female opinion for them. "You damn old b——," they said to her. "Go to the house." She also ordered Confederate men out of her house and in doing so, said one soldier, "got a little lippy." West of town, a young girl did her best to voice her protest and be patriotic at the same time. When Confederate soldiers began to set her furniture on fire—her house had been used by Union sharpshooters—she leaped out of the cellar and tried to smother the flames. Then she got mad. She told the intruders that her mother, who was no longer living, had been a Southern woman and that she "would blush for her parentage" if these men torched the house. One of the soldiers offered her a deal. If she would attest to her Southern loyalty by "hurrahing for the Southern Confederacy," he would "see what could be done." The girl, though, refused to speak disloyally. She was then told to "get out or . . . burn with it," and, faced with a choice between a house on fire and a field full of shooting soldiers, she chose the field and ran.[30]

As this account makes clear, the Confederate presence could galvanize women's patriotism and anger. And as it also reveals, women tended to fight back at Gettysburg by using gender conventions. This girl alluded to her expectations of Southern chivalry. While the strategy did not work for her, other women had more success taking action against their enemies with gendered assumptions and domestic "weapons." They also drew on traditional notions of women's skills and weakness to get what they wanted and employed the power of their female youthfulness or seniority.

Borough women had used cooking to barter with occupying soldiers, and they also used it as a means of protest. The family that entertained Confederate General Richard Ewell did not bother with delicacies or hospitality; they gave him "plain fare and no welcome." The woman who handed a soldier some tough ham actually *wanted* to give him a second-rate supper. She could have served him a better meal with the chickens she had hidden.[31] Since it was hard for the intruder to distinguish between this woman's cooking skill and her noncompliance, all she had to endure was his insult.

Women who did cook meals for Confederate soldiers may not have been compliant, either. They were trying to mollify enemy anger, certainly, but they may also have been trying to slow down the invading army. When Harriet Bayly and her family chased down their chickens and served them up as soup, they did so not only because they felt they had to but because they hoped to encourage desertion from the Confederate ranks. When they saw the same soldiers appear at consecutive mealtimes, even as fighting was in progress, they had a sense that their strategy worked.[32]

Women used cooking as a powerful means of negotiation and protest, and soldiers were aware that women could carry their culinary ability even further. Confederate soldiers were sometimes nervous about Pennsylvania cooking, knowing what might result from a hostile woman in the kitchen. When some infantrymen entered Pennsylvania, in fact, they heard a rumor, strengthened by the sight of a house burning, that there had been an attempted poisoning. In a separate incident, two Southern men entered a borough house, asked for something to eat, and the owner complied. She brought out a pie that she had made. Putting it down for them, with a knife, she said: "Now you cut it the best way you can." One of the soldiers cut it but hesitated and said: "You eat a piece." She said," Do you think it is poison? The women here don't poison people." They both refused to eat.[33]

In addition to deploying (nontoxic) domestic skills to counter Confederates, Gettysburg women found other "female" ways of protesting enemy occupation. Women and girls both put their presumed defenselessness to good use. Catherine Garlach, who helped hide Union General Schimmelfennig, accosted a Confederate soldier who had pushed into her house and was climbing her stairs. She "caught him by the coat . . . and asked him what he was doing there." He replied that the house would be used for sharpshooters. "You can't go up there," she said, without releasing her grip. "You will draw fire on this house full of defenseless women and children." She prevailed. Confederate soldiers, of course, could call women's bluff. The young woman who harangued enemy soldiers about setting fire to her house and claimed that they were a disgrace to Southern manhood also tried to shame them by referring to herself and her aunt as "defenseless females" who were being thrown out "in the midst of a battle." Soldiers did not appreciate her protestations, or did not believe her, and they brought out the torch.[34]

Women directed simple and authoritative rebuffs at soldiers as frequently as they played to a tenuous chivalry. When enemy men demanded a condiment for their biscuits, one young girl told them, "If you are hungry you can eat them as they are." Another Gettysburg girl, fourteen years old, told a soldier who wanted his canteen filled with water that the well was "within sight" and "he didn't look like a cripple." And an older woman confronted soldiers who demanded that she finish baking bread for them. "There is the stove," she told them, "put it on and bake it." The next day a young man came in and asked her if she would cook some bacon and onions for his officer who was asleep in the barn. She was even more emphatic. "You can cook and there is the stove," she told him; "fry it yourself." He did.[35]

Perhaps their ages relative to young soldiers helped older women dictate to these men and younger girls insult them. Or perhaps all these women were more comfortable issuing commands or refusing orders than people expected. Whatever the reason, women protecting the houses of Gettysburg and advocating for hurt and dying men could be fearsome. One woman shook her fist in the face of a Confederate soldier as he was taking the cow that fed her family. "You can't take this last cow!" she asserted, with success. Confederate soldiers who had ignored Union wounded men on the first day's battlefield finally responded to a local woman who "rose up in [her] wrath" to demand water. And men who rang a doorbell to demand a search of a house met a woman who, "having no fear" and acting "very bold," insisted that she conduct the search herself.[36]

To claim that the women's story of the Battle of Gettysburg was a tale of resistance, protest, and the creative and improvised use of power is to tell the truth. But it is not the entire truth. Women did not choose the time, place, or nature of the violent fighting. They must also be acknowledged, at times, to have been victims of the battle. The shooting death of twenty-year-old resident Jennie Wade underscores this fact better than any other.

When the battle began, Virginia Wade, better known as Jennie, had taken up temporary residence at her sister's home on Baltimore Street, near the southern end of the borough. Her sister, Georgia Wade McClellan, had given birth to a son a week earlier and was still bedridden. Located just within Union lines and prey to Confederate sharpshooters, the house provided little refuge. Even at night, when the firing quieted down, thirsty and hungry soldiers knocked on the front door, and the shouts and cries of wounded men made sleep close to impossible.[37]

Jennie Wade made the best of the battle's chaos. Besides caring for her sister and other family members, she baked for the men who begged for bread, wrapped soldiers' wounds, and, at night, when the crying became too pitiful to bear, she got down on her hands and knees—she did not want to be hit by stray gunfire—and crawled outside to provide men with fresh water.[38]

On the morning of July 3, soldiers continued to take shots at each other in the area around the house. The Wade women did what they could to protect themselves. Thinking that the west side of the house was more dangerous, they moved Georgia's bed around to face the north. It was the wrong move. A spray of bullets from the north hit the side of the house and shattered the windows. One of the bullets hit Georgia's bedpost.[39]

At about eight o'clock in the morning, Jennie began to mix up a new batch of dough. Commenting on the firing outside, she said that she hoped if anyone was killed it would be her and not her sister with the new baby. Half an hour later, a soldier to the north of the house, probably positioned dozens of yards away, took his loaded rifle, hoisted it to his shoulder, and fired. His bullet shot down through the street, flew across the threshold of the McClellan house, and moved through two doors. It had enough velocity, still, to enter Jennie's back and to penetrate her heart. She died, it seems, within seconds.[40]

The inadvertent shooting of Jennie Wade provoked an immediate outcry and launched accusations of blame that went on for years. Such a response suggests the way that conventional war was not utterly overthrown at Gettysburg— nobody expected the death of "innocent" civilians. There were other ways, too, that gendered divisions of war were upheld. There is no record of a Gettysburg woman taking up arms and defending herself or her house. And soldiers, including the man whose bullet killed Jennie Wade, did not take aim at civilians. Furthermore, as we have seen, both women and men drew on convention in order to take advantage of the crisis and to negotiate with or outpower the enemy.

But as Jennie Wade's death also makes clear, and as this essay has argued, the battle did indeed go out of bounds, blurring the much discussed boundaries between home front and battlefield and challenging ideals of wartime behavior. Women, fearful as they may have been, were agents of influence in this battle. They entered the conflict surging around them to counter the enemy, protect their homes and families, and comfort soldiers. They acted with courage and self-possession. Their presence during the battle elicited varying responses from soldiers. Some men looked for sympathy and social warmth and indulged their sentimental sides. Other men squared off with women, face to face.

Gettysburg was not the only Civil War battle that engulfed female civilians. The Battle of Fredericksburg and Vicksburg were two notable occasions on which women were actively implicated in the tumult. Yet the discrepancy that exists at Gettysburg between the narrow battle that has been so publicly celebrated and the wide events that took place may be unique. The purveyors of Gettysburg's memory have consistently acknowledged the death of Jennie Wade, according her the role of female battle victim, but she has stood in for all women at the site. Narratives of the battle have obscured women almost entirely, just as they have rendered soldiers one-dimensional and limited to circumscribed geography.

It was not always thus. The men who actually fought at Gettysburg in 1863, who shared stories of their experiences in memoirs, at monument dedication ceremonies, and at widely publicized reunions, helped generate a vision of the battle as a fight between brave men. At the same time, however, many of them acknowledged women as a salient part of their experiences and sought them out years later to thank them. The veterans tailored their memories to fit contemporary ideas about gender, to be sure, and emphasized women's nurturing work at the battle and their own chivalry, but they also recognized women's courageous and self-possessed efforts.

Some soldiers claimed such powerful feelings about the women they met during the battle that they went to great lengths to locate them after the war. One Confederate soldier in General Henry Heth's Division, for example, published a plea in 1911 to help him locate a woman he saw near the Cashtown Road nearly fifty years earlier. She had been "near our line," he said, when Confederate forces had advanced down the road and were about "to take their places in line of battle." She had children clinging to her skirt. He "often wondered if the woman was safe." Another veteran, cavalryman Merritt Lewis, sought a young girl named Anna Hoke. Lewis, who had been fifteen years old in 1863, had had a double amputation and was sent to the Hoke house to recover. Anna had been a seven-year-old at the time and had visited Lewis and other wounded soldiers every morning with a pail of milk, and then she had played at the piano for hours with "pure, childish tones." Lewis had lost sight of Anna's family after the war but finally succeeded in tracking them to Illinois decades later. The meeting of the grown-up soldier with the grown-up Miss Hoke was described as "joyous."[41]

Many veterans came back to Gettysburg to hunt for these individuals personally. One local woman recalled that ten years after the battle a soldier returned with a compelling memory of a farm he had marched past "where a lady stood by the roadside with two brimming buckets of milk, and her hands full of tin cups. [He had] gotten one of those cups of milk." And now he could say that "in all his life nothing had ever tasted so good." He wanted to thank her. General Oliver Otis Howard likewise claimed he could not forget the sight of a young woman on the first day of the battle as his Union troops were pushing through to the north of town. A young girl seemed to be the only soul in sight, he said, and she stood on her porch waving her handkerchief. "A vision like that," Howard remarked, "had in it a tender, tearful inspiration; but it gave heart and firmness of tread to the marching men." After the war, he claimed he went from one borough house to the next "to get the name of the brave girl who did us such a service." Howard finally found her father living—the man was in his eighties—but the daughter had died years before.[42]

Another girl served as the subject of a national—and nationally recognized— search. Sadie Bushman had been a nine-year-old girl at the time of the battle, had been rescued from crossfire, and had gone on to assist amputations in a field hospital.[43] In 1880, a veteran of the battle wrote a letter to a newspaper editor in St. Louis, Missouri. He described how he had had his "leg shattered" by a shell and how he had been cared for by a young girl. She had done "all she could" for the sick and wounded, he said, and the men, in turn, "loved that innocent little girl." He ended his note with a plea: "Now, boys, see justice done her, the heroine of Gettysburg." But the old soldier never finished or signed the letter, and it remained unread until another man discovered it and published it in a Chicago newspaper. Other papers carried the story.[44]

Sometime after that, a man living near San Francisco read it and realized that he had come to the end of a long search. None other than the surgeon who had put the plucky girl to work as an assistant, he claimed he had also been looking for "the little nurse." And what surprised him most was not the discovery of her name but her present location. She lived in the Bay Area just as he did, and they were "almost within range of each others' voices."[45] The elderly physician arranged a reunion with Sadie and thanked her with a generous gift. When he discovered she was relatively poor and her husband was sick, he provided her with a "cozy" little home on his large estate. "I am happy," he wrote, "to be of service to the little nurse of Gettysburg." She demonstrated during those trying times, he said, "all the qualities of American womanhood."[46]

Veterans seeking to honor the women they remembered from the battle did so most easily at the Pennsylvania site itself, particularly at ritual celebrations in the era of soldiers' reunions, from the 1870s to 1930s. While most of the reunion events focused on soldiers tenting together, banqueting together, speechifying, and reminiscing, women were not infrequently asked to play a part in reunion moments.

Twenty years after the war, for example, soldiers located Josephine Miller and brought her to Pennsylvania for a monument dedication ceremony. They decorated her with badges and spoke of her courage in baking bread for soldiers even as her house was racked by gunfire and then caught in the surge of Pickett's Charge. Miller was recognized with a poem, too, about a "maiden fair" whom "battle terrors failed to scare" and who served the bread as a "sacrament." She was also asked to "cook a special dinner" for General Daniel Sickles at the reunion of the Third Army Corps Association.[47]

At the fiftieth reunion of the battle, women were feted in similar fashion. One journalist described the scene along Cemetery Ridge: Confederate and Union veterans gathered in clusters under trees, and in many of the circles sat a woman, wearing a badge, talking. In one case, white-haired Sarah Weikert, who was seventy-one years old, sat on a stone wall and reminisced with Pickett's men about how she had baked bread for soldiers nonstop at her house at the foot of Little Round Top. Just as she finished recalling her battle days, a veteran took Weikert's hand. "I remember that bread very well," the veteran said, "and the women of this town were just as heroic as any man who ever led a charge across this valley or stormed this ridge."[48]

Of all the women who inspired tender recollections at Gettysburg and who were called on for an "appearance," none elicited more nostalgia than the young women of the borough who had greeted Union cavalry troopers the day before the battle began. At a regimental reunion in 1891, a captain of the Eighth Illinois Cavalry related in nearly rhapsodic terms how some of these women had appeared. "I remember a balcony where stood a bevy of young ladies dressed in white, waving their handkerchiefs," he said, "and I verily believe that the effect upon our troopers would not have been intensified had they been veritable angles [sic] waving their white wings and beckoning them on." The sight, he added, "awoke every feeling of chivalry in our souls. It recalled to memory all the dear and loving ones we had left at home. It brought back with overwhelming force that love of country which had first impelled us to enlist. It inspired [us] to heroic deeds."[49]

The force of this particular inspiration was so powerful that these women were called for repeatedly at veterans' reunions and asked to sing again and again. At the fortieth anniversary of the battle, the "Singing Girls"—who were now solid old women—moistened eyes with their renditions of "Just before the Battle Mother," "When This Cruel War Is Over," and the "Battle Cry of Freedom."[50] At the fiftieth reunion the "girls" were called on again. Gray haired, with "tears in their eyes" and in "quavering tones," they sang the wartime melodies. "I'm afraid we can't sing like we sang fifty years ago," apologized one of them. It doesn't matter, the veterans said, and everybody cried.[51]

The girls and women whom soldiers honored tended to be those residents who had done domestic caretaking during the battle: they had made bread, passed out refreshments, dressed wounds, soothed and comforted. They were also women who, dressed in white, had inspired troops, or they were mothers or young girls who had asked for help and elicited men's protective feelings. The women who had assisted or harbored soldiers during active fighting or who had bargained with them or challenged their authority slipped more easily from memory. Although Alexander Schimmelfennig's relatives came to visit the woman who had helped shelter the Union general, and even took pictures of his hiding place, other Eleventh Corps officers chose not to recognize the site, associated as it was with "unsoldierly" behavior. And General Oliver Otis Howard, commander of that corps, had an especially well-edited memory. For years Howard was reminded by civilians in the borough that Elizabeth Thorn had showed his officers Gettysburg's layout—under fire no less—and that she had served him and other generals a meal. He would eventually acknowledge the meal—even claiming it as one of the best he had ever tasted—but he never publicly recognized Thorn's work during the active battle. Most soldiers had memories like Howard's—they honored women who cared for them and who underscored their own protective fortitude.[52]

Soldiers also obscured their own sentimental histories. Regimental histories and memoirs stressed combative prowess, not emotive social moments in residential settings. Echoing a cultural trend toward a hard, martial, stoic masculinity, they culled domestic experience from their memories. And popular culture, including literature, history, and memorialization, did the same. By the early decades of the twentieth century, most veterans had passed away, and with them went concrete memories of women at Gettysburg. Even bread bakers, inspirational women, singing women, and nurses disappeared. Historic Gettysburg itself became an eerie place. Visitors to the National Military Park could tell a battle had happened in and around the borough—the houses had plenty of bullet holes marked—but, with the exception of Jennie Wade, the residents themselves seemed to have been strangely absent.[53] The houses where women had assisted soldiers, the streets they had crossed, the sites where they had protested and resisted invading men never became part of the federally authorized park. The scope of the battle, as it was publicly known, was limited to hillsides and fields and its length relegated to three days, not to the long months during which local women labored to help save injured men.

There are many reasons why women and the unruly battle that their presence implies were eclipsed from popular memory at Gettysburg. A battle that went beyond its "field" and that was inconsistent with the ideals of gendered spheres of wartime was jarring to nineteenth-century sensibilities. Even as those spheres were regularly contested and those boundaries were crossed, they were talked about as real. And in the twentieth century, changes in prevailing notions of masculinity helped strengthen the notion of Gettysburg as a female-free zone. In the era of sectional reunion, when moral differences between the Union and Confederacy were deemphasized, Gettysburg became revered less as a site that dealt a body blow to slavery than as a supreme test of manhood—north and south. Those who fought in Pennsylvania were seen as furthering a new masculinity: brave, battle hardened, unsentimental, and protective of, but distant from, home and family. As Gettysburg gained national attention with its growing battlefield park and repeated visits from American presidents, it became seen as an event that not only advanced manhood but defined it. Gettysburg soldiers told Americans what men—as opposed to women—should truly be.[54] It is hardly surprising, then, that battle accounts that blurred battle and home fronts, that highlighted women's presence, fortitude, and agency, and that revealed soldiers' "softer" sides were cast from the historical record.

And there are other reasons why women and the domestic battle of Gettysburg might have been eclipsed. Women were civilians. Throughout the twentieth century, the American way of warfare has been to focus on what it held were moral ends as much as practical means. Civilians have increasingly been caught in war's crossfire or, depending on the conflict, targeted as a path to a faster or more decided victory. At the same time, their involvement and their expanded casualty rates were and are edited out of the picture—revealing ongoing beliefs in or wishes for chivalric warfare.[55]

The depiction of Gettysburg over time certainly reflects prevailing ideas about limited warfare. These ideas are so deeply entrenched, in fact, that even when Gettysburg has been viewed as a "just" battle, serving the cause of emancipation, women's partisan efforts and their energetic commitment to a Union victory have been unacknowledged. In the twenty-first century, the story of Gettysburg may change. With more women fighting in the American armed forces, and with embattled home fronts made more visible thanks to a democratic and global media, we may see civilian involvement recognized and discussed, not only in the present but in the past as well.

"She-Rebels" on the Supply Line

Gender Conventions in Civil War Kentucky

KRISTEN L. STREATER

In June 1864, in the midst of defending against Confederate General John Hunt Morgan's raid into Kentucky, Union Lieutenant T. J. Hardin received the following orders from authorities in Lexington: "Fifty men will reach you [in Midway, Kentucky] in an hour. . . . Send them after she rebels."[1] By this time, Union military commanders fully appreciated Confederate women's importance in sustaining the Confederate war effort in Kentucky with physical and emotional support. When the war began, women on both sides demonstrated their political loyalties by providing domestic supplies to their men. As the Union gained military control over the state, clashes arose between Confederate women's domestic duty to continue to support their men and the Union's need to eradicate the rebellion in all quarters of the state. By 1863, when guerrilla forces became the principal threat in Kentucky, Confederate women's significance in the war made gender conventions a central tenet of the Union's civilian policies.

During the Civil War, the relationship between women's domestic duties and the public realm of politics and war increased in importance. Both the Union and the Confederacy considered their women "indispensable as allies."[2] Women's value in the war in providing men, supplies, and emotional support for their cause spoke to the connection between the home and society at large. Wartime home-front activity was intimately connected to public affairs. Throughout the Civil War female patriotism was expressed through the expansion of traditional domestic boundaries for the larger war effort.[3] Women's wartime activities were done in the name of service to their men on the front lines, and women understood themselves as "supporters and helpmeets of men."[4]

Nonetheless, the war politicized these traditional domestic actions, especially as they crossed into the realm of public patriotism.[5] From sewing uniforms to preparing food, women provisioned their men and their country. Indeed, the military depended upon this domestic supply line; without women's contributions, the war for either side would have ground to a halt. In the border states like Kentucky, as guerrilla warfare took over military operations, the Confederacy relied more heavily on women's domestic contributions for support. Confederate victory required all its citizens to participate, and Kentucky women's domestic patriotism shaped the war in the state. By transferring their traditional private acts to the public domain of war support, women became active political participants in the national struggle.[6] As the home front increasingly served as the battlefield, the distinction between the political and the domestic blurred. The war magnified the importance of the home and its occupants, politicizing the domestic sphere to the point that both sides believed that it could influence the outcome of the conflict.[7]

Confederate women realized that even if they were not engaged in overtly political acts of fighting or voting, their continuation of traditional duties, done now for a nation rather than for one family, contributed to the political cause. In Kentucky, Confederate women consciously politicized their traditional duty of providing men's basic needs into a patriotic support for their country. Women's benevolent spirit, coupled with their desire to fulfill their wartime roles, produced a domestic outlet for their political sentiments.[8] In 1863, Amelia Bourne of Somerset, Kentucky, noted, "I've been knitting *hard all* day—hope I'll finish my *rebel* socks this week."[9] Her description is revealing. By connecting the knitting with the Confederate cause, Bourne demonstrated Confederate women's own domestic rebellion. The way a woman could be a "rebel" was to sew socks in support of Confederate men's political cause. Confederate women understood such provisioning as part of their patriotic and traditional duties. These women were extending their domestic duties into the public realm to create a type of "public household."[10] A woman's responsibility was to attend to her husband's and son's needs. With her own men at the front, a Confederate woman continued her supportive role with the Confederate men she did encounter.

Since women were unable to resist the Union invaders on the battlefield, their defiance of Union authority on the home front "offered the satisfaction of direct participation in attacks on enemy troops."[11] One woman manipulated gender conventions to boldly defy Union authority. The Union arrested Mrs. Cobb (referenced by one historian as "Old Lady Cobb") for repeatedly thwarting Union efforts in Lawrenceburg, west of Lexington. Even while in a Louisville prison, she continued to frustrate her Union captors. While guarded by a soldier, "clad in the repulsive blue Yankee uniform, . . . Mrs. Cobb sat patiently by, knitting long gray woolen socks for the Confederacy. She was bringing the gentlest of domestic endeavors into sharp conflict with the stern military discipline."[12] Cobb consciously confronted the enemy by blurring gender limits and using her domesticity as a political protest. Instead of being submissive in the face of Union authorities, she politicized the patriotic outlet available to her, defied Union military authority, and further extended her domesticity to serve the Confederacy's supply needs. Despite her efforts, ultimately the Union prevailed; she appears to have been confined for the duration of the war, only to be "released from arrest upon subscribing to the Oath of Allegiance to the U.S. Government."[13]

Confederate women's politicization of their domesticity conflicted with the Union authorities' needs and ambitions within the border state. Knowing that Kentucky's population was divided over the war and wanting to avoid exacerbating tensions, military leaders formulated an early policy toward civilians that was cautious in tone. Orders ranged from Brigadier General John Anderson's 1861 command "that no one will be arrested for mere opinion's sake" to General George B. McClellan's later clarification that "it is the desire of the Government to avoid unnecessary irritation by causeless arrests and persecution of individuals. Where there is good reason to believe that persons are actually giving aid, comfort or information to the enemy it is of course necessary to arrest them."[14] It was their roles as provisioners and comforters that brought Confederate women into conflict with the Union in Kentucky.

Confederate women's behavior in their own homes reflected their politicized gender roles. While they willingly extended domestic care to their own men, their enthusiasm waned when the Union armies made similar demands on them. When the enemy's expectations came to Confederate women's doorsteps, the domestic borders constricted. Women's domesticity was politically dependent, and Josephine Covington's experience vividly demonstrated how women's political devotions shaped their reactions to the Union's supply needs. As a loyal Confederate, Covington was "delighted with all the [Southern] officers & soldiers that we came in contact with," and her family was willing to assist those men in any way they could. In 1862, her family warmly received both Generals William J. Hardee and P. G. T. Beauregard during their stay in Bowling Green, and in one report she noted, "A whole regiment camped on our farm (cavalry too) stretched their tents against the fences, & all the damage done was to burn the wood. I do not think we lost a dozen rails."[15] However, Covington's demeanor changed once Union troops occupied the city later that year. According to her account, one group of soldiers stormed through their home, where "they began to open the safes & cupboards & carried off everything eatable." Such behavior continued throughout the city as Union soldiers "went from garret to cellar, . . . insulting persons in them, particularly those of southern proclivities in the lowest manner . . . they broke into the houses stealing every thing that they could possibly use, even taking womens & childrens clothes to send to their own families as they said."[16] For Covington and other Confederate supporters, the supplies the Confederates took were perceived as gifts served to honored guests, while the taking of similar goods by Union soldiers was viewed as theft.

Not wanting to infringe upon loyal supporters' means, the Union Army in Kentucky turned instead to Confederate households. Confederate women's reaction to Union soldiers' invasion reflected their constructions of military honor and its relationship to domestic parameters. The expectations existed that "[c]hivalric warfare proscribed attacks on civilians and their private property."[17] However, the demands of war necessitated that armies enter and occupy private homes; soldiers needed food and supplies, and officers needed local headquarters near the battlefields. For instance, in 1862, in the battle to control the strategic Louisville and Nashville rail line at Munfordville, Kentucky, orders were issued to "[p]ress homes from the rebel citizens in the different counties in your district" to supply two Kentucky regiments. "Let the pressing be done by the Commissioned Officers and the receipts show that the parties are disloyal."[18] Not only would the army get its needs fulfilled, but it would also punish Confederate sympathizers for their misplaced devotions. Thwarting the enemy's domestic support system was a military and political necessity. In another letter, a U.S. military surgeon explained that he was in need of a home to care for the increasing number of smallpox cases developing in Lexington. He noted, "There is a house on the Richmond pike three miles from the city owned by the wife of the Rebel General Preston which is very well addapted [sic] for that purpose. Col. King will seize the house if authorized."[19] In a subsequent order to Lieutenant Colonel William Fairleigh, Brigadier General J. Bates Dickson stated, "You are authorized to take possession of any buildings belonging to disloyal persons actually needed for Hospital purposes."[20]

While Confederate women in the state may have expected to be immune from military invasion—the home was to be separate from the battlefield, not made a part of it—by their supplying the Confederacy's domestic needs, they had violated that immunity and blurred any public-private separation that may have remained. If, as Mary Scott discovered in Frankfort, "defenseless women and little children [were] turned out of their homes—their homes desolated, property routinely destroyed,"[21] or their homes converted into Union hospitals— Union authorities made Kentucky Confederate women suffer for their political choices. The war altered the sacredness of the home, politicized its members, and changed gender expectations. When a Union soldier invaded Confederate women's homes for supplies, he perceived it as part of his military duty. In their efforts to defend Kentucky against the rebellion, the military rationalized "the use of force, even deadly force, against all enemies, regardless of sex, age, or status, and patriotic duty justified this use of force."[22]

The community of women the soldier interacted with, however, failed to see any honor in or rationale for his behavior but rather a violation of traditional gender expectations and borders.[23] This change shocked women; "the vandalism of their homes showed how war had become even more undiscriminating and brutal, even invading the recesses of private life."[24] Despite orders to the contrary, Union soldiers destroyed clothes and household items and took wood, livestock, and other supplies without payment.[25] Any protest would have been futile. "They will take no denial, sickness nor any other escuse [sic]," Ellen Wallace wrote. "They go to the kitchen if denied to see for themselves."[26] The war removed domestic immunity. Both sides politicized women's supportive roles in the home. Definition as the enemy necessitated a transgression of the domestic sphere because women had made the domestic realm politically significant. Because Kentucky's loyalties were divided into those who supplied the Union and those who supplied the Confederacy, the war politicized women's activities as domestic supporters. As Confederate women blurred the borderlines between the domestic and the political, they made themselves susceptible to attack from their Union enemies. The importance of home-front support had always been clear to women themselves, but as the Union military fought for control of the state, Confederate women's actions assumed more significance. When Kentucky Confederate women actively crossed into the public war domain to demonstrate their loyalty, many would confront new political consequences for this behavior.

With the state under Union military control by 1862, Union authorities paid more attention to Confederate women who continued to supply their men. One Union soldier who was escorting a group of rebel prisoners through Kentucky remarked that the "secesh" women "tried to get to talk to the prisoners and brought them things to eat and flowers &c giving a good deal of trouble."[27] To restore order to the state and nation, the Union had "no room for disorderly women,"[28] and by the summer of 1862, a series of orders were issued in an attempt to restrict interaction between rebel sympathizing women and Confederate military prisoners. One captain in Louisville asked Lieutenant Colonel Henry Dent, who was the provost marshal, "Has it always been customary for secessionists to send victuals to the prisoners? I understand it is being done today. Has Gen. [Jeremiah T.] Boyle given permission for provisions to be thus furnished rebels? If he has not given such permission, you will by his order, please put a stop to it. Part of the punishment is the restriction to prison fare."[29] Dent replied, "By order of Genl Boyle you will restrict the prisoners to prison fare."[30] Further explanation of the order stated: "No victuals or delicacies will be permitted to be furnished Military Prisoners by secession sympathizers and all such prisoners will be entirely restricted to prison fare. Requests and civilian favors will be strictly excluded. Newspapers and all publications and letters referring to current political matters will be strictly kept from the prisoners. Any one attempting to convey to any prisoner clandestinely or openly any of the articles herein proscribed will be unconditionally arrested and lodged in the Military Prison."[31] By 1863, General Boyle was further limiting prison visits. In an order to the Louisville provost marshal, he remarked, "[Y]ou will refrain from issueing [sic] papers to persons wishing to visit Political Prisoners confined in the Military Prison in this city and all papers previously issued will be immediately revoked."[32] By preventing Confederate women in the state from extending domestic comforts (food and emotional support) to their men, Boyle made efforts to destroy the enemy's gender conventions and made gender a point of attack. By removing Confederate women's ability to feed their men's bodies and spirits and encourage their men to continue the fight, Boyle imposed consequences on women's political wartime roles.

The tension between Confederate women's domestic need to supply their men and the Union's efforts to suppress such supply served as the foundation for Union reaction to the rebellion in Kentucky. In Union-held Kentucky, aiding the enemy, through supply or information or other domestic comfort, counted as treason. Once the Union military had removed the organized Confederate threat to control the state by 1862, it turned to face the guerrilla-style raids primarily made by Confederate General John Hunt Morgan from the summer of 1862 to 1864.[33] Since guerrillas relied more heavily on civilian support, the Union's need to suppress Confederate home-front support increased. Consequently, Union military policy regarding the civilian population in Kentucky conveyed a gendered tone. On April 13, 1863, Major General Ambrose Burnside issued General Order No. 38 for the Department of the Ohio. The order stated that "hereafter all persons found within our lines who commit acts for the benefit of the enemies of our country will be tried as spies or traitors. . . . This order includes . . . writers of letters sent by secret mails; . . . and, in fact, all persons found improperly within our lines who could give private information to the enemy, and all persons within our lines who harbor, protect, conceal, feed, clothe, or in any way aid the enemies of our country."[34] While this order did not specifically mention women, these activities were consistent with Confederate women's wartime supply duties. Subsequent reports reflected a growing awareness of a specific female threat. An 1864 report on the activities of a "rebel order" noted: "A considerable number of women in that State [Kentucky], many of them of high position in rebel society, and some of them outwardly professing to be loyal, were discovered to have been actively engaged in receiving and forwarding mails. . . . Two of the most notorious and successful of these, Miss Woods and Miss Cassel, have been apprehended and imprisoned. By means of this correspondence with the enemy the members of the order were promptly apprised of all raids to be made by the forces of the former, and were able to hold themselves prepared to render aid and comfort to the raider."[35]

The Union's ability to counter Confederate guerrilla attacks was compromised if sympathizing women helped facilitate the rebellion. Because of the increasingly public nature of Confederate women's actions, Union authorities took them to be more threatening.[36] Believing that women had great influence over the Confederate will and ability to resist, Union authorities knew that failure to suppress women's political actions would only perpetuate the rebellion. They needed to eliminate the Confederacy's domestic supply line to end the rebellion in the state. Such resistance represented "not merely a tiny breach in a symbolic wall"; unless the Union prevented Confederate success everywhere, "rebellion in one quarter might encourage rebellion in others."[37] In the minds of the governing wartime authorities, rebellious domesticity carried as much political weight as did taking up arms in sustaining the Confederacy. No longer were traitors defined as men who fought against the government; the official definition now included women. Indeed, if a traitor is one who "seeks to undermine the citizenry," the Union authorities in Kentucky branded Confederate women who supported the rebellion as such.[38]

Union authorities grew more aggressive in response to public and private expressions of disloyalty. Concern turned not only to physical supplies but also to emotional support given by women. Despite the increasing possibility of arrest as Union control tightened, Confederate women continued their domestic defiance. Union authorities began targeting women who supported John Hunt Morgan. The Confederate cavalry general, who was raised in Kentucky, made frequent raids throughout the state during the war and proved elusive to Union capture, much to the pleasure of his Confederate sympathizers. Lizzie Hardin dismissed all warnings about Morgan supporters' arrests in Harrodsburg, but the rumors proved well founded.[39] Union authorities arrested Lizzie, her sister, and her mother for waving their handkerchiefs at Morgan and his men as they rode through Harrodsburg in the summer of 1862.[40] While in prison in Louisville, Hardin reasoned that she had done nothing wrong; if Union women could salute their troops, Confederate sympathizers should have the same privilege.[41] Union authorities felt otherwise; support like the Hardins' would only encourage Confederate war efforts generally and perpetuate the hero worship of Morgan and his tactics.[42] The Hardins faced three options: they could take the loyalty oath to the Union and return home, be jailed, or be exiled to Confederate lines. Hardin's Aunt Lucinda plead with Brigadier General Jeremiah T. Boyle, military commander of Kentucky in 1862, to release the Hardins into her custody. She contended, "[T]he slightest verbal promise not to interfere with 'the government' would be as binding as an oath." When Boyle responded, "The women think they will rule Kentucky but I will show them they can't do it while I am military governor," he depicted the war as one in which women's actions were significant.[43] In their attempt to lend emotional support to the rebellion, Confederate women in Kentucky were manipulating gender expectations for political ends. Union authorities had to eliminate these gender conventions among the enemy to be successful in the war. If exposing Confederate women to the harsh realities of political consequences for their actions facilitated the war's end, then the arrests like those of the Hardins were warranted. As for the Hardin menace, Boyle sent Lizzie, her mother, and her sister into exile from Kentucky, and they spent the remainder of the war as refugees roaming throughout the Deep South.[44]

Guarding against the effects of Morgan supporters continued through 1863, as the guerrilla again raided Kentucky and invaded Indiana and Ohio.[45] Union Lieutenant Colonel Styles reported "two women soliciting subscriptions for the benefit of John Hunt Morgan gang one of them boasting of 'our late success.'" The provost marshal instructed Styles "to notify the women referred that no such demonstrations will be tolerated in this war[.] Persons with near relatives in military prison will be allowed to furnish them such articles as the comd'g officer under instructions from the comdg gen'l of prisons will receive. [N]othing beyond this will be allowed."[46] Any public protest against the Union was not tolerated. Arrests of sympathizers sometimes took place at seemingly innocuous events. At a Louisville concert in 1863, when the manager announced the playing of "national airs" and warned that "all those who were too much opposed to the Government to listen to them had now an opportunity to leave," several Confederate women "flirted out of the room, but at the door were met by the Provost-Guard who marched them off to jail."[47]

Not only were these women to be condemned for their political statements, but the manner in which they made them was unacceptable. The description of them "flirting out of the room" connoted the women's public use of their bodies as part of their defiance. This violated the image of women as pure and innocent, further justifying their detention as a way to condemn the lack of public morality associated with Confederate women and their support of the rebellion. Unionist newspapers frequently editorialized on the immorality of "she-rebel" behavior. In one instance, an editor of a pro-Union newspaper related the example of Mrs. I. C. Johnson of Mt. Sterling, Kentucky. In 1864, a Union squad came to Johnson's home in search of her husband, who was a member of John Hunt Morgan's cavalry. She denied her husband's, or any other man's, presence but allowed a search of the premises. As she was ill, Johnson returned to her bed, but her condition did not make her immune from a search. The incriminating evidence emerged when a lieutenant "hauled out from under the lower extremities of the woman, a burly rebel [not her husband either; *he* was not to be found], who was lying so as to be as much concealed as possible under the woman, his head in immediate contact with the lower part of her body." Such an intimate hiding place might have been acceptable had the fugitive been her husband; however, the admiration for the power of the woman's self-sacrifice failed in the face of the compromising situation. Women's loyalty to the Confederacy encouraged them to manipulate their gender in unacceptable ways for political ends. These actions branded women as traitors who had to suffer the consequences, whether social shame or political arrest, for their devotions.[48]

The Confederate outrage over the application of Union policy abounded. In 1863, a minister from Logan County, Kentucky, noted, "Heard today that Miss Almeda Mason had been sentenced & sent off to the military prison on Johnson's I[sland] to be confined during the war—for the crime of yielding to the dictates of common humanity & writing a letter to her brother in the rebel army! Genl Burnsides [sic] infamous order 38 can be enforced against helpless women in Ky!"[49] Confederate supporters used such professions of disbelief to try to win further sympathy for their cause. By manipulating the gender convention that "before she was an enemy, she was a woman, and more than that, a lady,"[50] Confederate women believed they could use gender as a protective shield to both comply with their duty to aid their men and cry foul against the enemy's treatment of "helpless" women. In Confederate minds, the women in the theater simply were giving voice to their emotions; certainly Mrs. Johnson didn't expect her boudoir to be the subject of military inspection.[51] However, as Union authority and presence grew in the state, power relations and expectations changed.

As Confederate women's expressions of sympathy continued, Union officials had to decide what to do with the women they confined. One option was to send offending female prisoners beyond the state borders, eliminating the domestic threat they posed. Any association women had with men in the Confederate military, especially in guerrilla units, could mean arrest or exile from the state. In May 1863, Special Order 111 issued from Louisville Headquarters stated:

> In compliance with [orders] from Head Qrs Department of the Ohio, the following named persons whose husbands are engaged in rebellion against the U.S. Government, will be conveyed beyond the Federal lines South of Nashville, Tenn:
> Mrs. Byrne and children, wife of Capt. Byrne, C.S.A.
> Mrs. Hawkins and children, wife of Col. Hawkins, C.S.A.
> Mrs. Burnett and children, wife of Sen. Burnett, Confed. Cong.
> Mrs. Jack Allen and children, wife of Jack Allen, C.S.A.
> . . . They will not return within the Federal Lines during the present war, under penalty of being considered and treated as spies.[52]

Even if these women professed to be loyal themselves, Union authorities could not take the risk of having high-ranking Confederate relations living in the state. As the wives of officers and politicians, these women were public figures in the community who would use their spouses' positions to foster additional support for the enemy.[53] Further portions of the order declared that "Mr. Curd and wife, engaged in contraband trade with rebels in arms against the Government of the U.S. and in aiding and abetting the rebellion, will be conveyed beyond the Federal lines, South of Nashville Tenn. under penalty of being arrested and tried as spies, if found within the Federal lines during the present rebellion."[54] While Mrs. Curd's role in the illegal trade is not clear, her support for the Confederacy was enough to earn her the same punishment as her husband. Any activities and associations Kentucky women had with the enemy, even if the enemy included their own husbands, brought the full force of Union authority upon them.

As the number of women arrested for their Confederate sympathies increased, Union authorities took an even more politicized stance by holding female captives in military prisons. As early as August 1, 1862, Lieutenant Colonel Henry Dent wrote to Brigadier General Jeremiah T. Boyle, "There was delivered to me last evening a female prisoner named Mary Hoffman. . . . Having no place suitable for her I respectfully request instructions."[55] Eventually, the volume of women detainees forced the Union authorities to establish a Female Military Prison in Louisville. The charges against women detained in the prison typically related to "harboring guerrillas," "aiding the enemy," or "smuggling,"[56] and prison records repeatedly reveal women being arrested for their assistance with the Confederate supply line in some form. According to prison rosters, Captain Hawes arrested Miss Lizzie Wood of Fayette County, Kentucky, for "aiding the enemy." She was confined in Lexington for two months before being sent to Louisville, where the provost marshal released her "to remain at her home during good behaviors."[57] In Louisville, where the Union military presence resided in full force, an extensive Confederate female network seemed to exist to support the rebellion. In sworn testimony that led to the arrests of Confederate sympathizers, John C. Gorin testified that he went to the Louisville home of Miss Hutchinson and "stated to her that I was an escaped Gurilla [sic]. I asked her for assistance and she gave me five dollars—she then referred me to other rebel citizens for help. Capt. Shelton of my Regt made his escape and told me that he stopped at Miss Hutchinsons and she gave him clothes and money, that is the reason why I went to her house for assistance."[58] Gorin also testified that he was "referred to Mrs. Wilson for help as an escaped rebel Prisoner. . . . She gave me 2 Pr. Drawers, 3 Shirts One Pr Pants and one Hat [?] and gave me a note to Mr. Charley Miller for money."[59] Union officials also discovered that an organized group of rebels had been involved in "[f]urnishing the rebels with arms, ammunition, &c. In this, too, the order, and especially its female members and allies, has been sedulously engaged. The rebel women of Louisville and Kentucky are represented as having rendered the most valuable aid to the Southern Army by transporting large quantities of percussion caps, powder, &c., concealed upon their persons, to some convenient locality near the lines, whence they could be readily conveyed to those for whom they were intended. It is estimated that at Louisville, up to May 1 last, the sum of $17,000 had been invested by the order in ammunition and arms, to be forwarded, principally in this manner, to the rebels."[60] Clearly, these women had the resources and connections to make such a supply system thrive. Confederate soldiers, whether in the field or as escaped prisoners, were increasingly dependent on their female supporters to provide them with food, clothing, money, and weapons. Even in the shadow of Union headquarters, Kentucky Confederate women eagerly used these gender conventions to further the cause.

To quell the rebellion and restore domestic order in Kentucky, Union authorities imposed policies that responded to Confederate women's politicized gender conventions. Martha Jones reported in her diary that General Boyle "intensified the campaign against dissenters, arresting innumerable persons for their opinions and presumed sympathies with the rebellion." In this quest, Boyle gave specific consideration to the problem of disloyal Confederate women. He apparently "ordered that a prison be set up at Newport [south of Cincinnati, Ohio] for the incarceration of 'disloyal' women, who were required to sew clothes for Union soldiers."[61] Lizzie Hardin confirmed the existence of such a prison for Confederate women. She related the story of a sixteen-year-old girl who had been arrested and whose captors "had threatened to send her to Newport Barracks, where there were none but men, and make her sew for the Yankee soldiers. She held out until they put her on the cars, when the terror of her situation overcame her, and she told them she would rather sacrifice her conscience and take the oath than sacrifice her health sewing for the Yankees."[62] Mrs. M. M. Givens of Cynthiana faced the same threat when she protested a Union soldier taking her horse. According to her account of the incident, "My indignation knew no bounds. . . . When the soldier was ordered to lead the horse away, I defied him to touch the horse or me. 'You would look pretty if I put you up behind one of these soldiers,' said Major Brocht, 'and took you to Newport barracks to sew on soldiers' clothes.' 'I would not do it,' I replied; 'you could not force me to.' At the same time feeling pride in fact that I had sewed on 'butternut jeans' more than once."[63]

These examples all demonstrate the politicization of domestic gender conventions by both sides. The young woman made a conscious decision to forgo her political loyalties rather than use her domestic skills for the enemy. Mrs. Givens acknowledged that her defiant domesticity was a significant form of Confederate resistance. Union authorities found such Confederate politicization of the Kentucky home front unacceptable and looked to reassert proper politicized domesticity. Sewing on "butternut jeans" rather than Union blues was inappropriate wartime domesticity. By incarcerating Kentucky Confederate women and requiring them to provision the Union Army, Union officials punished them for their political loyalties and forced them back into their proper place supplying the Union.

Union acknowledgment of Confederate women's importance in the Kentucky supply lines crystallized in 1864 following two years of guerrilla raids by Morgan. In an order to Brigadier General Stephen G. Burbridge declaring martial law in Kentucky, Major General Henry W. Halleck, who was the U.S. chief of staff, emphasized, "Any attempt at rebellion in Kentucky must be put down with a strong hand, and traitors must be punished without regard to their rank or sex."[64] In Union eyes, Confederate women's politicized domesticity, whether in deed or language, merited swift and thorough punishment. As Morgan made one final raid into the state in the summer of 1864, the Union wanted to ensure that civilians would think twice about offering assistance to the guerrilla leader. Information given by loyal citizens helped the military create lists of suspected Confederate sympathizers. For instance, a group of women living outside Maysville, Kentucky, on Hurricane Creek (near the route of the guerrilla raid), included Cindy Beard, who "cannot be trusted"; "Rebel Sympathizers" Widow Griffith, Mrs. Giles (also a widow), and Jane Powers; and Widow Wells, described simply as "disloyal."[65] In a directive to Provost Marshal Fitch in Louisville, Brigadier General Burbridge ordered, "[Y]ou will take whatever steps may be necessary to prevent the circulation in this city of Mrs. Sallie Rochester Ford's Book entitled 'Romances and Raids of Morgan and his Men.'"[66] The increasingly public nature of this emotional support for and romanticized portrayal of the traitorous guerrilla concerned Union authorities. Wanting to shame women into not providing any further Confederate support, editors for the *National Unionist* wrote a scathing article about Morgan supporters in 1864. The editorial remarked that the "*supposed* female . . . rushes into the wake of rebel prisoners with frantic strides and gingerbread. . . . And not a few of those we are describing have been baptized into their devotion to the South by the chaste kisses of John Morgan and his refined accomplices."[67] By patronizing Confederate women's domestic devotions, Unionists hoped to quell any lingering support.

Even while the Confederate physical supply line dried up, Confederate women's emotional encouragement continued to be a contentious issue for Union authorities. In a March 7, 1864, order from Brigadier General Stephen Burbridge, he stated, "When citizens are arrested, and sent to the Military Prison under charges of Disloyalty, the use of Treasonable language, Treasonable practices, or similar charges, which in your opinion do not justify a trial of the parties and yet merit punishment, you will send with them to the Military Prison, an order fixing the term of their imprisonment, which shall not exceed thirty (30) days."[68] Several women were arrested for uttering disloyal sentiments. An Indiana captain wrote a letter to Lieutenant Colonel Fairleigh reporting "the traitorous and disloyal conversation indulged in by one Miss Jennie Mann a boarder of the US Hotel in this city [Louisville]. The language used by her was so disloyal as to make the blood of ever [sic] true and loyal man boil. such as that she wishes the President was dead and that nothing would please her better and she hoped that Jeff Davis would soon be in Washington as President of the United States. That she would rather have murder on her soul than to have a Brother in the Federal Army and many other abusive and disloy[al] epithets which is not necessary to mention here."[69] Even after Robert E. Lee's surrender in 1865, Union authorities continued to react swiftly to disloyal sentiments. Intolerance increased in the wake of Abraham Lincoln's assassination in April. In several sworn statements, Louisville citizens testified to hearing women say they were pleased at the news. Mrs. Joshua McDowell, her husband, and her son stated "that they were glad that President Lincoln was dead and said that he ought to have been dead years ago." Mrs. Francis Smith was accused of having similar sentiments, and Eliza J. Wright swore to the provost marshal, "I heard Alice Atwell say that she was glad that Old Lincoln was dead, and that he ought to have had the ball in his head long ago, then we would have peace. I have often heard her make use of very disloyal language."[70] All three women were arrested and released upon swearing the oath of allegiance.

The Civil War in Kentucky demonstrated the significance of women's home-front activities. While nineteenth-century gender conventions called for all women to provide physical and emotional support to their men on the front lines, the Civil War in the border state politicized these roles. As the Union and Confederate militaries battled for control in the state, women demonstrated their loyalties through their supply line activities. In the Union's efforts to suppress a domestic rebellion based largely on guerrilla tactics, authorities recognized the vital role the "she-rebels" played and initiated policies that brought new consequences for the Confederates' politicized domesticity.

"Corresponding with the Enemy"

Mobilizing the Relational Field of Battle in St. Louis

LEEANN WHITES

On May 14, 1863, the *Republican*, the leading Democratic paper of St. Louis, Missouri, reported by order of the U.S. secretary of war the banishment of thirteen men and thirteen women south across the Confederate lines. The women were an apparently odd assortment consisting of the wives of two of the banished men, who voluntarily chose to leave with their husbands; the wives of prominent Confederate officers; six women banished in their own right as "secret rebel mail agents"; and one Miss Lucie Nicholson, banished for being a "volunteer in the rebel army." The newspaper article also noted that more women were in line to be banished but that "efforts made on their behalf have to led to the postponement of their names." Banishment behind the Confederate lines in the third year of a bloody and protracted civil war was, after all, a serious matter, virtually unprecedented for women, much less for ladies. Roughly a month later, however, on June 22, 1863, the efforts of their friends apparently having failed, another eight women were also banished. This second group included no less than the wife of Trusten Polk, briefly the governor of the state in 1857 and thereafter U.S. congressman prior to the war and a highly placed adviser to Jefferson Davis, as well as Mrs. Marion Vail and Mrs. Lucy Welsh, key rebel mail agents.[1]

Altogether this banishment of some twenty Missouri women constituted one of the largest cases of banishment of women by the Union military authority in the course of the Civil War. It brought to a close an important chapter in a long and hard-fought battle between Southern sympathizing women in St. Louis—and in Missouri in general—and the Union soldiers who occupied a border area critical to the Northern war effort. The charge brought against most of these women was "corresponding with the enemy." In the case of the actual mail runners, like Marion Vail and Lucy Welsh, not only were they guilty of corresponding with their absent male relations who were off fighting with the Confederacy, but they were also guilty of having facilitated other women in doing the same—a crime that was even more serious in the eyes of the Union military authority. These women were responsible for covertly collecting, processing, and sending the mail, not just in St. Louis but from across the state of Missouri, as well as seeing that it was transported down the Mississippi River to the Missouri men fighting in the Confederate Army. Some of the other women banished, particularly the wives of high-ranking Confederate officers, were also guilty of sending mail through this covert mail operation. Whether actually running the mail, sending correspondence through the mail, riding with guerrillas, or simply choosing to accompany their banished husbands, all these women were at root guilty of the same basic offense, that of "corresponding with the enemy." They were all guilty of maintaining their domestic relationships to their men, even to the point of violating the stated regional and political lines the Union military was in the process of fighting a war to sustain.[2]

This is not to say, however, that either these banished women or the Union military responsible for their banishment necessarily always saw themselves engaged in a direct battle. Certainly when the Union military authorities established martial law in Missouri in August 1861, they were concerned with the possibility of disloyalty among the citizens of that state, and of St. Louis in particular, but their primary focus was to minimize that threat so that the manpower and strategic location of St. Louis might serve the formal military objectives of the Union war effort more effectively. For the occupying Union military forces in that city, then, fighting the war was about moving men, not women, whether those men were the raw troops that drilled many thousands at a time at St. Louis's Benton Barracks before being deployed down the Mississippi River into battle; the "irregulars," that is, the Missouri State Guard and the guerrillas, rounded up in the thousands and confined to Myrtle Street and Gratiot Street Prisons in the city; the formal prisoners of war, who also arrived from downriver in the thousands and had to be routed through St. Louis to Northern prisons; or the wounded, who arrived in boatloads to fill and overfill St. Louis's five thousand hospital beds.[3]

And for the Southern sympathizing women of St. Louis, and of the state in general, the war also had little to do with them directly. Many clung with outrage to what they viewed as their properly noncombatant—that is, their relationally grounded—domestic status. The response of Priscilla Patton to the imprisonment and banishment of so many women illustrates well the sort of outrage such treatment could elicit from Southern sympathizing women. It was, she noted, "the most disgraceful thing on record of any nation. Only the acts of the mob in France during the reign of terror can compare with it." She was particularly appalled that the banished were not only torn from their family circle and their larger communities but were not even allowed to take their infants with them. "And why?" she queried rhetorically in her journal. "All this," she answered, "for no greater crime than writing or receiving a simple family letter from someone in the South," that is, for doing what women do and maintaining relational connections between kin.[4]

Since the Union military really had no desire to make war on women and the overwhelming majority of Missouri's women had no desire to make war on the Union soldiers, how did a war committed to fighting on the formal field of battle and to conciliating civilians devolve into what Mark Grimsley has termed a "hard war," a war in which women's very domestic relations would be rendered grounds for arrest and banishment? Civil War historians have suggested that the military adopted such tactics only as a last resort. Michael Fellman has pointed out that the Union soldiers in Missouri took up informal guerrilla tactics be-cause they were forced to match the bushwhackers and fight them the way the bushwhackers themselves fought. Nonetheless, Fellman argues that both the guerrillas and the Union military continued to try to recognize the "noncombat-ant" status of women. Fellman suggests that, as the soldiers set aside so much of what constituted honorable manly behavior, it became ever more critical to draw some line across which they would not cross. Gender provided them with that line, for as long as they treated ladies with respect, they could continue to think of themselves as honorable men, no matter the other cruelties they might find themselves engaging in.[5]

According to this line of analysis, the Union soldiers were forced to fight bushwhacking men the way the bushwhackers fought, but they were not simi-larly forced to fight Southern sympathizing women the way this latter group fought. While this approach may accurately capture the thinking of military men, it fails to consider the thinking of domestic women. In this essay, I am sug-gesting that we take seriously the Union charge against these banished women, that of "corresponding with the enemy," not simply in its literal description of their crime of writing to their men, or facilitating the writing of others, but as a larger descriptor of their location and significance as participants in a very real struggle for military control of the state. The story of the events that led to the mass banishment of these women in May and June 1863 is then the story of how women's relational position became, in the course of the war, political and even treasonous from the perspective of the Union military, while the Union military's occupation became ever more invasive and abusive of women and of gender conventions of both men and women.[6]

Marion Vail, one of the leading secret mail runners who was banished in the summer of 1863, left her own account of how her relational position came to correspond with that of the enemy in the course of the war. She began her account by noting that she was the resident of a border state, and as a consequence of that, "we were not spared, because of the fact that we had no southern army to protect us." Certainly the Missouri State Guard attempted in the summer of 1861 to resist the Union military occupation of the state, but by the end of the only large-scale military encounter in the state, the Battle of Wilson's Creek in August 1861, the Union military had successfully vanquished the formal Southern sympathizing military presence in the state. Many of the State Guard went on to fill the ranks of the Missouri Confederate regiments, but those men left behind, unable for one reason or another to join up with the formal Confederate forces, found themselves in the difficult circumstances of Union occupation. As Vail explained, they were no longer recognized as formal military combatants; they were now classed instead as "guerrillas," "bridge burners," or "political prisoners" and confined to the hastily established St. Louis military prisons, Myrtle and Gratiot. During the course of the war more than eighteen thousand men would move through those prisons.[7]

While Southern sympathizing women found that the formal military defeat of their men stripped them of "protection," the occupying soldiers in St. Louis and the state found that their victory on the formal field of battle did not amount to the end of war but rather to a reconfiguring of the point of engagement. That there was no more formal field of battle meant only that the war had shifted to an informal one, a field of battle that was particularly enjoined in, around, and over the prisons, for while the Union military struggled to round up and confine the informal Southern military forces in the state, Southern sympathizing women attempted to continue to meet their relational obligations and responsibilities to these very same men. As early as December 1861, when there were already some 1,200 men confined in the Gratiot Prison, a prison with a maximum capacity of 500 hundred, Southern sympathizing women virtually besieged the commanding officers for the right of access in order to assist these men with their basic needs. Women who would eventually be banished for mail running were frequent visitors to these prisons. Margaret McLure went to visit her son, Parkinson, while Marion Vail went to visit her nephew, Absolom Grimes. As Vail put it, "I visited both these prisons and found that a loyal southern woman could serve her country elsewhere than on the battlefield."[8]

The gravity of the struggle around the prisons was only intensified by the great Union victory at Fort Donelson, in Tennessee, in February 1862. Indeed, the very extent of the formal military battle at the front served to intensify the informal war to the rear. In the days immediately following the battle, one of the most pressing problems confronting Commanding General Henry Halleck was how to securely distribute the some 11,000 prisoners of war, many seriously wounded, among Northern civilians. Some cities, like Cincinnati, were immediately eliminated as too divided in political sentiment to safely take on such men. In the end, some 7,000 POWs were sent to Chicago, much to the distress of the mayor, Julian Rumsey, who wrote to Halleck in fear that the prisoners would break out and burn down Chicago itself. "I am assured," he wrote, "by men familiarly acquainted with these people that there is the utmost danger." And, as he somewhat ominously concluded, the destruction of the prison camp "would surely do away with the glorious victory at Ft. Donelson."[9]

Along with the problem of how to securely place the rank-and-file soldier, the question of the proper treatment of the captured Confederate officers was also at issue. Initially Halleck followed military custom and offered them parole. F. A. Dick, provost marshal of St. Louis, was infuriated at the way this open-handed policy gave these enemy officers the opportunity of "going freely among our wealthy secessionists." The result was that these "home grown rebels" ran after the officers and "dined and feted them, encouraged them to stand firm in their disloyalty." Indeed, wives of Confederate officers, like Mrs. Pallen, even bragged as to the number and rank of the men they had taken into their homes (Mrs. Pallen could claim two; other Southern sympathizing women who would later be banished, only one apiece). From Provost Marshal Dick's position, the "feting and dining" of these men was deplorable. "If the rebellion had been less formidable and soon put down" (as it was in Missouri), "these men would not have been treated as officers but as felons" (as they were in Missouri). That is, they would be in Gratiot and Myrtle with the other rebels, the "bridge burners" and so on, and not in the best rooms of some of the wealthiest women in the city. Dick certainly felt vindicated when Halleck came to see that the "bold and defiant" culture generated by his policy of parole was too threatening to good order and had all the officers rounded up and sent off to Alton Prison across the river in Illinois instead.[10]

As much as the issue of "home grown" prisoners served to activate the relational field of battle and the quartering of officers continued it, the rebel wounded from Fort Donelson presented the most intense point of conflict between Union military policy and Southern sympathizing women. After all, the very lives of these wounded men were clearly on the line. Halleck's initial response was, as with the quartering of Confederate officers, to attempt to be openhanded. "Sick and wounded," he reported, "have been sent to hospitals and cared for without distinction of states or counties, friends or foes. Humanity required this." Unfortunately for the success of this conciliatory policy, all available structures were already jammed with prisoners of the informal guerrilla war. The only available space big enough to accommodate such a large number of men was an unfinished building originally intended for a hotel. So it was, according to Marion Vail, that it was into this ramshackle structure, "without fire, without cots, or any comforts of life, these wounded and dying prisoners were taken."[11]

In her recollections, Vail described with some pride her own and other Southern sympathizing women's role in aiding these men. "It was my privilege," she explained, "to be on the spot when the first vehicles containing prisoners arrived." And by the next day, "as many as fifty ladies had reported for duty," armed with bandages, lint, and food stuffs. This military policy, however, as with the policy of officer parole, would not last long. On March 11, 1862, Halleck changed the rules of prisoner visitation, requiring that all women who nursed soldiers take the loyalty oath in order to gain admission to the hospital. According to coverage in the local press, this order was experienced as a "severe check" by Southern sympathizing women, and ever since, "heads have been racked with some new expedient to outwit General Halleck."[12]

Marion Vail claimed that many Southern sympathizing women simply lied, taking the oath so that they could continue to support their men. She herself found a different way around the loyalty oath requirement. She simply presented her school tax receipt to the inspecting guards at the hospital door. The tax receipt just happened to resemble the loyalty oath slip, and she was for some time able to avoid detection until one day the surgeon in charge caught her in the act of using the false pass. Being, from Vail's perspective, a "decent man," that is, a man who valued her assistance to the men more than matters political or military, he simply chose to ignore her deception.[13]

The problem with this loyalty oath requirement, then, was that it was too difficult to enforce at the point of entry. Some military men would weaken when confronted by these women; they cared more about observing gender conventions, or as Vail put it, about "behaving like gentlemen," than about "requiring ladies to take loyalty oaths for the Union." Many Southern sympathizing women also had little respect for the political, much less the military, authority, and so they were willing to engage in false swearing or simply manipulating the individual official they needed to circumvent. By June, Halleck was forced to issue an oath that the occupying forces were better able to administer and enforce. Now all "suspected disloyals" were required to report to the provost marshal in person and take the oath and post a bond for its observance. A letter supporting the new policy published in the *Republican* pointed to the "excessive attention" of secessionist ladies to rebel prisoners as a reason why this stricter loyalty oath was necessary. The behavior of these women—the smuggling of delicacies for Confederate soldiers, "forbidden even to Union soldiers," not to mention their apparent proclivity to "whisper news of false Confederate victories in the ears of prisoners of war, and get permission to take them to their homes"—was what made this more severe measure necessary. Indeed, this writer concluded that Southern sympathizing women, in giving their gifts only to the rebels, "manifest their hostility to the Union as much as their humanity to the prisoners."[14]

Buried in this battle over who was or wasn't behaving like a lady or a gentleman was a basic argument over whose behavior deserved standing as humane. Was it the Southern sympathizing woman, carrying out relational responsibilities, which during peacetime stood at the core of not just women's but benevolent behavior in general? Or was it the Union military authorities, who so wanted to claim equality in their treatment of all wounded men and render the Southern sympathizing women as those who were fighting a partisan domestic war? The loyalty oath requirement was an aggressive attempt on the part of the military to mark women's domestic labor with the enemy as inherently political and partisan and not simply a manifestation of their concern for their men. Nonetheless, even in the face of the expanded loyalty oath, some men, like the medical officer who allowed Marion Vail to visit the hospital with her school tax receipt, continued to look in the other direction—they continued to behave as respectful men, like "gentlemen," as Vail put it, and privilege the domestic over the military. After all, men, like women, had something to lose with the erosion of gender conventions, perhaps more, and the war would not go on forever.

Perhaps if the "gentleman" who continued to allow Marion Vail entry into the prisons and the hospitals had known the scope of her activities, he might have thought twice about admitting her. One of Vail's regular visits in the winter of 1862 was to see her nephew, Absalom Grimes, who would soon thereafter manage his first of many escapes from Gratiot Prison, make his way downriver to the Confederate Missouri regiments, and present the idea of running a covert mail operation to the commanding general, Sterling Price. Grimes would later claim the idea of running the mail as his own, but it might just as well have been the suggestion of Southern sympathizing women, like his Aunt Marion, who were already carrying mail to men like Grimes in the St. Louis prisons and hospitals. Certainly it was the relational network these women had already developed in their efforts to supply the wounded and imprisoned sympathizers that created the practical basis for the entire scheme.[15]

It is hard to know when the Union military in St. Louis became aware of this newly expanded form of Southern sympathizing women's relational activism. Military authorities certainly knew of the mail-running ring by September 1862 because they intercepted a bag of mail. Not only did the authorities know of the covert mail operation, but so did the reading public of St. Louis because the provost marshal published portions of the intercepted mail in the daily press. On September 10, 1862, the headline in the *Globe-Democrat* read: "Rare Revelations. Inside View of the Fashionable Secesh of St. Louis," followed by: "[T]he richest expose of the season will be found in the following letters, which were captured a few days ago in the rebel mail bag." One Southern sympathizing woman, Anne Lane, was so outraged at the publication of this private correspondence that she wrote to her sister about it, noting, "There is nothing in the letter except what anyone might write to an acquaintance. What petty spite does it not seem to you?" She doubted that the military's use of this tactic had succeeded in shaming Southern sympathizing women into compliance. As she concluded in her letter to her sister, "It would have been an awful thing to me to have a private letter published, but I don't think girls of the present day care for these things."[16]

It is not clear whether the Union military or the *Republican* editors seriously thought they could shame Southern sympathizing ladies into dropping their correspondence with the enemy through the publication of their intercepted mail. Perhaps they hoped to have as much success in wielding gender conventions against Southern sympathizing women as Southern sympathizing women had had in pressing their expectations of humane gentlemanly behavior against them. What is clear is that the relational war was intensified on both sides by the capture and publication of this mail. The domestic was rendered ever more public, political, and apparently partisan, and its lady combatants were presented as ever more "misguided." At the same time, in the private correspondence and conversation of Southern sympathizing women like Anne Lane, the Union military was perceived as ever more inhumane and badly behaved.

Certainly the provost marshal was well aware that this covert mail was not simply a matter of high-society gossip and the trivial pursuits of "ladies" as they attempted to present it in the public press. For example, there was the intercepted mail of John Crosswhite of Audrain County. The locale, deep in the heart of mid-Missouri guerrilla territory; the contents of the letter; and the difficulties involved in apprehending the mail runner serve to exemplify the problems that this corresponding with the enemy presented to the occupying forces. In the first place, it wasn't particularly easy to arrest a woman mail runner, any more than it was easy to stop a disloyal woman at the hospital door. So while the St. Louis authorities notified the local provost marshal in Audrain County to arrest the mail runner responsible for this intercepted bag, one E. L. Moberly, they were unable to follow through. As they explained, "EL Moberly proved to be a woman . . . her husband is S. L. Moberly." The officers simply could not believe that the mail runner was a woman and concluded that some spelling error had been made and that the husband, S. L. Moberly (and not E. L. Moberly) must be the guilty party. While these arresting officers were surprised and disarmed by the unconventionality of a female mail runner (war, after all, being men's business), the St. Louis provost marshal was increasingly confronted with mounting evidence of women's responsibility for the work. Marion Vail's own niece, Mrs. Ivins, was arrested at a train stop in Warrenton with a bag of mail in her possession. Mary Cleveland was arrested in her home in Moberly, in Randolph County, in mid-Missouri, with the contents of a mailbag that she was about to transport out of the state in her skirts.[17]

Along with the difficulties of apprehending mail runners, the actual content of the letters was disturbing. For instance, in Crosswhite's letter to a brother in the Confederate Army, he described the hard circumstances of his Southern sympathizing friends and relations in the county. "O. S. Ridgeway was taken prisoner two or three months and was kept by them, the feds, until almost dead." Another relation was "yet a prisoner in Alton. . . . Harrison was released . . . but Joshua was killed twelve miles south of Booneville on his way south. . . . Thomas Wolfe died in the Alton prison last summer." The damage done to local farms and businesses was described, and while the soldier was assured that his own house still stood, it was only because a friend had moved in to guard it. The letter both reassured the soldier that his family and his property were still intact and outlined the misery faced at home at the hands of the Union military occupation. Surely the Union interceptors must have read this "news from home" as stoking the fires of rebellion, inflammatory in its potential for motivating Southern sympathizing Missourians, now part of the formal enemy forces.[18]

Southern sympathizing women had already been banned from the prisons and hospitals for their contribution to the morale of guerrillas and prisoners of war. How much more serious, then, was this mail route that spread the news all the way to the men actually fighting in the field, on the one hand, and across the state to Southern homes deep in the highly contested, "guerrilla infested" areas of mid-Missouri, on the other? What could be worse? Perhaps the letter intercepted in a mailbag in March 1863, addressed to General Sterling Price, assessing the military condition of St. Louis and the state in general and the probable support for an invasion of the state by Confederate forces. The letter urged Price to consider such an invasion. "It is sir, the night and morning prayer of both men and women for your return to this state and believe, sir, 75,000 men and boys will rally your standard the hour you reach the west bank of the Missouri River. St. Louis alone will give you an army of 8,000 men." The letter goes on to discuss the "bitter and intense hatred" felt against the North, especially against the "diabolical, base and fiendish army" that occupied the state and had "proscribed the men and basely insulted the ladies." This piece of intercepted mail was not published in the local press, as was that of the young ladies, but was instead forwarded to the governor and the commanding Union general on March 14, 1863.[19]

Since the fall of Fort Donalson in February 1862, Provost Marshal Dick had been agitating for a more stringent policy against the activities of Southern sympathizing women. He was not one to think that the ladies were a matter of high-fashion fluff, and Commanding General Halleck had come around to his position and altered military policy with regard to the parole of officers and limiting the access to men in the prisons and hospitals, even going so far as a general loyalty oath by the summer of 1862. But the more the Union occupation succeeded in lopping off the head of the relational war, the more the covert manifestations seemed to grow and expand, traveling in ever larger numbers and frequency across the state—by rail, by house, in mailbags, sewn into skirts. In the war of gender convention, the Union soldiers appeared to be no match for a determined Southern sympathizing woman; they could not hold their own lines. They could only render the relational ever more public and proscribed. They could attempt to castigate these women as "misguided" and as "she devils," but even then they were unable to truly cut the gentleman out of their own hearts.

Provost Marshal Dick had long had a solution to this dilemma in mind. Remove the most troublesome of the ladies from St. Louis altogether. Banish them. And in so doing the military authorities could kill two birds with one stone: they could remove the leaders of the relational war, women like Vail and McLure, who had risen up with the demands of the war itself into positions of prominence through their work in the hospitals, the prisons, or now in running the covert mail, and at the same time banish the highly placed wives of Confederate officers and antebellum political figures, like Pallen, Frost, and Polk—women whose actual treasonous behavior might be limited to a letter in an intercepted Confederate mailbag but whose high social standing at home, not to mention in the Confederacy, had long made them difficult, if not impossible, for the Union military to securely occupy.[20]

Dick took his campaign to President Lincoln on December 19, 1862, when he wrote in response to a query from Lincoln concerning the advisability of maintaining marshal law in the state. Rather than relaxing marshal law, as some of Lincoln's advisers were suggesting, Dick advocated intensifying it. In particular he advocated the policy of wholesale banishment, including the banishment of women. The intercepted rebel mail of February gave Dick even more fodder for his campaign, and on March 5, he wrote to Colonel Hoffman, commissioner general of prisoners in Washington. He noted that while the interception of several rebel mailbags had now provided the "necessary evidence" for the conviction of these women, "the embarrassment is to know what to do with them." And by this, he literally meant where to put them because many of these women whose mail was intercepted were the wives and daughters of officers in the Confederate military; they were wealthy and influential women.[21]

Before the war, the overwhelming majority of women incarcerated by the city police were jailed for prostitution. It was therefore unthinkable to arrest "respectable" women, especially women with any kind of class standing, and throw them into the prisons. The provost marshal had sporadically arrested a few women for disloyal behavior prior to this point, but they were generally held only for the day at Gratiot Prison, or at worst for a night, and even then with a notation like "keep her for the night, teach her a lesson." After his correspondence with Colonel Hoffman, Provost Marshal Dick dealt with this issue by arresting one of the biggest mail runners, Margaret McLure, and confiscating her home as a female prison. The Union military authorities simply emptied her house of its contents, sold them, and fitted up the house with cots, hired a matron, and designated it the third military prison in the city, the Chesnut Street Prison. McLure, many of the other mail runners, and several of the generals' wives guilty of sending covert mail were also arrested and incarcerated in the prison. They were held there until the provost marshal received formal permission from the adjutant general, on April 24, to banish women across Confederate lines.[22]

The accounts of arrest and experience of imprisonment vary with the source. In McLure's account, it all began with her son, Parkinson, who, like Vail's nephew, was arrested in December 1861 and initially imprisoned in Gratiot Prison in St. Louis. He was then transferred to Alton, a Union military prison located across the Mississippi River in Illinois, and on September 5, 1862, he was exchanged and returned to the Confederate Army. According to her recollections, even after her son was exchanged, McLure continued to be a "constant visitor in hospitals and prisons, trying to forget her own deep anxiety, and in fond hope that some tidings might reach her of her absent one." Eventually when a Dr. Wright asked her if she wanted to send a letter to her son, she of course accepted. When questioned by the provost marshal, McLure even went so far as to volunteer the information that this was not the first time she had sent a letter to her son through this covert means. Indeed, she was insistent about locating her behavior on relational ground. As she concluded, "[T]he destitution of the rebel army would induce a mother to accept such an offer, without asking any questions." And she told the authorities that she sent along with her letter a warm blanket, a pair of boots, a toothbrush, and some other small items in the hope that her son would receive them as well.[23]

The military's file on Margaret McLure puts a different face on the case.

Rather than a concerned mother, she is described as a widow who for the past few years had run a boardinghouse—one with some questionable guests and with some even shadier practices. Indeed, while it was undoubtedly true, as McLure recalled, that she was warned on the street that the Union troops were on their way to her house to arrest her, she must herself have been well aware of what was coming at that point because one of her boarders, the mail-running Dr. Wright, had already been arrested in her house, under circumstances fairly incriminating to her. When the military arrived to arrest him, Dr. Wright was found in her room. His exact location was contested, the arresting guard claiming that he was found under her bed, McLure claiming he was sitting front of the fire. No one, however, denied that McLure herself was in the bed.[24]

Of course, at the time of the arrest of Dr. Wright, the provost marshal had already heard repeated allegations against McLure. They had long known that she was involved in running the mail, certainly as long before as the previous summer. And not just the mail—they knew she was involved in collecting supplies for Confederate soldiers and in facilitating Confederate recruitment in Missouri. But it was not enough to be objectively treasonous; she had to be domestically treasonous as well. The fact that Margaret McLure was a widow and the keeper of a boardinghouse—which was already halfway to being a public house—was helpful, then, and as a boardinghouse keeper who also kept men under her bed, she was deserving of imprisonment in her own relational terms. She deserved to have her house become a female prison because it was already verging upon being a brothel. No longer a home, a center of relational domesticity, it was now a holding pen for treasonous "she devils," a fitting transformation from the perspective of Dick and the Radical Republicans.[25]

There are no formal military records for the Chesnut Female Prison (or any other female prison for that matter). Perhaps this lack of formal military documentation reflects the ambivalent status of a prison for individuals who only "correspond with the enemy." Nonetheless, by the spring of 1863, Southern sympathizing women were not simply tending devotedly the men in the prisons and hospitals; some of them were actually themselves *in* military prison, however much that military prison may have appeared to also be a home. And even after this core of mail runners and Confederate officers' wives were banished from the city, the Chesnut Female Prison continued as part of the disciplinary apparatus of the Union occupation of the city and the state. Finally the Union military got on the right side of gender conventions, if only for the moment. But it was a critical moment, allowing the military to break up the mail-running operation and to remove the leading St. Louis relational activists and high-ranking Confederate officers' wives from Missouri.[26]

So no one—neither the Union military nor Southern sympathizing women—really wanted women's work to be viewed as partisan and political, and yet it was. And as the war progressed, these women found their activities increasingly rendered so. They found themselves swearing false oaths, forging passes, carrying information from kin that was also critical military intelligence; they were exposed, denigrated for it in the public press, and labeled "malignant" and "inhumane," that is, as "she devils." While this was distressing to these women, it did not alter the fact that as women they had relational concerns and responsibilities. It was war itself that transgressed that place and mobilized domesticity and gender convention. That women were more than good for it is evidenced by the only solution that worked—not even imprisonment but wholesale banishment from the community. Otherwise the objective approach to war was really no match for the relational field of battle that it had itself mobilized.

The Practical Ladies of Occupied Natchez

CITA COOK

I have since my departure pictured your pleasant parlour and the good friends
that have so often met and will still meet there. . . . [H]as the fair divinity of
Elgin crossed the impossible gulf that divides Natchez from the country and lent
her charms to her friends there?

—COLONEL LOREN KENT,
 U.S. Twenty-ninth Infantry, to Mary Ker, October 27, 1864

Before my arrival here the district had been almost completely swayed by . . .
money in the possession of cotton speculators and political adventurers, and
beauty in the possession of rebel females, once lovely and with delicate sensibilities, now cunning, crafty, traitorous, and dangerous.

—MAJOR GENERAL N. J. T. DANA,
 U.S. Sixteenth Army Corps, to General O. O. Howard, November 12, 1864

After Colonel Loren Kent left occupied Natchez, Mississippi, in 1864 for a new
post, he remembered with particular fondness the entertaining evenings he
had spent at the home of Mary Ker, a young unmarried woman from a planter
family. He certainly did not think of Ker or her friend Alice Jenkins ("the fair
divinity" whose plantation home, Elgin, was outside the picket lines from Natchez) as "crafty" or "dangerous." Nor did he believe that his friendship with
them had in any way interfered with the possibility of a Northern victory in the
Civil War. There is no evidence that either Ker or Jenkins ever used their travel
passes or any other privileges they gained from their relationships with Kent
and other officers to help the Confederate military, but, as General N. J. T. Dana
recognized, they easily could have done so, and other women certainly did.

In wartime, it can be both important and difficult to determine who is a potential ally. From the first face-to-face meetings between Northern soldiers and elite Southern civilians in Natchez, traditional upper-class ideology, particularly that calling for a chivalrous relationship between ladies and gentlemen, warred with assumptions about how patriots should treat their enemies. Sometimes the latter concern predominated, but every specific interaction required a decision by each person involved about how to define at that particular moment "Us" and "Them." When Northern and Southern believers in gentility used the terms "gentleman" and "ladies" to indicate whom they believed they could trust, they generally assumed that these individuals possessed more distinguished family roots, more refined manners and taste, and a better character than the majority of white people. Since many members of the rising middle class in the North were reading books about proper etiquette to reinforce their claim to higher social status, some of the occupying soldiers may have had a special interest in not being considered "vulgar" by people whose claim to gentility was well established.[1] Whether individuals on either side were motivated primarily by military strategy, the welfare of loved ones, economic insecurity, greed, or any other concern, the ability or inability to transform interactions into ones involving familiar chivalrous gender roles could become a new source of power.

Whenever elite officers and women temporarily escaped the tensions of war by socializing with each other in the way they might have done before the war, they were slipping back into the assumption of many Americans from the upper classes that they could always rely on anyone who was a true lady or gentleman. Others, however, decided that their personal or political needs and priorities justified abusing the trust of officers who helped them cross the picket lines. For General Dana and some other occupying officers, the willingness of women they had classified as ladies to perform deeds that might be considered treasonous threatened not only the success of their military goals but also their faith in genteel gender roles.

The history of Natchez during the Civil War has often been shrouded in Lost Cause mythology. In the 1930s, women in its two garden clubs organized an annual "Pilgrimage" during which tourists paid to walk through the dozens of antebellum mansions that had survived the war and occupation. A Confederate Pageant soon became one of its most popular features.[2] The books written for "pilgrims" from around the world have usually downplayed the extent of wartime Unionism and bargaining with U.S. officers in Natchez.[3] Most military histories of the Civil War do not mention the town, but some studies of the region over a longer period cover key wartime events,[4] and several scholars have written about the new freedoms and challenges experienced by the thousands of former slaves who flocked to Natchez once the occupation began.[5] Lawrence Powell and Michael Wayne found that members of the planter elite from the Natchez region switched their allegiance back and forth between the Confederacy and the United States because their sense of economic self-interest was detached from that of national loyalty.[6] Authors discussing the fraternization between Confederate ladies and occupying officers across the South have sometimes relied on a few of the journals and memoirs by young women from Natchez,[7] and they and others have used similar documents from other communities along the Mississippi River.[8] Only Drew Faust, however, has noted how much more common the cross-national socialization was in Natchez because of its pseudo-aristocratic culture.[9] While the diaries and autobiographies include much valuable information, the complex roots and results of the interactions during the occupation, including the impact of faith in gentility and chivalrous gender roles, become clearer when these sources are supplemented by the many letters available in the collected papers of some planter families, along with a variety of military orders, reports, and correspondence.

The Mississippi River port of Natchez, located about halfway between Memphis and New Orleans, had fewer than six thousand people in 1860. It served as an economic and social center for a planter elite whose vast holdings in slaves, cotton and sugar plantations, and investments in Northern businesses made them the richest community in the antebellum United States.[10] They maintained their wealth and social status in part by exchanging favors with the members of a network of friends and relatives in both the South and the Northeast who interacted almost as if they were a tribe. This system of mutual support worked so well that they generally put loyalty to their network ahead of any other commitment. Just as many in the earlier generation of Natchezians had chosen pragmatism and aristocratic identity above patriotism when deciding whether to support the Spanish, English, or early American governments, most people in the Lower Mississippi Valley planter society moved in and out of official allegiance to the Union or the Confederacy according to what seemed to serve their self-interests at the moment. A month after the occupation of Natchez began, the *New York Times* reported that about a half of the citizens of the town were Unionists.[11] Over the next year and a half, a growing number of elite Confederates there would decide to give up on their Southern nation and adapt as best they could to the new circumstances.

As people across the South were debating whether to secede in 1860, Natchez-region planters had disagreed about what political position would secure their wealth and power most effectively over the long run but not about their right to own slaves.[12] The Unionism that many ultimately chose tended to be more a version of neutrality than a sign of strong pro-American partisanship. Unionists could avoid some but not all of the special challenges of war. The ability of Unionist men to stay at home relieved their wives and daughters of the need to take on added responsibilities, and both the men and women could sometimes gain special favors from invading officers. Nevertheless, their relative flexibility meant that most Unionists socialized comfortably with friends who disagreed with them. None of their sons served in the U.S. military, but a number did join the Confederate forces. Some Southern supporters from the planter class were sincerely anxious to help their new nation; others just did not want to be disloyal to friends and relatives fighting for it. Believing that the Confederacy was, like the broader American society, divided into "Us" and "Them," most members of the planter class of the Natchez region considered themselves to be in opposition to anyone who might harm their own economic and social authority and privileges. Whoever won the war, some of them would end up on the right side, ready to help those who had chosen unwisely.

Most of the officers who would oversee the occupation of Natchez, men of various ages and backgrounds, arrived there after having experienced relatively serious battles. Serving at a post where they were not regularly facing danger tested their administrative skills and their judgment about the possible behavior of citizens rather than their bravery or their knowledge of military strategy. A number of those who had enjoyed relatively genteel social interactions at home appreciated the opportunity to step outside the war for a short time into a familiar world where they could exchange light banter with charming young women. Some officers used to considering themselves guardians of proper women found it difficult to accept that seemingly gracious and refined ladies might be trying to undermine the Northern cause through actions that deserved to be punished. Others were more suspicious whenever a local lady smiled at them and asked for a favor. All experienced times when their expectations about certain individuals turned out to be wrong.

A common genteel identity could draw some people together across political lines, but how much opportunity they had to form such connections depended on the specific military context. The physical environment of Natchez throughout the occupation suffered little damage because the officers on each side never considered fighting a major battle for the sake of holding the town. Confederate military strategists decided early in the war that since attackers coming from any direction could so easily flank Natchez, there was no point in setting up a fortification there.[13] When, on May 12, 1862, the commander of a U.S. ship called on the local citizens to accept his authority, General Charles Dahlgren, a local planter, was able to gather only fourteen troops and about a hundred unarmed Virginians to defend the city. The mayor therefore agreed to surrender, but the practical impact of his action was nothing more than promising that no one would attack passing Federal gunboats. The newspaper continued to print articles praising the Confederacy, ads for runaway slaves, and reports about benefits for Southern soldiers and their dependents.[14]

As news from the eastern front deteriorated in 1863, the citizens of Natchez hoped that they would be spared a full-fledged occupation dominated by what a local newspaper called an "infernal horde of savages."[15] Members of the upper class in the Lower Mississippi Valley had long distinguished their friends and relatives in the North from the people even the Unionists among them disparaged as "Yankees." Louisiana planter Randall Lee Gibson, for example, condemned "the vulgar, cunning & ranting Yankee" who was so lacking in "manners and . . . principles" that he held cruel thoughts "against our best people—against Families of culture and pride."[16] Dismaying reports of plundering and general mayhem in newly conquered areas of Mississippi,[17] as well as General Benjamin Butler's order demeaning the Confederate women of New Orleans, led many to assume that Union officers, regardless of their class background, would all behave as Yankees rather than following the genteel code that called on them to protect honorable women. One plantation mistress in Louisiana wrote her Natchez relatives, "I do not fear the Yankees but their insults. You know they do not respect ladies."[18]

The more barbarous the elite citizens of Natchez imagined their potential invaders, the more relieved they would be when any of them seemed to behave like gentlemen. Once Vicksburg surrendered on July 4, 1863, U.S. officials there decided that Natchez could be a useful post from which to attack Confederate soldiers in the nearby countryside who had been freely transporting supplies across the Mississippi River. The change of government in Natchez on July 13 occurred so swiftly and peacefully that according to the general in charge, Thomas E. G. Ransom, many local white people expressed their gratitude that there had been "hardly a case of pillaging, or, even of disrespectful treatment of a citizen."[19] In a letter to a Chicago newspaper, a member of his brigade, identified only as "Dan," reported that "leading citizens" had told him that they had expected the soldiers to have "no restraint in burning or destroying their property, or ravishing their wives or daughters" and seemed elated when they discovered "that the troops in their midst were not only commanded by a gentleman, but by a large majority, gentlemen themselves."[20] He apparently agreed with the local elite that pillaging and ravishing by any man would be "ungentlemanly" and that divisions between genteel people did not have to create overt hostility.

Since Ransom had captured thousands of cattle, numerous prisoners, and "a number of trains loaded with ammunition," Grant proclaimed his accomplishment "a heavy blow to the enemy" and then ordered him to keep the river open.[21] Confederate troops led by General Wirt Adams made a few feeble attempts to retake the city, but they succeeded only at escaping after skirmishes with Federal units sent to the countryside to capture them.[22] While Grant expected Ransom to cripple the Confederate military in the region, he also wanted him to pacify the local citizens and convert more of them to Unionism through a combination of economic restraints and a relative leniency sometimes labeled the "rosewater policy."[23] Until the end of the war, U.S. officials used Natchez as a regional military headquarters; a base for an ever changing number of white and black soldiers; a center for processing, assisting, and policing thousands of freedmen and women; and an economic metropole for any owners and lessees of nearby plantations who pledged their loyalty to the United States. All these concerns meant that the only homes destroyed during the entire occupation were two whose strategic locations overlooking the river put them in the way of the construction of a fort.

The lack of physical destruction did not mean, however, that the occupation had no impact on its citizens. As soon as the Union troops arrived, they captured about twenty "rebel officers and soldiers . . . attempting to escape," demanded that all arms be turned over to them, set up a strong provost guard, took over the post office and the courthouse, and met with the mayor and the city council to decide how to govern the town.[24] Kate Foster, an unmarried planter's daughter in her early twenties, recorded in her diary that "a great many" of her friends who lived in the country had been "made to stay in town all night by the Yanks."[25] Once the troops had commandeered a few homes for officers' housing, offices, and tent cities for the enlisted men, they began raiding nearby plantations, seeking primarily food, horses, and hidden bales of cotton.

The rougher activities of Natchez had traditionally been relegated to "Natchez-Under-the-Hill," below the main section of the town, so planter-class women were used to receiving respect from all pedestrians as they promenaded about the main park at the edge of the bluff or cruised downtown streets while shopping and engaging in impromptu visits. As these areas became crowded with men in blue uniforms who were sometimes rowdy and freedpeople asserting their new independence,[26] local ladies became so reluctant to leave home that they felt almost as if they were under house arrest. They wrote friends about how "Yankeeized" and distasteful downtown Natchez had become—in Kate Foster's words, "a hog pen."[27] When two sisters in their early twenties met on a downtown corner, about eighteen men, who may or may not have been soldiers, threatened to take them across the river to where thousands of African Americans were crowded into a "contraband camp." The young women were so frightened that they allowed "a very common looking soldier" to help them into their carriage while "a band of terrors surrounded" them, "whooping & yelling & cursing & beating [their] broken down team."[28] The fact that the gentlemanly behavior had been displayed by an enemy from the lower classes emphasized how much their social environment had changed. The absence of elite women in the public areas of Natchez continued to be so noticeable that sixteen months into the occupation a local newspaper praised "the nightly increase of ladies at the City Theatre" as evidence that the restoration of "good order" allowed decent women to feel safe enough to go out at night once more.[29]

Whether Unionists or Confederates, most local citizens did what they could to help their families lead as normal a life as possible, an aim that sometimes emboldened adult women to become involved in struggles and negotiations over the practical meaning of occupation. When particular soldiers threatened their freedom in any way, they had to decide whether to swallow their pride and file official complaints to superior officers or to refuse to cooperate and prepare themselves for the consequences. Elizabeth Conway Shields, for example, was a strong Confederate supporter who became even more so when her husband, a member of the Mississippi legislature, was temporarily imprisoned. The troops took all the family's horses and many of the valuables that had not been sent to relatives for safekeeping.[30] Shields decided to go to the occupation headquarters to demand rations for her family, but she refused to walk under a large U.S. flag that hung over the front entrance. She managed to enter the building from the back, but as she prepared to leave the same way, a double line of soldiers guarded that exit so she would have to go through the front—under the flag. According to family legend, she simply tossed her head and "marched out the rear door between the soldiers and their bayonets." The next day General Ransom issued Special Order No. 49 requiring Elizabeth Shields to leave the city with her family within twenty-four hours because her "public conduct . . . was insulting to the Flag of our Union and the officers and soldiers of this command." She and five children immediately departed for their Louisiana plantation, refugees only in the sense that they did not choose the time to visit their other home.[31]

Other elite women decided it was wiser to find a male patron among the U.S. forces. For them to accept any kind of assistance from men who were strangers, enemies, and sometimes from the lower classes, they had to set aside their usual sense of entitlement and display the demeanor of a deferential client—unless, that is, they could transform the interaction into the familiar one of persuading men to look after dependent ladies. One of the more typical privileges women without an adult white male in their household were able to obtain when they stressed their feminine vulnerability was a guard for their property, usually someone no longer fit for more active service because of injuries or age. Fanny Conner, the wife of a Confederate officer, took advantage of this possibility once she lost patience with the endless number of soldiers who kept pestering her or her servants for food because her house was located just outside the official boundary of Natchez. After her first appeal did not work, she composed a letter of complaint to a Union captain that was a model of genteel gender diplomacy, displaying a combination of grace and feminine dependency that might inspire him to feel responsible for her peace of mind:

> I must again apply to you on account of annoyances from the pickets. . . .
> [T]hey took nearly all the milk from my cows and . . . part of the bread.
> . . . I do not speak of the loss—that is not worth mentioning. But the
> annoyance to me is very great. The pickets are constantly in my kitchen.
> I know the soldiers are not allowed to do these things, therefore I apply
> to you, hoping you may have some means of preventing a recurrence

of them. As I am just outside the line I hoped the pickets would be a protection to me.

I am sorry to trouble you, Sir.[32]

By appealing both to the captain's sense of military discipline and to his chivalrous responsibility to take care of women, Conner gained protection that he did not actually owe her, since she was not living within the U.S. lines. Ten days later she wrote her husband that the pickets caused "but little inconvenience" because she now had guards around the clock.[33]

Just how effective such tactics might be depended to some extent on who was in charge of the occupation forces. A change in command from Ransom to Brigadier General Walter Q. Gresham in late August enabled a woman seeking rations for the Protestant Orphans' Home to be more successful than Elizabeth Shields at showing her patriotic devotion without repercussions. When the woman told Gresham that she could not possibly walk under the American flag, even to keep the orphans from starving, he expressed his admiration for her frankness and declared that he would not allow her sentiments to harm the orphans.[34] Gresham was a thirty-one-year-old lawyer from Indiana whose father-in-law was a supporter of secession from Kentucky. Members of the local elite invited him for dinner and praised him for his graciousness, especially during the two months when his wife was with him. But he did not always do as they wished. When Gresham commandeered the mansion of A. L. Wilson for Federal headquarters and his living quarters, the close friendship that developed between the families did not keep the general from banishing Mrs. Wilson from occupied territory for spying. His wife later claimed that he was well aware that a number of the "ladies who were receiving courtesies and rations at our hands were secretly aiding the enemy" but did nothing because he thought they were only "foolish, misguided women."[35] If this was an accurate report of what he thought, it indicated that potential female spies could protect themselves with flighty airs.

Smuggling or spying required the ability to travel or send private letters between what historian Stephen V. Ash has labeled the "garrisoned town" and a "no-man's land" where neither side held clear control.[36] Since the boundaries established for occupied Natchez delineated only a small section of the area within which members of planter families normally traveled, they were quite frustrated when told they could not cross picket lines without special permission. The primary way to find some reprieve from this and other strictures of martial law was to promise to be loyal to the U.S. government. Individuals who had always thought of themselves as Unionists took the loyalty oath quite willingly. Katherine Surget Minor, for example, swore allegiance to the United States as soon as Natchez was occupied,[37] and she then turned her home into "a complete resort for the Federal officers."[38] Some Confederate supporters refused to take the oath because they were determined to remain faithful to the Southern nation. A few avoided it by moving to plantations within the Confederate lines, while others set aside their traditional code of honor and took the oath without actually meaning what they vowed. This enabled them to visit, manage, or lease plantations, as well as to sell products such as cotton or bakery goods.[39] By early 1864, at least thirty-five women managing nearby plantations had agreed to report to officials whenever they crossed the picket lines.[40]

The occupation was especially challenging for plantation mistresses and their urban sisters who were overseeing their household economies because of the absence of any close male relatives. The change in currency forced women who could not earn money from plantations to make or find products to sell to the occupying troops to gain the greenbacks they needed to purchase food and other necessities. The Natchez newspaper described "[l]adies, in flowing skirts, and 'go to meeting fixins,' followed by negroes, large or small, carrying . . . cakes, pies, corn bread," and various other goods for sale. The anti-Confederate author added that some of these ladies, "before this cursed rebellion broke out, were the spoiled pets of wealthy families."[41] These women might not have been able to earn money without the help of the "negroes, large or small," as when Fanny Conner, in her early thirties, hired three men "to cut & haul wood" to sell. She wrote her husband, "[I]n this way I support our family," but it is likely that the black men took care of the sales as well because she did not take the oath of allegiance until the next May and therefore could not cross into Natchez whenever she wished.[42]

After about a month of occupation, Louisa Quitman Lovell, the daughter of fire-eater John A. Quitman, the wife of a Confederate officer, and the sister-in-law of the general who had retreated from New Orleans, felt humiliated by the thought that she might have to sell vegetables to the troops to survive.[43] By early 1864 she, her sisters, and their children were living primarily off the sale of what few goods had not been taken, previously sold, or shipped elsewhere for safekeeping, including clothes that they sold to buy milk for a child.[44] The news in February that one of her family's most important working plantations was in danger of seizure she took as proof that her enemies were not gentlemen, exclaiming, "Is it not cruel to place helpless women in such a position as this! None but a base grovelling covetous Yankee would do it."[45] Nevertheless, she and two sisters decided to take the oath so they could regain and lease their plantation.[46]

Some pro-Confederate women took the loyalty oath so they might use a travel pass to smuggle gray cloth and military buttons to Southern soldiers they knew, a variation of the wartime female activity of sewing clothes and knitting socks for soldiers. Store clerks sometimes assisted them by hiding the Confederate gray material inside packages of calico; the women would then baste it into their petticoats, sometimes hang pistols from their hoop skirts, and "smile serenely at the pickets" who inspected their cargo of "coffee, sugar & calico." Annie Harper, a new bride at the time, later described these practices as if they had been an amusing diversion that revealed how clever young women could be, whether by bribing guards with whiskey or "alighting from the carriage . . . with the air of an old woman of eighty."[47] Such activities could seem amusing only as long as the officials who had the power to halt them did not treat genteel female smugglers as traitorous foes.

Smuggling became more dangerous in early 1864 when General Gresham was transferred to Sherman's army, leaving Natchez in the control of a series of commanders often demeaned by the local elite as "non-gentlemanly." General James M. Tuttle, an Iowan in his early forties who took charge in early March, alienated people on both sides by actions such as pillaging from army accounts and demanding bribes from local residents. His corruption became so blatant that both Major General Henry W. Slocum and Secretary of War Edwin Stanton ordered him relieved of his post by late May and he responded by resigning. Although General Dana recommended that he be prosecuted, Tuttle managed to return to Iowa, where he served in the state legislature after the war.[48]

In July 1864, General Dana visited Natchez to see whether the rumors of rampant corruption were true. He found it extremely difficult to reform the behavior of many officers who, he believed, had been seduced into doing the bidding not only of "cotton speculators and political adventurers" but also of "rebel females" whose beauty and delicacy hid how dangerous they could be. According to him, the "sons and daughters" of the nation had been "debauched," as "supplies of all kinds, including even arms, were freely carried out to the rebels" and many military secrets were "well known in rebeldom."[49] Whether or not

Dana was correct about there being so many duplicitous women, his suspicions led to a clear tightening of the regulations that affected everyone in Natchez.

One of the officers who had taken advantage of less stringent enforcement of the regulations was Adjutant General Lorenzo Thomas, assigned to the Lower Mississippi Valley to oversee conditions for the freedpeople. He had lived in Natchez for a while before the war and looked forward to continuing his friendships with local planters, who he claimed were almost all Unionists.[50] Apparently some of these friends were not so Unionist as he had implied, for less than a year later, General Dana reported that Thomas had allowed Confederate females to pass through the lines without taking an oath, had supplied a member of the Shields family with ammunition for the Confederate Army, and had requisitioned and sold materials for his own profit. Thomas was never arrested, but his son and alleged accomplice, Lieutenant Lorenzo Thomas Jr., was.[51]

The general ordered by Dana to set aside the power of the profiteers and the Confederate sirens was Mason Brayman, a stern man in his early fifties who did not understand or respect those who were willing to put their personal welfare ahead of that of their natal nation. Local citizens who had become used to expressing openly their Southern patriotism under the more forgiving regime of Gresham were shocked when Brayman jailed ladies for nothing more than "saying something disrespectful," confining them "with common men and negroes" until their families paid a bail.[52] After the war, a former official of the Treasury Department in Natchez called for an investigation of Brayman for his "Reign of Terror," claiming that under him and General Tuttle "there was, for females, but two passports to favor, one was to fill their pockets, the other I leave to conjecture." He even suggested that Brayman tried "to rape females in his quarters" and that he was helped out in his underhanded financial dealings by a known prostitute.[53] Whatever the truth of these allegations, it is likely that such rumors were believed by at least some of the elite white women of Natchez. According to one, many people attended a "grand entertainment" hosted by the despised General Brayman because they had heard that "an invitation to the affair was almost equivalent to an order." She declared that she would have preferred banishment, a vow that others considered foolishly impractical.[54]

Soon after his arrival, Brayman ordered a series of raids against the plantations around Natchez to clear out Confederate troops, to break the spirits of the civilians, and to recruit African American men into the army.[55] On one of these forays a Lieutenant Earle was in charge of soldiers sent to arrest Gabriel Shields and take command of his home. Shields, probably concerned about his wife and children, consented to surrender as long as the soldiers discarded their weapons and behaved "like gentlemen." When Earle started to attack Shields again, his twenty-three-year-old daughter, Ellen, intervened, reminding him that he had promised to behave "like an officer and a gentleman." He apologized and told her that he was not a devil but was acting on orders. Unlike Brayman, Earle apparently cared whether Ellen respected him or not, a concern that gave her more power than she would have had otherwise.[56]

Because Brayman, unlike some of his predecessors, did not accept the word of a lady as if it were the truth, he ordered pickets to search the possessions of any female who crossed the lines with a permit and, if they found any contraband, to send her to the headquarters, where a woman could search her clothes.[57] In August 1864, a guard discovered that Augusta Fitzhugh, the wife of a Confederate soldier, had sewn gray cloth into a cushion in her buggy. An officer in charge reported that the "Colored girl" he ordered to search her person found military buttons hidden in her clothes. This African American woman, Sidney Collins, later testified that she had first "waited on" Fitzhugh in the jail, evidence that elite white women did receive some special privileges even after having been arrested.[58] Fitzhugh was tried, found guilty of violating her oath of allegiance to the United States, and fined one thousand dollars.[59] While this may have been an unusually high fine, trials of female smugglers were not rare at this time. Even a relatively severe punishment was not a totally effective deterrent, however, for Fitzhugh was caught smuggling again in November. At that point, Brayman called her "a very foolish and indiscreet woman" and ordered her "to be placed outside the lines . . . not to return under penalty of imprisonment during the war.[60]

In spite of the arrests, smuggling became so common that in late November 1864 Brayman suspended "all passes and permits" to enter or leave Natchez except those involving "military business upon the personal order of the General Commanding"; anyone who tried "to pass . . . clandestinely" would "be treated as spies."[61] A week later, Major General S. A. Hurlbut, based in Vicksburg, ordered the officials in Natchez "to close the lines there 'hermetically' especially against women" because he believed they were regularly sending to the Confederate military "information of all movements" by Federal troops. According to Hurlbut, women in other towns were even beginning to request passes to go to Natchez because they expected to be able to spy and smuggle so easily from there.[62]

Along with enforcing existing regulations more strictly and arresting women who smuggled supplies past the picket lines, Brayman berated local citizens about their rejection of proper gender roles. He did not want anyone to think that he was challenging "the ties that bind families together" and labeled "the home affections . . . the foundations of public morality as well as love of country." He considered it particularly "reprehensible" that men would ask "their Wives and Daughters to take the oath and transact business, while they remain enemies and prepared to fight the Government." When Maria Louisa Williams, like Augusta Fitzhugh, was fined $1,000 for having attempted to smuggle Confederate gray cloth to "the public enemy," Brayman lowered her fine to $100 because he believed that her brother, allegedly part of a "band . . . prowling about our lines," had taken advantage of her familial affection by asking her to help him. He still added, though, that Williams's expectation that officers would violate orders "with careless indulgence" because she had offered them hospitality was evidence that fraternization had "seduced" some men into ignoring their duty.[63] Brayman expected everyone to realize that "by human and Divine law the place of Woman is at the fireside; that of man upon the threshold," and changing places, "especially for bad ends, degrades both."[64] He was calling on Confederate men to behave like proper patriarchs but also to be honorable soldiers who took responsibility for their own actions.

Neither arrests nor moral statements accomplished the cooperation Brayman sought. By early 1865, a new commander, General J. W. Davidson, had become so upset about the fraternization, corruption, and general sloppiness he believed had occurred at many of the picket lines around Natchez that he requested two particular regiments be sent to assist him because he knew "most of the officers" and was convinced that, unlike too many others, these were "intelligent and honorable gentlemen."[65] For Davidson, as for many others, someone he perceived as a gentleman could never behave dishonorably or be duped by flirtatious belles. As the war did not last much longer, it is doubtful that the issue of controlling the behavior of either those guarding the boundaries of Natchez or those trying to go to and from the city was ever solved to the satisfaction of anyone.

While planter-class mothers were focusing on how to protect and feed their children and sometimes how to smuggle supplies or secrets to the Confederate military, their daughters and nieces of marriageable age were dividing their attention between helping out with some of the housework once done exclusively by slaves, writing supportive letters to Confederate soldiers in their social network, and deciding how to react to individual occupying officers who seemed so attractive and genteel that they might have become their beaux in peacetime. The more a young lady had expected the occupiers to be inhumane barbarians, the more ready she would be to label as an exception any man who surprised her with respect and polite manners. According to one member of the invading force, only six weeks into the occupation, "young ladies who, when we landed ran home, shrieking 'the Yankees have come, what shall we do?' . . . and bolted bed-room doors in their terror, are now, many of them, rather pleased than otherwise to receive a call from a Yankee officer."[66] This anonymous soldier was, in effect, implying that he might have been equally pleased to be a gentleman caller at the home of a charming young Southern lady.

At first, a number of young women were determined to treat even gentlemanly officers as their enemy. While confiscating valuables from the home of Joseph Shields, one man politely raised his cap as he returned to eighteen-year-old Mary a silver goblet that had fallen out of the wires of her hoopskirt. This kindness, however, did not restrain her from taking out her anger on another soldier who asked her how to eat a pomegranate. She demurely told him to bite on it as on an apple and enjoyed the "tongue lashing" he gave her when he discovered the bitterness of its skin.[67] Such a prank may have been a way for Mary to guarantee the maintenance of a comfortable distance between herself and genteel soldiers.

Some belles demeaned "Yankees" as a class, while also acknowledging that most of the commanding officers "could not find it in their hearts to deny the ladies anything."[68] Elizabeth Brown, an unmarried diarist in her early twenties, found it "a great consolation to find some gentlemen among the enemy" but was so concerned about seeming disloyal to the Confederate cause that she almost did not tell her mother when she noticed that one of their guards was sick. Reluctant to return good manners with bad, however, she sent General Ransom "a handsome bouquet" when he arranged for stronger protection for their property.[69]

In the early days of the occupation, Kate Foster hoped the soldiers might "remember that they have mothers, wives & sisters at home" so they might "treat us as they would wish them to be by our men." When she thought of the army as a whole, however, she could not imagine their respecting ladies and declared, "I know that I hate them." As she was living with her aunt near a road along which the troops traveled and where pickets were posted, a series of Union soldiers asked her for food and drink. After spending three hours talking to one officer who had seemed to share her opinion of Lincoln, she told herself that she had been true to her principles because she "did not ask him to take a seat."[70] Foster restrained herself somewhat in her attraction to the young officers by condemning young women who seemed less ambivalent than she, criticizing "some of the young ladies around Natchez" who had "*so little character*" that they could not "resist love of admiration" enough to refuse to receive "attention from the Yankees." She admitted, however, that she had, much to her surprise, "seen three or four" lieutenants who seemed to be "perfect gentlemen," concluding that she would be "happy . . . to entertain them" if they only wore a Confederate uniform.[71] After one officer offered to punish soldiers who were taking advantage of the local citizens, she pondered, "This man was a gentleman but we know not how long this *appearance* of kindness will be kept up."[72] The usual ways of evaluating who might be an acceptable acquaintance were causing more confusion than reassurance.

To some extent, so many officers appeared to be gentlemen because they had been encouraged to befriend local Confederates in the hope that they might change their allegiance, and many of the youngest may have been as anxious as the local belles to have some fun with the opposite sex. According to General Gresham's wife, several young officers, particularly a civil engineer in his mid-twenties, were so "popular with the young belles of Natchez" that "when it came to a flirtation there was neither blue nor gray."[73] One brigade gave a military ball in October 1863 "for the purpose of cultivating a social feeling between the citizens of this city and the Union officers."[74]

Belles sometimes convinced themselves that they could proselytize for the Southern way of life through their hospitality. After several entertained Lieutenant Richard Hall and one sent him roses every few days, he changed his mind about opposing slavery and came to enjoy being served by "a Black boy."[75] It is difficult to determine who was influencing whom, however, when soldiers told women they no longer wanted to fight people they liked so much and begged them to tell their men to end the war.[76] Like later historians, the women and men involved in these interactions may have found it difficult to distinguish between authentic and feigned feelings. So much of Southern elite femininity required wearing a pleasant social mask that fooling a Northern picket may have seemed much like a belle convincing an unattractive suitor that she was heartbroken that she could not dance with him that evening. Federal officers with roots in the same elite social circles were probably just as effective at hiding their true sentiments. When the sister of a local bank president tried to remove ten thousand dollars from the area, a "handsome officer" asked to search her carriage. She smiled sweetly, and he let her go. After the war, he told her at a party in New York that although he had assumed she was hiding something valuable, her "poise" had "completely disarmed" him.[77] There was probably a parallel dynamic with slightly different behavioral rules for interactions between soldiers and females from the lower classes, but those who were proud of their genteel identity were not apt to fraternize with anyone whose manners did not meet their standards.

Some elite young women and officers went beyond occasional casual flirting and developed relatively strong friendships. Twenty-five-year-old Mary Ker, a fervent Confederate at the start of the war, had made the unusual decision to live on her own after her widowed mother's death in 1862. Although a younger brother fighting for the Confederacy advised her "not to receive socially the yankee officers, even though they *might* be 'gentlemen,'"[78] by January 1864 she had turned her home into a social center for a select group of her Natchez friends and a few genteel Union officers, some of whom she corresponded with after the war. Lieutenant Richard Kent, one of her frequent guests, complained later that he had not enjoyed Mobile (which had not been occupied until April 1865) so much as Natchez because there was "none of that social feeling existing between the citizens and the army, such . . . as made the army give Natchez the name of 'Soldiers' Paradise.'"[79] One of the officers who habituated the Ker salon was Major George McKee. Whatever his official duties, he was comfortable bending the rules to maintain his new friendships. When he spent some time in Vicksburg, he became a friend of another member of the elite Natchez network, forwarding a message from her to Ker because "the 'blockade' precludes her from sending letters herself."[80] In Ker's parlor, everyone apparently felt free to set aside his or her wartime identities and to connect as fictive kin with a common social background. The experience was so pleasant that she later complained to a friend in New Orleans that the end of the war made her life "dull . . . on account of the change of society." Her friend reminded her that the poor belles of New Orleans had experienced "no society at all during these four long years of warfare,"[81] indicating that they had been less willing to become friendly with the occupying soldiers than their peers in Natchez had been.

While enjoying the company of charming young officers, many young women were also cultivating a protective patron. Colonel Loren Kent, one of Ker's frequent visitors, asked a doctor to give her his "official and personal consideration" because he considered her a "very particular friend, deservedly so from the many kindnesses she has returned to me."[82] With the assistance of Kent and other admirers, Ker received a general travel pass for the Natchez area in September 1864, a "quiet and gentlemanly" guard for her house in October, a gun permit for self-protection in January 1865, and a permit to sell ten bales of cotton from the plantation she owned with her younger brother in March. The revolver permit stated that she was a "loyal citizen," an indication that she had agreed to sign the oath.[83] Mary Ker, like many other women in her class in Natchez, was pleased when she could pass pleasant evenings with friendly gentlemen, even though they represented the army that was fighting against her brothers. But her desire to own a gun indicated that she was willing to stand up for herself if the gentlemanly guard and the even more genteel visitors did not turn out to offer her sufficient protection.

At times the occupation of Natchez challenged the social assumptions of both women from the planter class and U.S. officers who thought of themselves as gentlemen, and at other times it reinforced their traditional prejudices. The discourse of nationalism, whether Confederate, Unionist, or American, did not always harmonize with that of genteel femininity and masculinity. While perceiving some men in U.S. uniforms as "vulgar" and dangerous, many planter females decided that others were gentlemanly, as well as conveniently able to help ladies in ways even most of their male relatives could not at that point. Elite females who used their gentility in a pragmatic way helped their families endure occupation with their economic and social privileges more or less intact, while those who chose to take the Confederate moral high road were apt to experience more economic loss. Young women may have been glad to find a beau in a uniform of any color, but they—and their mothers—also wanted guards and travel passes. All had to learn what it meant to choose between principles and personal welfare. In various ways, women from the planter class had called for a genteel occupation in which officials would recognize their rights as ladies. Enough Northern officers were willing to accommodate them to frustrate other officers who, whatever their class background, were focused solely on the war.

[III]

OCCUPATIONS WITHIN
OCCUPATION

Race, Class, and Culture

Between Slavery and Freedom

African American Women and Occupation in the Slave South

LESLIE A. SCHWALM

Because their wartime occupation occurred as part of their transition from slavery to freedom, enslaved women experienced it as no other Southern women did. Their occupation was further distinguished by its chronology and by the impact and consequences of military policy. Unlike that of Southern white women, slave women's occupation began before shots were fired at Fort Sumter. Even as the secession crisis developed, enslaved women's communities were subject to intense scrutiny, a surveillance far more acute and violent than the South had known since Nat Turner's rebellion in 1831. When secession led into war, enslaved people would also be occupied, metaphorically, by slave owners, who came to regard their slaves, including women, as "enemies in our own households."[1] South Carolinian Mary Chesnut eventually feared the "Yankees in front" but also the "negroes in the rear." After the murder of an acquaintance by slaves, her sister became suspicious of the close attentions she received from slave women in her own household: "Is this to protect me or murder me," she wondered.[2] In this context of both imagined threats and demonstrated rebellion, slave owners became self-conscious "occupiers," closely monitored their slaves, and increasingly resorted to imprisonment, physical coercion, and even executions of the suspected enemies in their midst. In addition, enslaved women were "occupied" by the Confederate provost guard and civilian militias, who policed slave populations and punished those who were suspected of rebellion or who attempted to flee, at precisely the moment when the numbers of enslaved women running away—and toward the Union lines—exceeded every precedent, including the massive flight of slaves during the American Revolution.[3] Finally, enslaved women were occupied by the Union Army, with its evolving, unevenly enforced, sometimes liberating, and often dangerous policy toward female fugitives from slavery. Enslaved women were initially targeted for exclusion, removal, and relocation, and it would be the third year of the war before occupying forces settled on a role for them in the war effort, one that commodified their productive labor: as field hands on abandoned plantations and as laborers in the wood camps that kept navy ships fueled. While their experience of occupation fell far short of the freedom they hoped for, it was nonetheless a staggering, welcomed difference from being chattel property, held and seized as collateral, loaned, or bought and sold on the open marketplace.

Each stage of their occupation dramatically altered the circumstances of wartime bondage for enslaved women. When they were under the occupation of slave owners early in the war, the material conditions of daily life declined. As wartime shortages reduced provisioning, enslaved peoples' suffering increased proportionately. With fewer resources at hand, enslaved women's central role in reproductive labor became increasingly important and increasingly difficult in the slave quarters as well as in the homes of their owners. In addition, the cost of waging war, as well as the social and economic instabilities that war visited upon the Southern home front, had an unanticipated and corroding impact on the institution of slavery. Mastery began to lose its power and resiliency.[4]

The wartime erosion of slavery under Confederate occupation had mixed consequences for enslaved women. They faced numerous obstacles to surviving with their families intact, as their families were separated by Confederate impressment agents seizing slave men to labor in defense works, as their communities became targets of officially sanctioned terror and violence, and as they faced dispersal when planters were required by local authorities to send their slaves away from advancing Union armies. At the same time, when Confederate and state government restrictions disrupted the cycles of cotton agriculture that had regimented slave life, and when white men withdrew from daily management of farms and plantations to be enlisted or drafted into military service, enslaved men and women carefully exploited the weaknesses that began to appear in the system of slavery. Even when reinforced by Confederate soldiers and civilian militia, the relations of power and domination that had once sustained the institution of slavery began to wither.[5]

Enslaved women became occupied by the Union Army when they made an active decision to exchange slavery for the freedom and relative safety they hoped to gain under the protection of Union forces.[6] Their flight to Union lines (or their refusal to flee as Union forces approached) was a tactic in their war against slavery and a stage in their journey toward freedom. As the Union Army drove deeper into the Confederacy over the course of the war, an unprecedented number of slaves, particularly women and children, came into Union lines. Roughly 320,000 enslaved people (out of a population of about 4 million slaves) became "occupied" by Union forces during the war, and more than half of them were women and children.[7] With the onset of war, sex, age, and family status were no longer useful predictors of who would or could flee.[8]

Most significant, women's flight from slavery to Union lines was an effort to transform the meaning of reproduction in their lives. As they led their children out of bondage, African American mothers rejected slaveholders' claims on their progeny and absolved themselves of the terrible burden that enslaved motherhood had forced upon them—of adding to the wealth of slave owners by bringing a child into the world as a slave, subject not only to punishment, deprivation and discipline but also to the looming likelihood of family separation by sale, seizure, punishment, or estate disposal. The ecstatic relief and victory of that moment were sometimes observed by Union soldiers, including an Iowa soldier during his march through Alabama: "Some of the negros came out to meet us, and I Shall never forget one old Woman. I heard her shouting 1/4 of a mile away. When we came up to where she was She was jumping up and down and Shouting Glory to God and the Yankees forever. She said my ten Chilen all free haliluyah."[9] But despite the primary importance enslaved women placed on emancipating the meaning of motherhood and reclaiming their reproductive labor, it was their productive labor, and its commodification by Northern employers and then military authorities, that would guarantee their protection from reenslavement and secure for them a place behind Union lines.

Although gender played a critical role in shaping their experience of occupation, African American women who exchanged their status as slaves for the status of occupied women shared little in common with Southern white women who also came under Union occupation. Choosing to flee slavery meant that black women, like white prostitutes, female bread rioters, and female refugees, were moving into the public sphere in an unmediated and unprecedented fashion. But the risks of occupation were far greater and vastly different for former slave women, who seemed poised to gain the most from their Union allies in the war against Southern slave owners yet were accorded so very few gender-specific privileges or protections by those allies. Southern white women feared that the enemy's occupying forces intended to "Butlerize" them—deny them the prerogatives of their womanhood, as General Benjamin Butler threatened while commanding the occupation of New Orleans.[10] But historian Drew Gilpin Faust has demonstrated that Confederate women used their womanhood as a weapon, as a political tool, and as a disguise during the course of the war, deploying the prerogatives of their gendered immunity to violence in order to "manage their occupiers," demanding and often receiving privileges and protections as women.[11] For fugitive slave women, however, their womanhood attached only disabilities to their experience of occupation. Until the spring of 1863, the only consistent recognition of their womanhood that the occupying Union Army offered to fugitive slave women was to exclude them from the policies they developed that allowed the army to maximize the use of slave men as military laborers. Not only were women excluded, but they were also warehoused in contraband camps and with Northern employers. Only in 1863, after the combined impact of the Emancipation Proclamation and the Union's victory over Vicksburg allowed an unprecedented number of slaves to make their way to Union lines, and only after Northern employers found former slave women's labor a serviceable substitute for the workers they had lost to the army, did the Union finally identify a specific role for former slave women in the Union-occupied South. The army turned to commodifying former slave women's productive labor on abandoned plantations and in the wood yards that kept the navy in fuel.

From the perspective of most white military officials, African Americans lacked the innate characteristics that would allow them to attain the highly differentiated gender roles that marked white civilization.[12] This view of inferior black manhood and womanhood would directly impact Union policy; it encouraged the exclusion of black men from military service but also rationalized a widespread pattern of maltreatment of fugitive slave women and disregard for the familial connections and responsibilities that marked their womanhood.[13] White Union soldiers and their commanders frequently shared with white Southerners a disdain for bondswomen, regarding them as salacious "public women," undeserving of masculine respect or protection and unfit for social proximity to white women except as their servants. With the somewhat sympathetic term "refugee" reserved for displaced whites, contemporary observers found themselves lacking even the terminology to describe self-liberating slave women.[14] The label that came into wide contemporary usage—"contraband of war" or "contrabands"—grouped slave women and men with the wagons, horses, and miscellaneous enemy property seized by the Union Army. The term simultaneously dehumanized fugitive slaves and reflected technical military usage that bore little resemblance to the acts of courage and desperation that prompted women, men, and their families to risk all with their flight to Union lines. But most important, the term indicated the Union Army's dual difficulty in reconciling popular racist caricatures with the women who fled to their lines and in reconciling military policy with the humanitarian needs of a steadily increasing civilian, noncombatant population coming into Union lines.

Whether in the eastern or western theater of war, in towns, in cities, or on the barrier islands off the southeastern coast, on plantations or farms, in Union or Confederate slave states, enslaved women found that the arrival of occupying Union forces brought potentially liberating but also ambiguous and sometimes dangerous consequences. In the complex evolution of legislation, articles of war, presidential proclamations, and military edicts that marked the Union's changing policies toward slavery and enslaved people over the course of the war, enslaved women's experience of occupation was marked more by the fact that they were not men than by the fact that they were women. Official policy toward enslaved people was gendered, but primarily to the extent that those policies reinforced traditional notions about war as a masculine endeavor. As a result, the story of enslaved women's occupation under the Union Army is as much a story of exclusion as it is a story of how the army finally envisioned black women as people whose labor could be commodified to support the war effort.

The invasion and occupation of the South by Union forces would place enslaved women intent on gaining their freedom in open conflict with the policy directing the army's contact with enslaved people. Early in the war, with the support of white Northerners as well as the loyalty of four slaveholding border states in the balance, President Lincoln directed his commanders to conduct the war without interfering in the practice or legality of slavery.[15] General Benjamin Butler was one of the first Union officers to demonstrate what that policy could mean. In Maryland, Butler offered his forces to the governor to aid in the suppression of a rumored slave insurrection.[16]

But no sooner had Butler's forces headed south and taken possession of Fortress Monroe in Tidewater Virginia in May 1861 than the policy of noninterference was tested first by enslaved men and soon by large numbers of women and children who believed that the war would determine the fate of slavery and hoped that Union soldiers would be their liberators. Within a matter of days after Butler's arrival, the number of fugitive slaves approaching his forces grew in magnitude.[17] With the Confederate Army impressing local slave and free black men to aid in the war effort and slave owners threatening to remove enslaved women and children from the proximity of Union forces, slave families chose flight to the occupying Union Army and an uncertain guarantee for the future over their certain fate under wartime slavery. Despite Lincoln's instructions, Butler accepted the fugitive slaves into his lines. He grouped them with other "contraband of war," enemy property that, because it was being used in the Confederate war effort, was a legitimate target of confiscation.[18]

This first departure from Lincoln's initial policy of nonintervention had come from one of the Union's most conservative officers on the question of slavery. Even so, Butler, a shrewd peacetime lawyer, understood that in the matter of the disposition of fugitive slaves he was faced with an issue of considerable magnitude with complicated military, political, and humanitarian ramifications. Because President Lincoln and his commanders insisted that the war could and should be fought and won with slavery intact, the army was left ill prepared for its role as an occupying force, particularly in light of the large proportion of women and children among black refugees. But wars require laborers nearly as much as they require soldiers, and even at this early point in the conflict, Butler relaxed the "hands-off" policy toward slavery demanded by the Lincoln administration and allowed fugitive slave men who had been employed in the Confederate war effort into Union lines to deprive the enemy of their labor and to gain it for the Union.

But Butler also accepted women and children into his lines; after all, as he noted at the time, how could he accept "the services of a Father and a Mother and not take the children?"[19] At this early point in the war and in the evolution of Union responses to the determination of enslaved people to free themselves, Butler separated fugitive slaves into two groups: those "able-bodied men and women" whose labor was an important commodity in the Union war effort, and families—primarily mothers with their children—whom he categorized as "nonlaborers" and proposed to support by taxing the able-bodied laborers.[20] Butler showed no qualms about putting fugitive slave women to work in support of his army; he had no misgivings that feminine frailty might disable these African American women from physical labor. Yet Butler also seems to have been guided by some concern for gender conventions, since there is no evidence that fugitive slave women were employed in the construction of batteries or the digging of trenches. They may, however, have been among those sent to work in local hospitals to help with the wounded after the local battle at Big Bethel on June 10. Soon they would also be employed as regimental laundresses, while others set up cake stands and marketed food to soldiers and fugitive slaves alike.[21]

By the end of July 1861, nearly nine hundred fugitive slaves—two-thirds of them women and children—had taken up residence in and around Fortress Monroe. The women, Butler noted, "were earning substantially their own subsistence," affirming his decision to accept them into Union lines as laborers in support of the Union cause, but the large numbers of children who came under his control were another matter. Never impressed by the Confederates and unable to subsist themselves, the children "must be considered an encumbrance rather than the auxiliary of the army" and fell outside his own definition of "contraband of war." Yet Butler felt his "duty as a human man is very plain." He would admit and take care of the men, women, and children.[22]

Unfortunately, neither the army nor Congress would embrace Butler's initial deployment of slave women as military laborers; they also did not endorse his attention to the humanitarian issues involved when fugitive families confronted the occupying army. The result was the First Confiscation Act, signed into law in August 1861, in which Congress adopted a significantly circumscribed version of Butler's policy for Union commands throughout the South. Rather than take as its premise Butler's willingness to accept all the families who approached his lines and use the labor of all those who were able bodied, female as well as male, Congress approved a far narrower policy that authorized the punitive seizure only of that enemy property directly employed in the rebellion.[23] Women and children were a large proportion of the fugitive slaves approaching Federal lines, but they were excluded from the provisions of the First Confiscation Act—both because the Confederacy rarely impressed slave women and because the First Confiscation Act was an intentionally moderate response to a potentially revolutionary problem. White Northerners were not prepared to support an emancipatory policy, and Congress sought careful rationalization for any policy that authorized the seizure of personal property.[24] Furthermore, Northerners had already begun to weigh in with their fears that the "great mass of recently emancipated slaves" might become "idlers, marauders, and 'a curse to the community,'" as one New York periodical put it; many white Northerners associated black emancipation with the northward migration of former slaves and were opposed to both prospects.[25] Seizing only those slave men impressed by Confederate authorities provided Congress and the president with a legal rationale that sidestepped any suggestion of Union interference in slavery. Congress thus steered Union policy clear of any discussion of the legal status or future condition of confiscated slaves beyond negating all claims by rebel owners to (men's) productive labor. The act was notable in its recognition that the labor of former slaves might become an important resource in the war, but the Federal government's new policy was nonetheless more noninterventionist than it was emancipatory, especially for enslaved women.

In only three months, Fortress Monroe had become an important staging ground for the collision between the confiscation policy newly adopted by the occupying Union Army and the pursuit of freedom by enslaved women and men. The drama that unfolded there would repeat itself across the South as soldiers, Federal authorities, slave owners, and enslaved people battled over the role that occupying forces of the Union Army would play in the wartime collapse of slavery and the role fugitive slave women would play in the Union effort.

Given the narrow constraints of the First Confiscation Act, fugitive slave women and their children were key beneficiaries when Congress issued the Second Confiscation Act in August 1862. Because it authorized Union confiscation of slaves of all disloyal owners (as well as guaranteeing their freedom), the 1862 act dramatically broadened the grounds on which Union forces could accept the growing numbers of fugitive slaves into their lines. As one white soldier in the Mississippi Valley reported in the month following the passage of the act, "The entire negro population of the valley, which at one time constituted nineteen twentieths of its inhabitants, seems to regard our mission here to simply be their deliverance, hence I am constantly besieged." White Union soldiers varied in their responses to the growing numbers of fugitive slaves arriving at their camps. Some welcomed and valued their labor; having "2 boys and a woman to wait on us, and wash & sew" made camp life "quite comfortable" for one Minnesota company.[26] Other white soldiers, however, regarded women and children as a nuisance. The "problem" with the arrival of fugitive slaves in camp, complained another soldier, was that "every Sambo has his Dinah and maybe a litter of little 'pickaninnies' that we have no sort of use for, and don't know what to do with."[27] Although former slave women could and did perform essential and valued labor for Union soldiers and encampments, as laundresses, cooks, nurses, and servants, they were just as frequently regarded as an encumbrance at the same time that fugitive slave men were increasingly valued and welcomed into Union lines as military laborers. General Butler's initial solution, which recognized that some fugitive slave women could ably support the war effort while others with young children to care for would need to be supported, had been supplanted by the First Confiscation Act. Consequently, Union officials would struggle, over the course of the war, to "fit" slave women into Union policies that were driven primarily by an increasing reliance on slave men's contributions to the Union war effort. Many commanders in both the eastern and western theaters of war found it simpler to exclude fugitive slaves from Union lines and, later, to relocate them to contraband camps.[28]

One of the attempted solutions to emerge out of the conflicted juncture of women's pursuit of freedom and the restrictive policies of the occupying Union Army was the relocation of enslaved people—the majority of them women and children—to Northern states and to abandoned Southern plantations leased to venture capitalists who rented the land and hired former slaves.[29] Ironically, relocation was premised on the assumption of women's ability to work and an existing demand among Northern employers for them as laborers.

The relocation of occupied women was first proposed when the Northern public gained word of Union "embarrassment . . . felt with regard to a proper disposal" of self-liberated Southern blacks, men and women. In August 1861, it was abolitionist Lewis Tappan who initially suggested to Butler that a civilian committee could help to remove the "self-emancipated negroes" from Union lines to the "farms and workshops and families of northern citizens."[30] Although Butler rejected Tappan's proposal (as expensive, dangerous to the health of a people racially suited to a Southern climate, and contradictory to their desire to stay in the South if their safety could be assured), enslaved people in pursuit of both protection and freedom were already putting distance between themselves and their former owners by accompanying Union troops in their movement through the nation's capital during the early months of war and joining the fugitive slaves who gathered there in improvised camps. Also in this first year of war, a few Union soldiers had begun to arrange with individual "contraband" to send them to their own Northern homes or communities, where the wartime labor shortage was already being felt.[31]Relocation would evolve from these hastily improvised responses to a more coherent policy in the Mississippi Valley during the late summer of 1862 in the aftermath of the Second Confiscation Act.[32] With the expansion of officially sanctioned confiscation, as well as official encouragement for the widespread employment of male contraband as military laborers, growing numbers of black refugee families approached the occupying forces of the Union—which were still without the benefit of a well-considered policy or adequate resources to protect or subsist them. As a result, those families encountered commanders like General W. T. Sherman, at Memphis, Tennessee, who insisted, "We never harbour women or children—we give employment to men." "No instructions had come or could come to guide me," he explained, "and I was forced to lay down certain rules for my own guidance."[33] In a matter of weeks, Union commanders would begin organizing contraband camps, but conditions at those camps varied widely in different regions of the South and under superintendents of differing sympathies and capabilities. Of course, poorly considered or ineffectually developed policies were plentiful in other arenas of the military bureaucracy (such as medical care, purchasing and distributing supplies, and the disposition of prisoners). But the failure to respond more effectively and humanely to the determination of enslaved people to gain their freedom and aid the Union cause could not be laid to the challenges of modern warfare; racism and the very specific denigration of enslaved women were powerful forces among ill-advised commanders with deeply held beliefs about the mutually informed meanings of race and gender in American society.

The large-scale relocation of former slave women northward first began in September 1862, when several hundred people, mostly women and children, who had recently arrived at the contraband camp that had been established at Cairo, Illinois, were sent (under the authority of the secretary of war, at government expense, and with the assistance of secular and denominational charities) to employers in Illinois, Iowa, Wisconsin, and Minnesota, where wartime labor shortages were having a particularly significant impact.[34] Their numbers included "large lots" of women and children who had been sent to Cairo from Tennessee by Major General Grant, many of them the families of black men employed by the army.[35] Officers in the field welcomed the opportunity to relieve their camps of women and children; Minnesotan Lucius Hubbard, writing from northern Alabama in September 1862, noted: "I am constantly besieged by men, women and children, who apply for 'protection,' and facilities for leaving the country. . . . I was sorely puzzled to know what to do with them." Within a month, he sent five hundred former slaves north; "they flocked into my camp in great crowds, and I shipped them as fast as I could get transportation. They are in a free state by this time."[36] Hubbard's relief was shared by many other Union commanders; the army could now rid itself of a large and undesirable noncombatant population.

Contraband camps would become an important part of the mechanics of relocation. The camps were established, however, not to aid in relocation but rather to handle the overflow of female and child fugitives from slavery who came into Union lines.[37] For example, a contraband camp was established at Helena, Arkansas, in mid-July 1862 when General Samuel Curtis advanced into that state down the White River.[38] Within ten days of arriving at Helena, his quartermaster reported "a perfect 'Cloud' of negroes being thrown upon me for Sustenance & Support" as Southern slaves began abandoning their masters, some—including a considerable number of women and children—traveling long distances to make their way to the camp. Of the first 50 fugitive slaves the quartermaster had to feed, he noted, only 12 were what he called "working stock": able-bodied men who could perform military labor. "What am I to do with them," he asked.[39] Those 50 fugitive slaves who arrived in July had increased to 900 by September and to 4,000 by January, with the Emancipation Proclamation increasing the flight from slavery.[40]

Women and children encountered conditions at some camps that posed a significant humanitarian problem, while Union commanders felt that coping with the noncombatant population of women and children drained the Union war effort of resources and materiel and put post commanders in the vulnerable position of improvising on official policy.[41] Housing in the contraband camp at Helena, for example, consisted of cast-off army tents and roughly hewn cabins.[42] Close to the Mississippi River, the camp often flooded; drinking water was contaminated; and soldiers and contraband alike were vulnerable to Confederate attack.[43] As the superintendent of contrabands reported, Union soldiers often mistreated the contraband, sometimes taking over their cabins and robbing them of their few possessions. Women in the camp were sexually assaulted, and their defenders among the contraband were attacked and even murdered.[44] Hundreds of contraband men were employed to work on the fortifications at Helena and to transfer government stores from ships, but they were not paid regularly—if at all.[45] There were far fewer opportunities for women to support themselves or their children, and they often lacked the most basic necessities. The camp hospital was "notorious for filth, neglect, mortality & brutal whipping."[46] Suffering patients testified to "cruelties and barbarities perpetrated on male and female," including many who were "brutally beaten." A "notorious number" of deaths had occurred at the hospital.[47]

At Cairo, Illinois, some 800–1,000 people, "nearly all" women and children, were held "in a most miserable condition" by October 1862, suffering from a want of clothing and bedding, many of them sick.[48] By April 1863, 5,000 contrabands were reported to be in the camp, and more than 2,000 former slaves were still gathered at the camp at the end of the war.[49] Like Helena, Cairo occupied a very unpleasant location, on a low peninsula that was subject to flooding from both the Ohio and Mississippi rivers; it was muddy and rat-infested.[50] Most came into the camp with "very poor" clothing, "many of them hardly enough to cover their nakedness." Unlike the fugitives who occasionally arrived at contraband camps in the South with some personal possessions, those who were shipped to Cairo arrived with empty hands and empty pockets. Food rations were somewhat better than those provided in other camps—at Cairo they were given the same kind and quantity as soldiers' rations. Three hospitals were established, and Northern Quakers took up the work of organizing and teaching schools there. Local military officials seemed indifferent, offering little cooperation or opposition to the presence of the contraband.[51] But the former slaves were not safe from depredations either by soldiers or by local citizens, described at the close of the war as "bitter negro haters" who committed a series of "petty abuses and outrages" on the women there.[52] The attacks against women and their daughters "would shock the moral sensibilities of any well-regulated mind or community," according to one observer.[53]

Early in March 1863, as the Emancipation Proclamation increased the stream of Southern blacks to Union lines in the Mississippi Valley, a contraband camp was established at St. Louis, which also became an important gateway for organized relocation. Brigadier General B. M. Prentiss, then in charge at Helena, sent five hundred people—again, mostly women and children—by steamboat to St. Louis.[54] His superior, Major General Samuel Curtis—then commanding the Department of the Missouri—was unhappy with their arrival and warned Prentiss to send no more.[55] However, another observer—Samuel Sawyer, an Indiana chaplain escorting the boat and soon to be appointed the city's superintendent of contraband—encouraged Prentiss to send up as many people from the overcrowded camp at Helena as he wished.[56]

Despite the concern Curtis expressed at being overwhelmed with fugitive slaves in a location where slavery remained legal (and where he was obligated to protect it), St. Louis quickly became a major and purposefully temporary stopping place for African American women who hoped to leave slavery behind them. Curtis (among the most empathetic of Union commanders toward the uncertain status and experience of former slaves) seized the abandoned Missouri Hotel to house the arrivals, and within two weeks, hundreds of women and children were being sent north and west to Wisconsin, Illinois, Iowa, and Kansas. With thousands of applications from potential Northern employers directed to St. Louis, Sawyer enthusiastically expected the Missouri Hotel to become "the leading contraband intelligence office for the great Northwest."[57]

The women and children sent to St. Louis benefited from the very efficient and unusual organization that local military officials turned to when the first steamer arrived from Helena: the city's all-female, interracial, and abolitionist Contraband Relief Society. The society had first organized in late January 1863, initially to collect donations for contraband at Cairo, Helena, and Memphis, but soon turned to the caring for the former slaves arriving daily in its own city. Working with a small staff of soldiers, the society managed to provide for the constant flow of people, including meals, clothing, two schools, and a hospital for sick and dying. Finally, society members also took on the work of organizing the relocation to the North. They screened potential employers and covered the costs of transportation for many of the estimated 2,500–3,500 freedpeople who were housed at the hotel.[58] They worked closely with the provost marshal's office in making sure that employment contracts were properly drawn up and that each person obtained a certificate of freedom and was outfitted with appropriate clothes and shoes for the climate of the Northern states.[59]

Of the three major camps through which female fugitives from slavery in the Mississippi Valley were likely to pass in their difficult, complicated, and sometimes desperate journeys north, the conditions within the "camp" at St. Louis were by all accounts the safest of the three—at least in part because local civilians, rather than the occupying forces of the Union Army, took primary responsibility for their well-being. Still, city slaves, fugitive slaves, and free blacks in St. Louis were all vulnerable to kidnapping and sale south. Slave owners and slave traders alike supported an active business with "professional man-hunters" in recapturing runaways (or men and woman the traders claimed were runaways) and sending them out of state where they could be sold.[60] African Americans in the city were also at the center of an open and ongoing contest among slave traders, city police, provost marshals, and Union soldiers over the status of the city's slaves, suspected runaways, and contrabands. An extension of the internecine struggle in Missouri between radical and conservative Unionists and pro-slavery Confederate sympathizers, the tug-of-war between anti- and pro-slavery forces in St. Louis had dire consequences for African Americans.[61] This ongoing political turmoil prompted President Lincoln to appoint a new commander in May 1863, and General John M. Schofield soon implemented changes in the occupying army's handling of fugitive slaves sent to St. Louis.[62] By early September, Schofield ordered the centrally located Missouri Hotel closed and the fugitives relocated to Benton Barracks on the outskirts of the city. The Contraband Relief Society continued its work, aiding the contrabands—who were now largely women and children, as black enlistment ushered thousands of fugitive slave men into the Union Army.[63] Between the fall of 1863 and early 1864, more than nine hundred additional women and children came into Benton Barracks; most would be relocated north.[64] That period also saw the resumption of relocation efforts (now by civilian groups) in the eastern theater of war. Civilians would continue supporting relocation efforts after the war, from the eastern seaboard to the middle and upper Midwest.[65]

Relocation relieved the occupying army of the burden of protecting and subsisting a noncombatant population within its lines, and many midwestern farmers and employers whose workers had enlisted or been drafted into the Union Army were eager to make arrangements to hire the black refugees. When shiploads of former slave women disembarked at Mississippi River towns, they were often outnumbered by the employers who anxiously awaited the opportunity to hire them.[66] Many of those employers were Northern white women, eager for both household help and farm laborers. Northern white women flooded military officials and civilians involved in the war effort (including Annie Wittenmyer) with requests for "employable" black women. The possibility of obtaining black servants, according to one white Minnesota family, "had given house wives all around the wench fever," suggesting that many Northern white employers were simply desperate for domestic and farm help and some were attracted to the elite status that would accrue to them as white householders who could afford black servants.[67] There is little evidence to suggest that these employers were motivated by abolitionist sympathies. Rather, Northern white civilians seemed more than willing to commodify the labor of former slaves.

Government-sponsored relocation of former slave women and children to the North also provoked extensive opposition from white Northerners who feared that a flood of black migration might upset the well-established dynamics of white supremacy in the North. Relocation drew strikes and protests by white workers, who refused to work side by side with black workers or feared being replaced by blacks willing to earn less pay. Relocation shaped partisan politics in both the 1862 and 1864 elections and provoked meetings and mob actions by farmers and villagers who insisted on defending the racial purity of the white domestic sphere, while others protested that emancipated slaves would be unwilling to work and would become a burden to the public treasury. Whites who employed the relocated former slaves were visited by angry neighbors and mobs and were targeted for threats and violence. Rarely enforced laws limiting and prohibiting black migration into midwestern states were suddenly resurrected.[68]

Former slave women's perspective on the opportunities presented by relocation to the North are harder to document. They were removed from the threat of reenslavement, but they often had to leave spouses, family, and friends behind. They were also dependent on the trustworthiness of their Northern employers and faced long, complicated, and risky journeys to completely unknown locations to live with white strangers, some of whom were violently opposed to their arrival. Elizabeth Estell, a fugitive from Missouri slavery, traveled by steamboat, train, and stagecoach to Cleveland, Minnesota, where her employer's family resided. Restless throughout her stay in rural Minnesota, Estell especially missed her husband (who had enlisted) and her two children, who remained in Missouri. Perhaps the cooking, sewing, laundry, cleaning, and farm chores that she was expected to perform for a family of four were harder or more tedious than she had expected, or the isolation starker, or the lack of a firm arrangement concerning her wages too disappointing for her to appreciate the lessons in reading and writing and the occasional sleigh rides she received in exchange for her labor. Certainly her experience was not unique among the thousands of African American women who came to the rural Midwest under similar circumstances.[69]

Former slave women found their relocation northward brought to an abrupt but temporary stop during in the fall of 1862, on the orders of Secretary of War Edwin Stanton, who feared that vigorous Northern opposition to black relocation might undermine support for Republican candidates in the upcoming election. After the election, relocation was quickly resurrected, and women and children were once more transported north from Cairo and St. Louis.[70] But by 1863, military authorities (under pressure from the Lincoln administration) looked instead to black enlistment and the employment of contrabands on abandoned plantations in the South as a solution to the flow of fugitive slaves into Union lines and Northern anxiety about Northern relocation—although organized relocation would continue under civilian control and Northern whites kept up the demand for black laborers.[71] Many of the army chaplains in charge of contraband camps used their association with denominational and freedmen's aid societies to continue assisting in the relocation of large numbers of former slaves to Northern employers.[72] And at Fortress Monroe, three years after Lewis Tappan first suggested it, the commander in charge of contraband began planning with civilian agencies to relocate freed families to the North.[73] Tens of thousands of African American would continue to be relocated or independently migrate to Northern states during and immediately after the war.

But the Union's occupying forces turned their attention to another area of relocation for former slave women, their children, and men unable to enlist or work as military laborers: the free labor experiments on abandoned plantations, in wood yards, and in contraband camps throughout the occupied South. Although in the first months of the war the Union Army had regarded enslaved women as an encumbrance, by late 1862 women's publicly acclaimed value to Northern employers, their demonstrated ability at self-subsistence, and Northern white opposition to relocation appear to have persuaded Federal authorities that freed women's productive labor might be a valuable commodity in the occupation of the South and the transition to free labor. The Emancipation Proclamation and the enlistment of slave men as soldiers created a turn of events and a new context in which the army reexamined its dispossession of African American women.

General Grant's 1863 assault against Vicksburg drew thousands of Mississippi Valley slaves from Mississippi, Louisiana, and Arkansas to Union lines. Irrespective of the army's ambivalence about the presence of fugitive slave women in and around its camps, for most enslaved people the arrival of Union troops and the defeat of Confederate forces at Vicksburg in July 1863 offered a compelling opportunity for freedom that they pursued at all risk. In response to the determination of former slaves to gain their freedom, General Lorenzo Thomas was sent to the Mississippi Valley to begin mobilizing Southern blacks on behalf of the Union war effort. Thomas pursued a policy of enlisting African American men (more than seventy thousand African American men from the Mississippi Valley freed themselves by enlisting); lining the crucial river ways of the valley with a loyal population by putting women and children to work on the plantations abandoned by Confederate owners and leased by Northern entrepreneurs; and establishing temporary quarters for thousands more contrabands (again, mostly women, children, and the elderly) in camps. The fall of Vicksburg opened the Mississippi Valley to the war's full and devastating impact on slavery, multiplied as Union troops launched campaigns into the interior of Arkansas, Louisiana, and Mississippi and reoccupied northern Alabama.[74]

Under Thomas, the Mississippi Valley provided the Union's occupying forces with a new wartime experiment. Rather than turning fugitive slaves away or relocating them in the North, the occupying army now enlisted African American women into the initiation of free labor on abandoned plantations and work camps. Their work would not only provide their subsistence and contribute to the Federal treasury but would also introduce former slaves to the rigors of free labor. Simultaneously, former slave women found increased opportunities for employment at military hospitals and in supporting roles to black regiments—as cooks, laundresses, and servants to white officers—as they struggled to support their families in the absence of their husbands and male kin who had joined the Union Army.

By February 1864, for example, Martha Thompson had managed to escape slavery with her small baby, make her way with her brother to Helena, and live in a nearby woodchoppers' camp, where she worked piling the cord wood that Union steamboats so desperately relied on. Every morning she left her small baby with a neighbor and went to work. As was the case with so many occupied black women, both her own and her baby's subsistence depended on her own labor; her husband had been enlisted, and her brother had been impressed as a military laborer. But as the Helena superintendent of freedmen observed, "she seemed cheerful and determined." Martha was one of 180 residents at the camp, where just under 50 percent of the residents were regarded as able-bodied workers and 58 percent of those workers were adult women.[75] Here, former slave women were once again regarded as "able-bodied" workers, just the way Butler had earlier viewed (and sought to commodify) them.

From Virginia to the Mississippi Valley, former slave women like Thompson had taken up a new role in the occupied South: they had become central to the army's endeavor to see former slaves self-subsisting on the abandoned farms and plantations and in the wood yards of the occupied South. Fugitives but not refugees, slaves but not workers, women but not entitled to the prerogatives and privileges of gender enjoyed by white women, an encumbrance to the Union Army but valuable field hands and servants in the North, former slave women would finally be welcomed by Federal and military authorities who decided, as the war drew to its denouement, that these displaced and denigrated women were strong enough to usher in the successful transition from slave to free labor across the South. Yet despite the army's reliance on women in these new free labor experiments; despite the fact that women frequently accompanied men in their military service, working as nurses, laundresses, and cooks; and despite the fact that women often were the sole means of support for their families while husbands and brothers and fathers were occupied elsewhere, African American women's occupation—and subsequent war work—would be dismissed in popular culture and neglected in popular memory.

Many enslaved women would not survive their occupation by Confederate and Union forces. Yet if the history of enslaved women's wartime occupation seems largely a history of what was done to them, it is also important to remember that it was their resistance that provoked slave owners' and Confederate surveillance; that it was their flight that contributed to the wartime collapse of slavery even as it confounded Union military authorities; and that it was their determination to be free women and free mothers that fueled their willingness to endure the challenges of survival in contraband camps, during relocation to distant towns and farms, and while performing hard labor on behalf of the Union on plantations and in wood yards. In contrast to the many Southern white women whose wartime experience led them to chafe against the restrictions of womanhood, African American women endured a great deal in order to live to see the day when they might claim the prerogatives that they hoped and expected their gender might secure.

Occupied at Home

Women Confront Confederate Forces in North Carolina's Quaker Belt

VICTORIA E. BYNUM

Early in 1864, near the county seat of Carthage in Moore County, North Carolina, Franny Jordan followed a "squad of soldiers" who had seized her teenaged son with the intention of forcing him into the Confederate Army. Fearful of what lay ahead, she stopped at the home of a neighbor and enlisted the aid of two young women to retrieve her son. As the women approached the Confederate soldiers, the soldiers cursed them for daring to challenge their authority. When one of the women retorted that they intended to do "no such thing," the soldiers surrounded her. Crying out "god dam her," one man urged the others to "take her along too."[1]

At first, the young woman stood her ground, warning the men not to touch her. But when they drew their bayonets and one pretended to drive his through her, she bolted and ran. As she scrambled over a fence, another soldier grabbed her dress, ripping it before she could escape his grip. "Shoot her," a man's voice rang out, prompting another to cock his gun and take aim. In the end, although the same man continued to holler "shoot her," none of the soldiers had the stomach to kill an ordinary white farm girl. They held their fire as the three women ran away.[2]

During the Civil War, such home-front skirmishes occurred regularly in North Carolina's "Quaker Belt," so named because its counties, stretching from Surry in the west to Orange in the east, had been centers of Quaker settlement during the eighteenth century. A stronghold of Unionism during the Civil War, the Quaker Belt has received renewed attention during the past twenty years from historians of Southern Unionism and the Southern home front. As a result, we now know that women such as Franny Jordan did far more than wonder and wait while husbands marched off to war or hid in the woods.[3]

Although historians now recognize women as active participants in the war, forced as wives, mothers, or slaves to protect home and family from intruding soldiers and deserters alike, the very nature of women's wartime struggles makes it difficult to view them outside their biologically and socially constructed roles, or as anything other than victims. Because white women such as Franny, emotionally and economically devastated by the loss of husbands and sons, appear in past records mostly as wives and mothers, they are rarely viewed as individuals—that is, citizens—who publicly asserted opinions or influenced the course of wartime policy.[4]

We should not discount, however, the possibility that Franny acted as both a mother and a citizen when she and her female companions contested the right of the Confederate state to impress her child into military service. Franny lived in the heart of the Quaker Belt, where more than fear and suffering motivated many women to oppose the Confederacy. This region, labeled the "Randolph County area" because it encompassed parts of Randolph, Montgomery, and Moore counties, exhibited immediate and fierce opposition to the Confederacy, compelling military occupation by late 1862.[5]

A strong sense of cultural solidarity, nurtured by nonconventional religious traditions, characterized the Randolph County area. Quaker Belt women developed a public voice in response to the Civil War's violation of their cultural values and traditions, and particularly to Confederate military occupation. Yet because occupying forces are typically understood to be enemy soldiers who have seized control over a rival government's lands, it is easy to overlook the Confederacy's occupation of disloyal regions and its punishment of pro-Union citizens. As a result, Civil War tales about occupation of the South regularly recount harassment of citizens by Yankees and deserters but rarely include women like Franny Jordan, who were abused by their own government's forces.

Race and class, as well as culture and religion, influenced many people throughout the South to view the Confederacy as an illegitimate, occupying government. Certainly, few enslaved, free black, or landless poor white Southerners expressed much affection for the Confederacy. Free African Americans, a visible reminder of the possibility that all blacks might soon be free, were more stringently policed, sometimes harassed, by methods resembling those of an occupying force.[6]

The case of Elizabeth Burnett, of Goldsboro, Wayne County, demonstrated the dangers of open resistance to Confederate authority by women of color. During the war, Burnett's home was a popular meeting place for blacks. Goldsboro's mayor, worried that she might be involved in a theft ring, ordered Officer Blount King to investigate. During King's investigation, a fight broke out between him and Elizabeth Burnett. After the war, the reconstructed court charged King with assault and battery. In October 1867, however, in what presaged coming race relations, about 120 white citizens protested the indictment of Officer King. They praised the officer for keeping free blacks in their "proper place" during the war. Citing Burnett's "rude and insulting" behavior toward the officer and her well-known "high temper," these white members of the community argued that a beating was just what Burnett deserved. They accordingly petitioned Governor Jonathan Worth to drop all charges against Officer Blount.[7]

White people's fears of black women like Elizabeth Burnett symbolized the Confederacy's difficulty in mobilizing support for the war, especially among certain segments of the South's population. Like free black women, poor white women—especially those who lacked husbands, or whose husbands lacked property—were not particularly loyal to the cause of war. Unlike yeoman farm-wives such as Franny Jordan, however, such women rarely dared to openly defy the new government.

Women's wartime behavior in Orange County, located northeast of the Randolph County area, reveals the effects of race and class in producing different sorts of female unruliness. In contrast to the Randolph County area, where women boldly and publicly confronted Confederate forces, Orange County's women frequently complained about food prices and shortages but rarely challenged Confederate authority. As conditions worsened, thefts, rather than political protests, became increasingly common. Such striking differences among women of the same general region reveals much about the intertwined, but varied, effects of gender, class, and culture on women's reactions to the war.[8]

Although Orange County was included in the Quaker Belt and Quakers were among its earliest settlers, by 1860 their influence had long been overshadowed by migrating Virginians, Scots-Irish, and German settlers. Here, religion and class had different cultural and political effects than in the Randolph County area. Slavery grew more rapidly, creating larger gaps in wealth among citizens and enabling Orange's Confederate leaders to more easily suppress Unionist sentiment.[9]

By mid-1861, Orange County's pro-secession politicians had asserted control over the local population. As Mager Green of Durham Township later commented, Unionists like himself "were not very plenty there in those times."

Those in the Chapel Hill region likewise mostly kept their mouth shut. Joseph Ivey, William Lloyd, and Cannon Bowers were reputed to be the only three men in their neighborhood who dared vote against secession. Commented Lloyd, "[I]t was considerable of a secession corner where I lived."[10]

If it was dangerous for propertied white men to express Unionist views, it was doubly so for African American women. Nelly Stroud, of Chapel Hill, remembered that "colored people" such as herself did not discuss the politics of the war, at least not publicly: "A still tongue made a wise head." Stroud was a washerwoman, and her livelihood depended upon the willingness of whites to hire her; thus she dared not shoot off her mouth about politically charged issues. Even her friend Nancy Brewer, a rare economically independent black woman who owned her home and had purchased her husband out of slavery, agreed with Stroud that blacks generally kept quiet. She felt compelled to add, however, that they always sympathized with the Union cause, believing it was "God's will for the colored race to be free."[11]

Orange County's laboring people faced great hunger and need during the war, despite public officials' efforts to supply grain to the destitute. Significantly, the county had an unusually large number of female-headed households whose average per capita wealth was lower than that of single women in surrounding counties. This fact, combined with the wartime deaths of so many men, sapped the vitality of neighborhoods in which most farmers were self-sufficient at best before the war.[12]

Crime dockets swelled with the names of poor white women in Durham Township, noted for its unruly population even before the war, as hunger threatened to unhinge Confederate authority. In the spring of 1864, Rebecca Davis, Nancy Bowers, and Nancy Carroll were charged with forcible trespass after helping themselves to government flour stored at William McCown's mill. Similarly, in winter of early 1865, William McCauley charged two poor white women, Elizabeth Gilbert and Hawkins Browning, with stealing bed clothes and blankets from his home.[13]

The women mentioned above, linked by kinship, class status, and neighborhood, lived precarious lives even before the war. All were from families of small farmers and laborers whose ability to support themselves was severely strained or broken by the war. Such women did not dare assert their rights as independent citizens who happened also to be wives or mothers; dependency defined the core of their existence.

Being female brought an even greater likelihood of poverty to women such as these from economically marginal families. Dependent upon marriage for economic support yet sexually vulnerable, all except Gilbert had diminished their chances for marriage by giving birth to illegitimate children. Nancy Carroll lived much of her adult life with her parents. The mother of a mentally deficient illegitimate child, she was unable to support herself or the child adequately, forcing her to request aid from the county wardens of the poor in 1845. Nancy Bowers, like Carroll, was granted a cash payment of ten dollars per year by poorhouse officials for support of her illegitimate child.[14]

Hawkins Browning (whose legal name was Hawkins Hicks) lived with Jefferson Browning, her neighbor since childhood, until his death during the Civil War. The couple had three children together, causing the courts to charge Hawkins regularly with bastardy and illegal fornication. The poorhouse was also familiar to this couple. From 1846 to 1857, Jefferson's mother, Nelly Carroll Browning, received aid from the wardens of the poor for support of his brother, David, who was blind.[15]

Elizabeth Gilbert was also from a network of poor families. Most of the male Gilberts who lived in Orange County during the 1850s were laborers; a few were small farmers. None owned slaves. Like Carroll, Bowers, and Browning, Elizabeth was familiar with the wardens of the poor, at least indirectly. A decade before the war, in 1852, two Gilbert women, Tabitha and Eady, died in the poorhouse. Another Gilbert relative, Penny Gilbert, struggled to make a living during the war by operating an illegal tavern. Arrested in 1862 for operating a "disorderly house," Penny may also have engaged in prostitution. The Civil War drove such women ever more deeply into the precarious underworld of petty crime and illicit sexual affairs merely to survive.[16]

Women's reactions to Confederate authority in the Randolph County area, where some broke laws in broad daylight, provide a vivid contrast. By early 1865, for example, a white farm woman openly threatened the life of the Montgomery County sheriff if he did not supply her family with wheat and corn. In a letter that revealed both gender and class consciousness, Martha Cranford Sheets raged at Sheriff Aaron H. Sanders, a wealthy slaveholder, for having done nothing for the "pore wiming" of the neighborhood and for telling lies to keep his sons home, while "my husband is gon, and he has dun work for you." Calling Sanders a "nasty old whelp" who cared nothing for the county's suffering families, Sheets issued a final warning: "[I]f you don't bring that grain to my dore you will sufer, and that bad." She then signed the letter with her full name.[17]

The ease with which Sheets threatened to "send" deserters to punish the sheriff attested to neighborhoods where deserters, civilians, and Confederate forces met one another on the "battlefields" of their own farms and nearby woods. Whether Sheriff Sanders obtained military exemptions for his sons, as Sheets implied, is not clear. What is clear is that his twenty-year-old son, Romulus, was home in the fall of 1864, assisting the sheriff in identifying and harassing deserters. Both father and son served as state's witnesses against several men arrested for desertion. Young Romulus's suppression of disloyalty may have exceeded legal boundaries, however; during the same court term, he was charged with stealing the horse of Malinda Beaman, wife of deserter John Beaman and cousin to Martha Sheets.[18]

Sheets's subsequent threats against the sheriff would not have surprised distinguished educator Braxton Craven, who warned Governor Henry Clark from Randolph County in early 1862 that "it was a great mistake to leave [punishment of the disloyal] to the County authorities. Deep, inveterate hate to [sic] this government abounds and the authorities of the county will never crush it." By March 1865, Randolph County alone was estimated to harbor six hundred deserters, many of them members of armed bands.[19]

The Quaker Belt's potential for class conflict was grounded in the non-slave-holding landed majority to which Martha Sheets belonged. Throughout this region, reciprocal economic relations, kinship, and relatively isolated, cohesive neighborhoods diminished the potential for class conflict among slaveholders and non-slaveholders before the war. Class differences were soon laid bare, however, by Confederate conscript policies that favored slaveholders, tax-in-kind laws, and military impressment of vital farm goods that drove non-slaveholding families to the brink of starvation. Any semblance of class reciprocity was soon destroyed, as Sheets intimated when she commented to the sheriff that her husband had "dun work" for him, yet there he was, claiming privileges for his own sons that were unavailable to her family.[20]

The persistence of Quaker and Moravian traditions added moral force to resentment of the Randolph County area's small but powerful slaveholding class. Although Quaker antislavery convictions had faded over time, the emergence of Wesleyan Methodism around 1848 planted outright abolitionism in this portion of the Quaker Belt. Martha Sheets's evident sense of moral authority over the sheriff was no doubt reinforced by her own religious connections. Many of her Cranford kin had intermarried with the founding members of the Wesleyan Methodist Lovejoy Church, where in 1851 the Reverend Adam Crooks was mobbed for denouncing slavery from the pulpit. As part of this Wesleyan Methodist circle, Martha was likely familiar with the views of pro-Union leaders who seamlessly blended religious antislavery views with republican free soil ideologies.[21]

Such leaders included militant Unionist Bryan Tyson, of Moore County, descended from Quakers, and Daniel Wilson and Daniel Worth of Randolph County, both of whom were Wesleyan Methodist abolitionists. Likewise, Hinton Rowan Helper, of Davie County, and John Lewis Johnson, of Forsyth County, combined political class consciousness with religious principles of equality to become two of the most important political leaders from the Quaker Belt. Helper wrote the free soil–abolitionist tract *The Impending Crisis of the South,* and Johnson founded the state's most important underground Unionist organization, the Heroes of America (HOA).[22]

More so than in the North, where women like Lydia Maria Child and Harriet Beecher Stowe carved out public careers as abolitionists long before the war, the political protests of antislavery Southern male leaders may appear distant from the world of women. Indeed, Helper belittled the abolitionism of "yankee housewives" like Stowe in favor of his own sturdier (i.e., masculine) economic analysis of the horrors of slavery. Yet Martha Sheets's confrontation with Sheriff Sanders exhibited a sense of moral and economic outrage equal to that expressed by Child, Stowe, or Helper.

So determined was Helper to distance himself from Northern abolitionism and, by extension, feminized abolitionism (since his primary audience was nonslaveholding Southern men) that critics often dismiss him as a Southern racist who objected to slavery only because he wished to rid the South of blacks or because of the white class divisions it perpetuated. In fact, Helper objected to slavery on the same grounds as did most Northerners: because it was morally wrong to enslave human beings and because it privileged one class over another, creating an economically backward society in the process.[23]

Helper's racism, as well as his effort to distance himself from Stowe's "feminine" critique of slavery, was typical of Northern abolitionist men, too. Throughout this patriarchal society, politics was the province of men and their efforts to prove masculine fitness a work in progress. Nevertheless, religious training, considered the special province of women, had an enormous impact on their behavior, adding special urgency in the Randolph County area to perceptions of the Confederacy as an alien, intrusive force.[24]

Buoyed by local political leaders who refused to be silenced and a powerful secret organization, the HOA, non-slaveholding families in the Randolph County area only grudgingly supported the rebel government, if at all. By 1863, many of the area's men refused altogether to serve in the Confederate Army. North Carolina had the highest desertion rate among Confederate states; Randolph County had the highest desertion rate in the state.[25]

The enforcement and abuse of Confederate policies further deepened people's disaffection. The military seizure of Franny Jordan's son, for example, was a direct result of Governor Zebulon Vance's proclamation of September 11, 1862, in which he condemned Confederate disloyalty and desertion. Soon after, Vance authorized the use of military campaigns to suppress Unionist activities. Major Peter Mallett, head of North Carolina's Confederate Conscript Bureau, ordered militia officers to take charge of such efforts in the Randolph County area. On February 1, 1863, Captain Nathan A. Ramsey requested that Governor Vance authorize him to lead North Carolina's Sixty-first Regiment into Chatham, Randolph, and Moore counties to aid in "exterminating all enemies to our great and glorious cause." Ramsey would head the forces that captured Franny Jordan's son in Carthage the following year.[26]

Confederate arrests of resistant conscripts and those who harbored them, forced enlistments, and executions of deserters occurred over and over again in the Randolph County area as local and state Confederate forces worked together to suppress dissent and desertion. Captain Ramsey's forces were accompanied by fifty-four-year-old Adams Brewer, a self-appointed vigilante who roamed the woods in search of men disloyal to the Confederacy. It was Brewer who commanded Ramsey's soldiers to shoot the young woman who confronted them after they captured Franny Jordan's son. A slaveholder, he lived just across the Moore County border in the Brower's Mills neighborhood of Randolph County. Brewer was part of a distinct minority in a community noted for pro-Union, even abolitionist, families. Militant Unionist Bryan Tyson, who lived in Moore County, was born in the Brower's Mills neighborhood and maintained contact with friends and kinfolk there. Tyson and Brewer's neighbors considered Brewer a "hot head secesh" and kept close track of his movements.[27]

In a letter to Governor Vance, Thomas W. Ritter, a prosperous non-slaveholding farmer who served in North Carolina's House of Commons, reported Franny

Jordan's confrontation with Adams Brewer and the Sixty-first Regiment. Aware that the reputation of any woman assaulted in public was immediately suspect (hence the euphemism "public woman" for prostitute), Ritter assured the governor that Franny's assaulted companion was from as "respectable a family as any in the country." Adams Brewer, he explained, was a menace to civil society, a pro-Confederate zealot dedicated to hunting down and killing his less-than-zealous neighbors even though he was not enlisted in military service. Rather, Brewer was "piloting" Captain Ramsey and his men through the woods, directing their depredations on local citizens. A few days before the soldiers seized Franny's son, claimed Ritter, the same group shot to death a seventeen-year-old boy accused of having evaded conscription. Ritter reminded the governor that Brewer had also murdered another Moore County man, George Moore.[28]

Assaults and murders in the name of Confederate loyalty were common enough that women like Franny had every reason to panic when their menfolk were seized. Franny certainly would have known about the murder of Neill McDonald, a young man who, shortly before the war, worked on a farm just two households away from her own. In separate letters to Bryan Tyson, two of Adams Brewer's neighbors claimed that Adams and his son, Stephen, were "behind" the murder of McDonald, who had deserted the army and was accused of robbing and pillaging his neighbors (common activity among deserters). According to H. K. Trogden, Stephen Brewer pulled the trigger, shooting McDonald after he refused to reveal the whereabouts of other deserters. "They shot him through the Boddy," wrote Trogden to Tyson. "Hiz foalks heard the gun. They went out in the woods wher they [had] taken him and found him Shot." Soon, Adams Brewer himself became a hunted man. Another of his neighbors told Tyson in late 1864, perhaps more wishfully than accurately, that Brewer had been murdered by deserters.[29]

Vigilante murders and military executions of men accused of desertion intimately involved women, who surely were among the "foalks" who heard the shot that killed Neill McDonald and retrieved his body in the nearby woods. Less murderous efforts by overzealous militia and home guard to police pro-Union men and women in this section of the Quaker Belt sometimes even spilled over into abuse of women of the slaveholding class. Henry W. Ayer, state agent on contracts, wrote a lengthy letter to Governor Vance after a visit to Randolph County, during which he learned of numerous abuses committed in the Asheboro region under command of First Lieutenant William A. Pugh. A crisis ensued after Pugh's cavalry burned the distilleries of several men accused of providing whiskey to conscripts and deserters. In the process, Pugh's soldiers appropriated hogs, tobacco, and various goods from the citizens of Asheboro.[30]

Although this confrontation began as a clash between male soldiers, deserters, and moonshiners, women were soon drawn into the fray. One of the accused men, non-slaveholder Loton Williams, countered the Confederate charge of illegal bootlegging with an image of innocent woman's work. Williams insisted that he had not produced any liquor since January 1862 but that his wife was "in the habit of washing her clothes in the still house, and using the kettle to boil them, which accounts for the fire under the kettle." Although Williams's explanation sounded plausible to Agent Ayer, Lieutenant Pugh scoffed at his explanation, commenting that Mrs. Williams must wash clothes in "hot swill." Pugh and his cavalry proceeded to burn Williams's still, and several others, to the ground.[31]

In need of food and rest after the day's activities, the troops next entered the home of "Esquire Foust" over the objections of his daughter, even though there was not "another white male person on the place at the time." Foust's daughter watched helplessly as the soldiers cooked a hog they had taken from yet another citizen. Ayer seemed particularly disturbed by the cavalry's dishonoring of a wealthy patriarch's daughter and equally so by the disrespect shown to Nancy Hoover, a slaveholder and the proprietor of a hotel located in Asheboro.[32]

Hoover fell victim to what Confederate sympathizers today would term "collateral damage." Their stomachs full, the soldiers prepared for an evening's rest by appropriating a quilt and four blankets from Hoover's hotel. As a result of their behavior, reported Ayer, the people of Randolph "say the deserters and conscripts do them less injury than those sent to take them do." Lieutenant Pugh defended himself and his men against these accusations, proclaiming the guilt of every man whose still or mill they had burned and denying that Foust's daughter had been treated with disrespect. In regard to Nancy Hoover's complaints, Pugh insisted that after a diligent search of his troops' supplies, her goods were not found.[33]

Governor Vance was infuriated by Pugh's "plundering" of Randolph County citizens but stopped short of dismissing him from his post. In fairness to the Confederate troops, rounding up deserters and those who sheltered them was a thankless task. They were sent to restore order in a region they were told was under siege by lawless bandits. What they found were neighborhoods of families and extended kin who resisted with arms the authority of what *they* considered to be a lawless government created in defiance of the will of the people. Never truly understanding the perspective of these Unionists, Confederate officials routinely dismissed them as merely ignorant. Commander Pugh's most revealing statement came near the end of his letter of defense. After carefully addressing each and every charge against his unit, he denigrated Randolph County as a region where few "respectable people" lived and where people displayed "little or no refinement."[34]

Pugh's use of the word *refinement*, with its feminine connotations, justified his men's harsh treatment of Randolph County citizens by conflating class and gender. His cavalry was assigned the task of punishing disloyal lawless men, not that of defiling or robbing helpless women. By presenting the people of Asheboro as neither loyal nor culturally refined, Pugh suggested that neither its men nor women deserved his soldiers' respect.

Lieutenant William Pugh was hardly alone in caricaturing rural plain folk as degraded, ignorant, or unrefined when it served his purposes. Even Confederate congressman Andrew C. Cowles, a "peace man," referred to leaders of the HOA as "still house orators" because of their popularity among common people. Thomas Morris, described as "extremely poor" on his petition for a military exemption, was dismissed by enrolling officer D. C. Pearson as belonging to a "class of individuals in Montgomery County noted for their thriftlessness and want of energy." Captain Pearson cavalierly proclaimed the benefits of Confederate service for such a poor man, ignoring the probable effects of Morris's lengthy absence, or death, on his dependent wife and children.[35]

Politically and socially, military occupation encouraged people in the Randolph County area to accept desertion and evasion of Confederate service as appropriate behavior. Shortly after Captain Ramsey and his men cut a swath through Moore County, Congressman Thomas Ritter joined other leading members of the county in sponsoring a peace meeting in Carthage on February 10, 1864. Less than six months later, Moore County enrolling officer P. H. Williamson described Ritter's voting precinct as "one of the worst holes in the Confederacy." Deserters, he reported, were "stealing a good deal. . . . Still, the citizens don't care about arresting them." It was not that men and women did not care; many lived in neighborhoods that openly approved of desertion. As one citizen commented in a personal letter, "deserters and conscripts" in Moore County were "doing a bout the same" and could be seen "at the Sunday School every Sunday."[36]

John Milton Worth, relief commissioner of Randolph County and brother to state senator Jonathan Worth, refused to accept that churchgoing and otherwise law-abiding people supported disloyalty to the Confederacy. In August 1864, Worth complained to Governor Vance that "more than half of this county, Moore, and Montgomery are now in the hands of *desperadoes.*" How otherwise to explain why Randolph County's voters would elect as sheriff Zebedee F. Rush, a member of the Heroes of America and the recommended candidate by Bill Owens, the most notorious leader of deserters in the region? On Christmas Eve of the same year, Moore County slaveholder Iver D. Patterson likewise expressed his disgust with Lincoln-loving "tories" and recommended to Vance that the state legislature strip deserters of their right to vote and confiscate the property of their families.[37]

Forced to admit that women abetted men's avoidance of Confederate service, many of the same men viewed torture and deprivation of deserters' wives as simple necessity. Torturing the wife of deserter-band leader Bill Owens, after all, had resulted in his capture and imprisonment. In some counties, pro-secesh millers also denied deserters' wives government grain even though there was no official Confederate policy to that effect.[38]

Women who sheltered male kin in the nearby woods eagerly told their side of the story. In separate letters to Governor Vance, Phebe Crook and Clarinda Crook Hulin, daughters of a Montgomery County Methodist schoolteacher and kin to numerous deserters, blasted their Confederate occupiers. Clarinda, who had three "outlier" brothers-in-law (she did not mention this in her letter), implored Governor Vance to consider the plight of farm women. "I hav three little children to werk for and I have werk[ed] for ever thing that I have to eat and ware," she wrote. But military men sent to the region to restore order were "destroying every thing they can lay hans up on." Troops had taken her "last hog" and poured her molasses all over her floor. "It ant only Me they air takeing from," she added; "they take the women'[s] horses out of the plows," she explained, for their own use.[39]

Ten more months of armed warfare between militia and deserters brought a more detailed letter from Clarinda's sister, Phebe. As a single woman, Phebe Crook could not anchor her protest in the time-honored trope of the soldier's wife or mother. She seemed eager, however, to describe herself as "a young lady that has Neather Husband, son, father, no[r] Brother in the woods" (although she did have male kin hiding in the woods). Invoking the moral authority of republicanism rather than motherhood, Crook informed Governor Vance of the "true" conditions of her community. Calling on him to "protect the civil laws and writs of our country," she denounced the militia and magistrates of her county for arresting "poore old grey-headed fathers who has fought in the old War and has done thir duty."[40]

Enraged by members of the home guard who, Crook insisted, had no intention themselves of fighting in the war, she condemned their physical abuse of women and children and their burning of barns, houses, and crops, all done in the name of fulfilling the governor's directive to force deserters in from the woods. Following such orders was merely an excuse, she wrote, for pro-Confederate men to "take their guns and go out in the woods and shoot them down Without Halting them as if they war Bruts or Murder[er]s." Once again, Crook emphasized rights of citizenship rather than victimhood by assuring the governor that her motive for writing was that "I always like to [see] people hav jestis."[41]

Despite the sisters' separate appeals to Governor Vance, they could not prevent the killing of their three brothers-in-law on January 28, 1865. Jesse, John, and William Hulin were executed along with James Atkins, who had been identified as a draft evader by the hated Sheriff Sanders during the previous fall court term. The Hulin brothers, like Martha Sheets, belonged to the county's network of Wesleyan Methodist families who opposed slavery and refused to fight for the Confederacy.[42]

Was it mere coincidence that Sheets's threatening letter to Sheriff Sanders was dated only one day before the executions, probably on the very day that the Hulin brothers and Atkins were thrown in jail? Not likely. It would also appear that ten women from the Wesleyan community charged with rioting at the Sanders Mill in May 1865 had revenge as well as the acquisition of grain on their mind.[43]

In an 1867 letter to Colonel M. Cogwell, commander of the military post at Fayetteville, Hiram Hulin described how two county justices of the peace had delivered his captured sons and their companion, James Atkins, into the hands of "murderers who were home guard troops." Rather than taking the men to prison to await trial for evading Confederate service, the home guard "deliberately shot and beat to death with guns and rocks my three sons and Atkins while tied with their hands [sic] and handcuffed together." Although the elder Hulin pleaded for justice for his sons and their companion, the Reconstruction government failed to convict anyone for the murders.[44]

The regular claim by Confederate leaders that the war was fought on behalf of the South's "fair women" clearly was meaningless rhetoric to plain farm women of the Randolph County area. Jesse, John, and William Hulin left behind numerous kinfolk, including wives, children, and their father. James Atkins left behind his widowed mother, Sarah, who was charged the previous fall with harboring him as a deserter. The trauma of so many deaths likely explains why Nelson and Clarinda Crook Hulin moved to Kentucky shortly after the war, along with numerous members of the Crook family. Jesse Hulin's widow, Caroline, who had long aided her husband in hiding in the woods, remained with their children in Montgomery County. Carefully saving the shoes, socks, and cap that he wore on the cold morning of his death, Caroline passed them on to descendants, for whom they became grim reminders of a war that turned Southerners, sometimes even neighbors, into cold-blooded killers of one another.[45]

Governor Vance's policies in regard to deserters and those who harbored them found its harshest expression in orders issued by Lieutenant Colonel Alexander Carey McAlister, commander of a detachment of soldiers assigned to break up deserter bands in the Randolph County area. In March 1865, McAlister directed his forces to scour the country for seven miles around for "deserters, absentees, and recusant conscripts," adding that they were "empowered to impress citizens for guides." If citizens (who inevitably included women as well as men) refused to obey orders, the soldiers were told to administer "punishment as you may think necessary to protect you from betrayal." To any who resisted their authority, or the authority of the government, McAlister advised his soldiers that "no quarter will be shown; they will be shot down wherever found."[46]

What did Lieutenant Colonel McAlister mean by these words? Did he actually intend for soldiers to shoot down civilian women as well as men? Probably not. The dilemma faced by Confederate occupiers, epitomized by vigilante Adams Brewer's insistence that Captain Ramsey's soldiers shoot Franny Jordan's female accomplice, emanated from contradictory attitudes about "womanhood." Typically, lower-class and black women were considered dissipated and potentially dangerous, while women of the white propertied classes were imagined to be timidly reposing in their homes. In forming their policies, Confederate leaders had difficulty imagining the wives, mothers, and daughters of propertied white men on the front lines of home-front "battlefields." But there they were. And there, too, was Adams Brewer, "ordering" Captain Ramsey's soldiers to shoot a female civilian suspected of treason. Although no woman accused of disloyalty appears to have been executed by the Confederacy, arrests and tortures of Unionist women were regularly reported throughout the war.[47]

On the one hand, Governor Vance regularly deplored the ill treatment of women and children by militia, magistrates, and home guard. On the other hand, as Phebe Crook's letter made clear, such abuses were a predictable result of his proclamations and policies in regard to deserters and those who abetted them. Just three weeks after Crooks wrote her letter, prominent lawyer Thomas Settle, a supporter of peace candidate William Holden, informed Vance that roundups of disloyal women in the Randolph County area had "terrified" some pregnant women into having "abortions almost under the eyes of their terrifiers." Yet it was Governor Vance who ordered the arrest and detention in prison camps of all citizens, irrespective of gender and age, who harbored deserters or evaders.[48]

In line with the Confederacy's policy of detention, Major J. G. Harris, headquartered at Asheboro, requested on March 27, 1865, that Lieutenant Colonel McAlister send Mary Jane Welch and Christiana Wilson to him "under guard," since Welch had admitted that she and Wilson had participated in two robberies committed by deserters.[49] But Lieutenant Colonel McAlister, who lamented on March 16 that deserters "possess so generally the sympathy of the inhabitants [i.e., women] that we are laboring under great difficulties," now had an about-face in regard to detaining women. On March 30, just three days after the arrests of Welch and Wilson, he advised Major Harris that extorting confessions from captured women and children was "productive of more evil than good" and ordered the practice ended. Of course, by that time the war was almost over.[50]

Deeply felt class, cultural, and religious values animated women's resistance in the Randolph County area, presenting Confederate authorities with a qualitatively different home front than that of Orange County. No inner war raged in Orange, although civil disorder increased dramatically during the final year of the war. The obvious cause of that disorder was abject poverty. By 1864, many women of Orange County were stealing from their wealthier neighbors and merchants, but none dared openly threaten a Confederate official as did Martha Sheets of Montgomery County. Although both classes of women struggled for personal survival, women like Sheets also fought to restore the justice they believed was threatened by the Confederate government.

As discussed earlier, Nancy Carroll and Elizabeth Gilbert were among the Orange County women driven to theft by the war. Such women and their families often became the maligned "poor white trash" of the "New South" as wartime devastation ushered in postwar impoverishment. Nancy Carroll kept house alone in 1870; her eighty-seven-year-old father, widower Archy Carroll, lived with three grown women (Nancy's sisters?) in a propertyless household. The sixty-two-year-old Betsy Gilbert who lived in Hillsboro in 1870 with Louisa Gilbert Pearson, a propertyless widow with two children, is likely our Elizabeth.[51]

Although it did not constitute an inner civil war, Orange County's breakdown in civil order did revitalize political opposition to the war. As more and more soldiers deserted their units, local peace candidates emerged to challenge Confederate policy. After the war's end, pro-Confederate Conservatives would vie with pro-Union Republicans for local power. By 1868, a fiercely violent white supremacy campaign would dominate that struggle throughout the Quaker Belt as the Ku Klux Klan terrorized white Republicans, black citizens in general, and even poor people who dared cross the color line. A "New South" would institutionalize segregation and rewrite the Confederate Lost Cause as a noble effort by the Southern "people" to resist the tyranny of the North.[52]

As for the Randolph County area, well into the twentieth century both professional and amateur historians portrayed Confederate occupation of pro-Union regions of the South in positive terms. In 1901, Captain Ramsey wrote a brief history of North Carolina's Sixty-first Regiment in which he described the very expedition that resulted in the kidnapping of Franny Jordan's teenaged son. Using the language of the Confederate Lost Cause, Ramsey lauded his troops for their unsurpassed bravery in battle and gave special credit to Company D for having "restored peace" to the citizens of Chatham and Moore counties, where they were sent to protect "life and property against lawless deserters and conscripts." To Ramsey, and to Confederate leaders in general, Southerners who resisted or defied the authority of Confederacy were lawless bandits to be hunted down; if a few of their "leading spirits" were killed by his men, well, so much the better for the larger community.[53]

Captain Ramsey could not conceive of white Southerners who opposed the Confederacy on principle or women who did not seek his soldiers' "protection." Southern Unionists appear nowhere in his narrative, and white married women were subsumed within his reference to protecting communities. Other Lost Cause historians regularly presented such women as damsels in distress, threatened on all sides by Yankees, runaway slaves, and deserters—but never by Confederate forces. Thus women who fought against the Confederacy, as did those of North Carolina's Quaker Belt, rarely appeared, until recently, in Civil War accounts as anything other than the deluded female arm of a "lawless gang of marauders."[54]

Widow in a Swamp

Gender, Unionism, and Literacy in the Occupied South during the Civil War

JOAN E. CASHIN

Among the Unionists residing in the South in 1860 was Ann Smith Mew, a widow, of St. Peter's Parish, Beaufort District, South Carolina. She lived in the swampy northern reaches of Beaufort, and she was old by nineteenth-century standards, in her mid-seventies. She was so old that her father had served in the American Revolution and her husband had served in the War of 1812. Because of their military service, she declared, she maintained her loyalty to the United States when the war broke out. According to one of her peers, she was loyal for another reason: she was illiterate and therefore unaffected by pro-slavery and secessionist propaganda. Mew, who was a rather direct, straightforward person, blamed the war on what she called the "aristocracy of South Carolina." She stuck to her views even though her family lived through a perilous occupation by both armies during the war. All this emerged when she applied in the 1870s to the Southern Claims Commission for reimbursement for property taken from her farm. She made her statement under oath, and she signed it with an X.[1]

Ann Smith Mew's biography gives us a fresh perspective on the persistence of Unionism in the cradle of secession, South Carolina, on slave-owning widows in the antebellum and wartime eras, and on the struggles of women who lived through occupation during the war. Some historians have investigated Unionism in the South, to be sure, but they concentrate on military and political actions by men or on the handful of women who engaged in espionage. Widows have been the subject of some research, but historians tend to agree that these women rarely, if ever, challenged the social and political hierarchies of the slave-owning class. Furthermore, there is no scholarship on the very old, which is itself a category of experience. As we will see, Ann Mew maintained her own opinions about the war because of her family history, her geographic location, her age, her illiteracy, and her forthright personality, and she was able to exercise some degree of agency in the unstable, unpredictable world of occupation.[2]

Beaufort District in South Carolina, where Ann Mew spent her life, was settled by the British in the seventeenth century. Plantation owners from the Barbados moved to the Carolina low country in the 1670s, and the town of Beaufort was founded on the Atlantic shore in 1711. Planters bought slaves to cultivate the rice crop and, in the eighteenth century, indigo. During the American Revolution, some local planters served in the Patriot army, and one of them, Thomas Heyward, signed the Declaration of Independence. Some hard fighting took place in Beaufort after the British invaded the South in 1779, but the local economy recovered, and by the 1790s planters switched to long-staple cotton. The flat earth near the shore was exceptionally fertile, and the sandy roads were lined with ferns, palmettos, live oaks, and magnolias draped in Spanish moss. There were more than sixty islands in Beaufort District, most of them strung along the coast, and the mainland was crisscrossed with shallow, muddy streams. Four saltwater rivers, so brackish as to be black in color, ran north to south through the district, the water levels rising and falling with the tides. The labyrinth of waterways proved a challenge even for seasoned pilots. The human beings living in Beaufort had to contend with a physical environment that was unyielding and sometimes overwhelming.[3]

By the late antebellum era, the slave-based economy had made the planter class in Beaufort District quite rich. In 1860, bondsmen outnumbered whites by a factor of six to one, with approximately 32,000 slaves and 6,800 whites. Only seven counties in the United States had a higher concentration of slaves. The area had a higher wealth per capita in 1860 than Massachusetts, New York, and Pennsylvania. Planters in the Beaufort low country demonstrated their wealth with luxurious houses, grand entertaining, fancy carriages, thoroughbred horses, and elegant clothes. They became notorious, one visitor said, for a pride that was typical of European aristocrats. Other writers north and south chose the word "aristocracy" to describe the coastal elite, and one remarked that they disdained other white people. The townspeople of Beaufort organized some private academies for their children, and coastal planters took it for granted that girls too should be educated. Almost all the adult white residents of Beaufort town were literate, and some of them had impressive private libraries.[4]

Beginning in the eighteenth century, rich men from the coastal area dominated politics in Beaufort District. These men held an array of public offices,
from mayor of Beaufort, to presidential elector, to U.S. senator. They became
ardent exponents of slavery and, after the 1820s, secession if they deemed it
necessary. Vociferous in advocating their ideas, they spoke repeatedly in favor
of the peculiar institution, defending it from all criticism. The planter class in
Beaufort contained some dissenters, such as Dr. William Henry Brisbane, who
decided slavery was a sin, freed his bondsmen, and moved to Cincinnati. But
very few whites in this part of the South were capable of making such choices.
By the late antebellum era, most political figures in Beaufort were increasingly
outspoken in their advocacy of disunion to protect bondage.[5]

Families such as the Mews were not part of this universe. Ann Smith Mew
resided about forty-five miles inland, geographically and culturally far from the
coastal elites. In the late eighteenth century, Anglo-American, Scots-Irish, and
Swiss farmers settled the northern section of the district, what might be called
the frontier of Beaufort, and the area filled up with subsistence farms, modest
houses, and little towns. Ann Smith was born in Beaufort District near the Coosawhatchie Swamp in 1785. Her father Samuel Smith affected her political views
long after his death. His family, yeomen farmers from the British Isles, lived in
Beaufort by the 1750s, when Samuel was born. He served in the Revolutionary
War for seven years, indicating a deep commitment to the Patriot cause. When
he died in 1815 in South Carolina, he owned sixteen slaves and about a thousand
acres of land. Ann's mother passed away in the 1840s, and five of Ann's seven
siblings died before 1861. One brother moved away, and one brother James, several years her junior, farmed nearby in Beaufort. In the world in which she grew
up, many people died before middle age, and only a few survived to old age.[6]

This part of Beaufort District was hallowed ground for American Patriots.
After the British invaded the South in 1779, troops from both armies camped in
Beaufort on the mainland, and they fought a battle on the banks of the Coosawhatchie River. When the British captured Charleston in 1780, English soldiers
overran the Carolina colony and occupied Beaufort District, after which Patriots
such as the "Swamp Fox" Francis Marion organized guerrilla attacks and hid out
in the Coosawhatchie Swamp. The remnants of a Revolutionary fort were visible in the area more than fifty years later. In these places, Ann Mew passed her
childhood, her youth, and her adulthood. After the British evacuated Beaufort
in 1781, a fierce internal war broke out. Patriot and Tory partisans engaged in a

murderous cycle of raids that left villages and farms in ruins. The War of 1812, in contrast, left no mark on Beaufort. Some troops were posted in the district, but there were no battles like those of the Revolutionary era.[7]

Sometime in the early 1800s, Ann Smith wed Maccamee Mew, a local farmer some ten years her senior. He did not own any slaves, and she brought some land, but no slaves, to the match as her dowry from her father. Her husband's given name, the title of a Scottish clan, suggests that his ancestors hailed from that part of the world. Nicknamed Kemmy or Kimmy, he was a North Carolina native, born around 1775 in Craven County, where his relatives had lived for at least two generations. His family and many kinfolk migrated to Beaufort when he was young. Kemmy and his wife had eleven children, and their last child was born when Ann was in her forties. In the War of 1812, Kemmy served as a private in the Fifth Regiment of the South Carolina Militia After the fighting ended, he came home to farm, and by the 1820s he owned twelve acres of mediocre land in St. Peter's Parish, taxed at four dollars an acre, and six bondsmen. (In 1820, half of the whites in St. Peter's Parish owned slaves, and most of them owned fewer than ten bondsmen.) A small number of rich slave owners—which did not include the Mews—dominated politics in St. Peter's Parish. Most planters advocated secession during the Nullification Crisis in the late 1820s and early 1830s, but Kemmy Mew did not share their political outlook. He was "always against" disunion, Ann recollected. Before he passed away in 1832, Kemmy made her the executrix of his will, which was increasingly rare among South Carolinians, revealing that he trusted his wife. Unfortunately, the will burned in the courthouse in 1865, so there is no evidence on how much property she received.[8]

The widow Mew never remarried, although she outlived her husband by more than four decades, and she stayed in St. Peter's Parish. She seems to have led a secluded life, bound by family duty and the routines of country life. Six of her eleven children were alive in 1860, with two daughters and two sons in Beaufort. Unlike the sons of the planter gentry, her sons worked in the fields alongside the slaves. A local judge noted that the Mews were "not strictly needy" but not rich either. Three of the four children married into local families in Beaufort, where they farmed, while Alexander, the youngest, a bachelor, and Ann's favorite, lived with her. Her farm was located north of Cypress Creek and west of the Coosawhatchie River, one of the black-water rivers, on a patch of solid earth called a "hammock" near a river crossing, Mew's Ford. She raised cotton and food crops, as did most of her neighbors. The courthouse at Gillisonville stood about ten miles to the south, and the nearest post office, which had the evocative name of "Horse Gall," was about ten miles to the north. Her home was surrounded by forests, creeks, and dense swamps, which natives traversed on foot on low-lying bridges constructed of earth and wooden planks.[9]

Ann Mew prospered after her husband's death, for she was listed in the 1860 census as the owner of eighteen slaves. How she acquired these slaves is unknown, but four were adults, two males and two females, and the rest were children, so they may have constituted two nuclear families. She also owned some fourteen thousand dollars' worth of land. She may have managed her property herself, or she may have been assisted by her son Alexander, her brother James, or her in-laws, two of whom were small-scale slave owners in Beaufort. Nothing is known about her role as the mistress of eighteen slaves. Her native state, South Carolina, had a tormented history of race relations. The Stono Rebellion, the largest slave uprising in American history, happened in Carolina in 1739, and during the Revolution, slaves from Beaufort ran away to join the English army. Rumors of slave revolts persisted in Beaufort into the nineteenth century, and fugitives from the area fled to the North. Mrs. Mew must have exploited slaves much as other whites did, although she may have been somewhat more humane than some whites, for two black people testified in her favor in the 1870s when she applied for compensation from the Federal government.[10]

One of the most striking features of Ann Mew's background is her illiteracy. Most of the planet's current population is illiterate, and it has always been a sociocultural issue. Literacy rates have increased across Western society since the eighteenth century, and by the time of the American Revolution, three-quarters of white American men could read and write, but some groups have lagged behind, including white women and blacks of both genders. In the United States today, there are many illiterate adults over age sixty-five. Although the exact number is contested, most of the unlettered are white and native-born. Most illiterate adults feel powerless, unable to participate in society, immobilized in every way.[11]

In the case of Ann Mew, it is unclear why she never learned to read or write. The assumption that women should be literate, one consequence of the Revolution, somehow passed her by. Part of the explanation may be the lack of schools in St. Peter's Parish during her youth, which had no academies open to female students until 1820. South Carolina's public schools were underfunded for another reason: legislators, many of them planters, believed that learning in the hands of the wrong people could be dangerous. After Ann Mew's marriage, she may have been too preoccupied with eleven pregnancies and the attendant household duties to learn to read and write. When her husband named her his executrix, he may have hoped she would become literate. Their daughter Harriet Mew McDonald was literate, and likely some of the other children too. Maybe they tried to teach Ann to read and write, and they failed, or maybe they did not make the attempt. By the 1870s, when Ann Mew testified before the Southern Claims Commission, she did not seem ashamed of her illiteracy, and during the war she did not act as though she felt powerless. She may have perceived literacy as an abstraction that had nothing to do with her daily life, whatever the practical skills or the transcendent benefits it offered. In some communities, literacy is neither expected nor rewarded. St. Peter's Parish in Beaufort District in antebellum South Carolina seems to have been such a community.[12]

In the election of 1860, South Carolinians voted for John Breckinridge, the pro-slavery, states' rights candidate who was threatening to break up the Union. The extremists in the state had grown more influential since Nullifica-tion, and some of the worst firebrands, such as Edmund Rhett, hailed from the Beaufort coast. He had talked so vehemently about leaving the Union that his place of residence was called Secession House. In the late antebellum years, some planters from the Beaufort mainland began to agree that secession might be appropriate. A Southern Rights Association based in Gillisonville issued a statement denouncing abolition, socialism, and communism, with the fillip that the U.S. Congress had "virtually dissolved" the Union already. The victory of Republican Abraham Lincoln in November 1860 terrified many slave owners, and at South Carolina's secession convention in December 1860, every delegate voted for disunion. But there was not complete unanimity in Beaufort District. Some wealthy families split over the war, such as the Draytons: one Drayton brother served in the Union and another in the Confederacy. Yet other Beaufort slave owners were initially against secession, such as William Elliott, but chose reluctantly to support the Confederacy after the war started. Other low-country whites never supported rebellion. John Meriman, the tax collector at George-town, was imprisoned because of his Unionist sympathies.[13]

Within Ann Mew's immediate family, political opinion was sharply divided. Ann remained fiercely on the side of the Union. She stated later that she "was for the Flag and stuck to it" because her father fought for it during the Revolu-tion and her husband in the War of 1812. In her old age, she had to protect their legacy. She did not support the Confederacy "at any time," and she was "glad" when it collapsed and "the old Flag restored." Her son Alexander, aged thirty-four in 1860, volunteered for the Southern army in 1861, although she was "bitterly opposed" to his decision. She told Alexander that he was "doing wrong," but since he was an adult, she could not stop him from leaving. She did not try to keep him out of the war altogether; rather, she did not want him to serve in the *Confederate* military. They had quite a debate, for her relatives stated that she "tried her best" to keep Alexander out of the rebel army. She must have realized that some white men from their neighborhood fought for the Union, one of the estimated several hundred South Carolinians who fought in the Federal army or paramilitary units. Nevertheless Alexander returned to his mother "disgusted," which sounds as though he resigned or deserted the army. He was forced back into the service, presumably by Confederate provost marshals, and became a sergeant in the Eleventh South Carolina Infantry. The Confederate Army drafted Ann's thirty-eight-year-old son Abraham, a farmer in Beaufort, and he served as a private in the Third South Carolina Cavalry. One wonders what Ann's sons would have done if their father, Kemmy Mew, was still alive.[14]

Ann Mew's other relatives differed on the war, although the documentation does not explain their individual motives. Her daughter Harriet McDonald, a widow in her mid-thirties with a daughter of her own, resided close by and shared her mother's Unionism. Another daughter, Rebecca DeWitt, a widow in her early thirties with two children, lived nearby, but her political attitudes went unrecorded. Ann's brother James R. Smith voted for what he called the "Union ticket" in 1860, either the Republican Lincoln, the Democrat Stephen Douglas, or the Southern Unionist John Bell, and he commented that Ann was "always" against the war. Two of her husband's relatives (probably her nephews) volunteered to serve in the Confederacy Army, Samuel in the infantry and John in the artillery. One of Ann's in-laws, identified simply as "Mrs. Mew," supported the Confederacy so ardently that she gave information to rebel forces in early 1865.[15]

Seven months after the war commenced, Union forces invaded Beaufort District. In November 1861, they captured the town of Beaufort and surrounding islands to use as a supply depot. Most whites fled the town for other parts of the state, while some planters burned their cotton to prevent it from falling into Northern hands. Federal soldiers and slaves looted some of the mansions until Union General Thomas (not William T.) Sherman put a halt to it. The polarization among whites continued during the Federal occupation. A few whites in Beaufort welcomed the Northerners, such as a slave owner, Mr. Ben Chaplin, who was denounced in the Confederate press as a "traitor," and a storekeeper, one Mr. Allen, while local Unionists allegedly burned some of the planter mansions. The national press celebrated the taking of Beaufort, but Yankee reporters did not comprehend the range of political opinion. In November 1861, one journalist described all plantation owners in Beaufort as "venomous traitors" and slaves and free blacks as the only "loyal" residents. Throughout the war, Federal officers who passed through Beaufort tended to ridicule white Unionists in the South. William T. Sherman, a conservative Unionist, derided the cowardice of white male Unionists, while Thomas W. Higginson, a dedicated abolitionist, referred to white female Unionists as "old crones" who pretended to be loyal but actually supported the rebels.[16]

With the appearance of Union soldiers on the Beaufort coast, profound changes happened in the district with whirlwind force. More slaves ran away to the Union lines, and in May 1862, Robert Smalls piloted a vessel out of Charleston and took it to the Yankee fleet at Port Royal, making him famous nationwide. That month, U.S. Major General David Hunter issued his own emancipation decree for the coastal regions of South Carolina, Georgia, and Florida, which President Lincoln overruled before issuing his own proclamation in September 1862. The president abolished slavery only in those areas in rebel hands, but slavery in all sections of Beaufort District began to break down as yet more bondsmen ran away. The Emancipation Proclamation was celebrated in a public ceremony in Beaufort in 1863, attended by none other than Dr. Brisbane of Ohio, and abolitionists began teaching former slaves in the coastal district. The Federal authorities took over abandoned lands, which freedmen purchased at public auction in Beaufort in 1864. As Union soldiers made occasional forays onto the mainland of Beaufort, they burned rice on plantations still in operation and constructed earthworks in the interior.[17]

The war began to encroach on the Mew family soon after the Northern army established its headquarters on the coast. Although the Mews resided on the mainland some forty-five miles away, troops from both armies occupied their part of the district at various times. In November 1861, Confederate Lieutenant General Robert E. Lee reached the town of Coosawhatchie, about twelve miles southeast of the Mew farm, preparing to fight the Union forces if they invaded the mainland. (The Federal commander Thomas Sherman chose not to invade because his men were inexperienced and the landscape so formidable.) During his ten months in South Carolina, Lee ordered the waterways to be obstructed to prevent Northern vessels from moving inland; Confederates also built several batteries on the rivers, and in 1863 they destroyed a Yankee gunboat near Coosawhatchie. Rebel units were stationed in the interior of the district, and soldiers often traveled through the Beaufort mainland near the Mew farm. The two armies fought the occasional skirmish, which left dead soldiers and military debris scattered across the fields in the neighborhood.[18]

The Mews stayed on their farm, hunkered down. They continued to work the fields, much as other whites did on the Beaufort mainland. Ann Mew now managed the farm herself, and she had four fields planted. In this volatile situation, she somehow raised enough food. The Mews had "plenty of provisions," one of her neighbors said. Many of the slaves eventually ran away, although one, a young woman named Hannah, stayed throughout the conflict. The plenty did not last, and then whites and blacks on the Mew farm "fared the same," according to another bondsman, sharing the same diet. Ann explained that because of her family's isolation on the swamp, they knew little about the course of the major battles. Her daughter Harriet McDonald agreed that the family felt isolated living by the swamp, and she added that since she was a woman she did not travel about much. The family seemed to be cut off from other Unionists.[19]

Harriet McDonald and her mother often discussed the causes of the war, however, and Harriet related that Ann "always said" that "if it had not been for the aristocracy of South Carolina we never would have had the war." There may have been a Confederate soldiers' relief society in St. Peter's Parish, such as existed in other parts of Beaufort, but Ann Mew did not join. Her white neighbors were aware of her political convictions. People gossiped at the courthouse, the post office, or wherever civilians encountered each other on the roads. Ann's neighbor James W. Grimes, a native of Beaufort who was too old to serve in the war, favored secession, and he knew, as did most of her white neighbors, that she was pro-Union. They "frequently talked about [her] behind her back," he acknowledged, but she was "not troubled" by these vigilant neighbors because she was just "an old widow lady" and therefore, they seemed to believe, insignificant to the war effort.[20]

The toll of war escalated dramatically for the Mew family in the summer of 1864. Alexander Mew died in Petersburg on August 21, 1864, and was buried somewhere in Virginia. His death devastated Ann Mew, not least because she thought he died for an unworthy cause that betrayed the ideals of his father and grandfather. In the fall of 1864, while she was reeling from this blow, rebel soldiers turned up at her farm. Whether they knew of her pro-Union sympathies is unclear, but they appropriated forage outside the house, food (corn and potatoes) and livestock (cattle and about fifty head of hogs), as Confederate military regulations permitted. The troops had an angry exchange with the widow about the forage: she "would not give it to them," Mew recalled, so they "took it" without her permission, and she was never compensated. At the same time, William T. Sherman's army churned through Georgia in his famous March to the Sea, capturing Savannah in December 1864. In January 1865 he invaded South Carolina, heading for Columbia, the state capital. His soldiers were eager for vengeance, Sherman admitted. He believed that the state was responsible for the war and its white citizens deserved "extirpation." In January 1865, some rebel forces composed of boys and old men fought Union troops near Cypress Creek, the Coosawhatchie River, and other places in Ann Mew's neighborhood, falling back before the Northern troops. Guerrilla bands also prowled the area, harassing Federal soldiers.[21]

In February 1865, the Union forces showed up in Ann Mew's front yard. Members of a foraging party appeared one day, part of the thousands of Federal troops crossing the upper half of Beaufort District, going west to east from the Savannah River to the Combahee River. Union soldiers torched some private homes in this part of Beaufort, and they burned the towns of Gillisonville, Lawtonville, Loudenville, and Robertville. Military records indicate that the contingent at the Mew farm was the 123rd New York Infantry. The unit, which included a long train of wagons and artillery, had great difficulty crossing the terrain. The weather in January and February 1865 was severe, with weeks of heavy rain, and many bridges had washed out or been deliberately destroyed by Confederates. Some of the rivers were nearly impassable. Union soldiers had to wade through chilly, waist-deep waters and chop down trees to build new bridges. During the second week of February 1865, men from the 123rd of New York bivouacked near the Coosawhatchie Swamp for a day and a night.[22]

The foraging party at the Mew farm numbered about one hundred men. Again, we do not know whether they were aware of Ann's political sympathies when they arrived. She was sick in bed, tended by her daughters Harriet and Rebecca, and the slave Hannah was at the house. As Federal military regulations allowed, the soldiers took a saddle, a harness, and livestock, filling several wagons. Then some thirty men entered the house, which violated regulations and Sherman's Special Field Order No. 120 of November 1864, still in effect. They took food (meat, salt, honey, and syrup) and crockery from the kitchen and bedding from the bedrooms. Although Ann Mew welcomed the Union soldiers, she realized that the looting could hurt her own household. She sized up the character of the officer in charge, an unidentified captain, and complained to him about the soldier's conduct. He responded as she hoped he would, telling the men to stop swearing, and what was much more important, he "protected us personally," Ann recalled. The captain announced that the white women were "ladies," and he stopped the troops from taking Ann's bedding and her clothes. Her daughter Harriet asserted that the good captain "did what he could" but could not entirely control the men, who took clothing from the other rooms, although they did not assault any of the women white or black, which Southerners of all backgrounds feared from both armies. Then the soldiers crossed Mew's Ford and rejoined their unit bivouacked a short distance away. The Mews could hear their music and see their campfires, but no one thought to get a receipt or a voucher for the foraged property.[23]

While this was happening at Ann Mew's farm, one of her female relatives decided to pass military information to the Confederate Army. This "Mrs. Mew," no first name provided, visited the headquarters of rebel Colonel J. D. Kennedy on the Salkehatchie River, the Confederate line of defense some twelve miles east of the Coosawatchie River. She "came over the river" by herself, Kennedy reported, to tell him about Northern troop movements in the area, which he mentioned in his official correspondence in February 1865. Possibly this was Emily S. Mew, spouse of Confederate soldier John Mew, a slave owner in Prince William Parish, not far from the Salkehatchie River; John Mew's petition for postwar compensation from the Federal government would be denied because he also sold supplies to the Confederates. Whoever she was, Mrs. Mew did this at some risk to her safety, revealing a zealous loyalty to the Confederacy in the last months of the war. Did her relatives know what she did, and did it cause strife within the family? Which side did John Mew really support? On these points the documents are silent. But their conduct only highlights the political differences within the Mew family and the white populace during occupation.[24]

After 1865, Ann Mew stayed in St. Peter's Parish, most likely because she was too old and too rooted in the place to go anywhere else. The region underwent another series of profound transformations. The Thirteenth Amendment abolished slavery, white men came home from the Confederate Army, Federal troops occupied South Carolina, more abolitionists and reformers—the "carpetbaggers"—

came to the state, and the Ku Klux Klan began to attack African Americans and nonconforming whites. The old plantation elite rebounded, even though many of them were no longer rich, and they were determined to regain political power at almost any cost. Some former Unionists served in the U.S. Congress, even as conservatives denounced whites who were loyal to the United States rather than South Carolina. Traitors, they called them, or "scalawags." What Ann Mew deemed the state's "aristocracy" became engaged in a protracted political struggle with blacks, other white Southerners, and the Federal authorities.[25]

The struggle over land ownership was resolved more quickly. Most whites in South Carolina kept their land, and Ann Mew kept hers, partly from sheer luck and partly because she recombined her household. William T. Sherman's Special Field Order No.15, issued in January 1865, set aside for freedmen the abandoned and confiscated land in coastal South Carolina and Georgia up to thirty miles inland, but the Mew farm was not included, being forty five miles from the coast. Then the new president, Andrew Johnson, rescinded the order. Some whites in Beaufort lost their land for nonpayment of taxes, but Ann Mew somehow kept hers, perhaps with the help of relatives, including her son Abraham, who returned to Beaufort to farm until his death around 1870. Ann's daughters Harriet McDonald and Rebecca DeWitt moved in with her, as did her daughter Mary Mew Perry, a middle-aged widow who resided in Georgia before and during the war. As happened in other white families after 1865, the widow Mew gave her children a "safety net," and they in turn cared for her as she entered advanced old age. The economy of the state, the region, and Beaufort District stagnated as a result of the Panic of 1873 and the war's damage to the region's infrastructure. By the 1870s, land cultivation in Beaufort had fallen below prewar levels.[26]

In these circumstances, the middle-aged daughters of Ann Mew may have done physical labor in the fields, just as her sons did before the war. If so, they labored alongside the former slave, Hannah, who was owned by the Mews before 1861 and was working at the farm in 1876. Her motives for staying with the Mews are unexplained—perhaps because of a lack of work opportunities, as was true for other ex-slaves in the low country, or because Ann was a good employer. Hannah adopted the Mew surname, much as other black Southerners occasionally adopted the surnames of former owners, for reasons unknown. In 1876, Hannah Mew was approximately thirty-seven years old, suggesting that she may have been the eighteen-year-old female slave listed in the 1860 census. Like her former mistress, she was illiterate.[27]

In Ann Mew's testimony before the Southern Claims Commission in 1876, she gave a plainspoken, unadorned account of her personal history. Her sorrow at Alexander's death is obvious, as is her hostility toward the South Carolina "aristocracy," her anger at the Confederate foraging party, and her gratitude for the Union captain who protected her. But if she appreciated the other ironies of occupation—living in a neighborhood that included Revolutionary battlefields, dealing with foragers from both armies even though she was a Unionist, the white women deemed "ladies" by the Federal captain even though she was illiterate—she gave no sign of it. Because she was seeking payment, it was in her interest to emphasize her Unionism, and her memory in old age may not have been perfectly accurate. But her testimony has the ring of truth, and the commissioners decided in Ann Mew's favor. They seemed touched by her advanced age, some ninety-one years, and the membership of her household, one of them exclaiming, "old widows . . . on a hammock in the Coosa[w]hatchie Swamp!" Another commissioner remarked that these white women had "little or no" education and were therefore immune to the "pernicious influence" of pro-slavery and secessionist literature. The fact that the Mews had only a few slaves left by 1865 meant that they would not have "felt" the end of slavery, he believed. The Mews were "self[-]working people," he concluded, and "truthful."[28]

The testimony of Ann Mew's neighbor James Grimes and her brother James Smith helped her case, since these white men took opposite sides during the war yet both declared her to be a Unionist. But the testimony by her black contemporaries Hannah Mew and Henry Newton almost certainly clinched it, since they, like other African Americans, tended to know which white people truly supported the Union. Hannah Mew confirmed that she witnessed looting by Federal soldiers, and Henry Newton, who was owned before the war by Ann's brother James Smith, stated that he heard other slaves talking about it afterward. Newton seemed to admire the Mew sons for working in the fields and the Mew family for sharing the slaves' diet during the conflict. After the commissioners proclaimed in 1876, "We find her loyal," she received $519 in compensation. Payment was by no means guaranteed, for the commission rejected more than two-thirds of the approximately twenty thousand claimants, including Ann's in-law, John Mew, living in Beaufort after the war. The commission denied him reimbursement because it discovered that he sold several hundred dollars' worth of supplies to the rebel army.[29]

The winter of 1876–77 happened to mark the official end of Reconstruction.

The Republican presidential candidate, Rutherford B. Hayes, took office even though the Democrat Samuel Tilden won the popular vote in 1876, and the unsavory bargain that brought Hayes to power, a classic backroom deal struck at a Washington hotel, stipulated among other things that Federal troops would leave South Carolina. The effort by the U.S. government to remake Southern society limped to a halt at the national level and the state level. Conservative Wade Hampton, a former planter and Confederate general, became governor of South Carolina in 1876 after a disputed election. The "aristocracy" had regained power in Ann Mew's home state. She probably did not live much longer, since she was about ninety-one in 1876, although the actual death date has gone unrecorded. If she left a will, it is not in the local courthouses. The household may have broken up with her death, since the other personalities fade from the historical record, except for Henry Newton, who lived on the Coosawhatchie in 1900.[30]

Ann Smith Mew's story reminds us that although we should not idealize the illiterate as happy simple folk, as some writers have done, we should not dismiss her convictions because she could not read or write. Nor should we discount her opinions because she was a widow and a very old one, at that. She had a powerful sense of American history, transmitted by oral tradition within her family. In fact, her Unionism seems to be related to her age, and it was only strengthened by her residence in a place where blood was shed for the Revolution. The Confederate leaders tried to enforce loyalty among white Southerners, but they did not succeed. The widow Mew never lost her ability to criticize the society in which she lived, during and after the war. In that respect, she maintained some cultural autonomy, as well as a canny ability to endure the chaos of wartime occupation—to run a farm while surrounded by troops, to think fast when soldiers entered her household, to appeal for help when necessary from a Federal officer, to survive.[31]

Epilogue

The Fortieth Congress, Southern Women, and the
Gender Politics of Postwar Occupation

JUDITH GIESBERG

The first issue facing the Fortieth Congress in the spring of 1867 was what to do about the threat of widespread starvation in the postwar South. Republican John Bingham proposed setting aside Freedmen's Bureau money to support poor white Southerners, many of them women and children, suffering from famine.[1] Bingham's proposal elicited a sharp rebuke from Benjamin Butler, Radical Republican congressman and U.S. Army veteran. "The men and women who stood by and viewed without compassion the miseries endured by our noble soldiers will, if they experience a little starvation, themselves, be able to realize what was suffered in Southern prisons by those who fought our battles," Butler fumed from the House podium.[2] Although the Confederate Army had been defeated on the battlefield, Butler believed that Southern white women had not yet been sentenced. Distributing Federal rations to disloyal Southerners was tantamount to issuing a blanket pardon for their wartime misdeeds. To Butler, a little starvation would be good for women who had waged a war of resistance against their occupiers. The money, he argued, would be better spent supporting widows of U.S. soldiers.

As one of the primary architects of the U.S. Army's war on Southern women, Benjamin Butler represented an extreme case of resistance to the changing role of the occupiers as the war dragged on into a postwar occupation, but he was not alone.[3] For Butler, U.S. policy toward Southern civilians had been set in 1862, when he issued General Order No. 28 declaring war on women who contested the authority of Federal occupiers in New Orleans. Although the formal conflict had ended in 1865, for Butler and others who held civilians responsible for the deaths of U.S. Army soldiers, the battle raged on. Now that the Radicals, many of them veterans, were preparing to launch an ambitious campaign of reconstruction, declaring martial law and placing the defeated South under direct military control, the occupation faced a turning point.

The debate about provisions highlighted the difficulties faced by soldiers of war who abruptly became the architects of peace, the impossibility of declaring victory in a battle waged against civilian hearts and minds, and how quickly wartime popular consensus among the victors (roughly hewn as it was) can fall apart. Between Bingham's plea to feed the hungry and Butler's willingness to let them starve there were likely many gradations of public opinion about whether and how to respond, many of them hinging on Northerners' personal experience of the war.[4] Northern veterans lost comrades in a war that was fought against soldier and civilian alike, a war that came to an end before the loyalties of either could be secured. And now that the fighting had ended, veterans like Butler found it difficult to give the war up, in the case of Southern white women, to "feed the hand that bit them."[5] Nevertheless, to win the peace, southern women had to be defeated, brought into dependency—if not within the household then to the state. To affect this peace, the 40th Congress was prepared to reinvent the federal government as paternal provider, to exercise a new moral authority when it came to southern women. In this context, Butler's opposition had an air of inevitability about it, for the general could neither lead this new Southern campaign nor successfully sink it.

Women's war has "a longer chronology," according to Margaret Creighton, one that does not necessarily correspond with the start of formal hostilities and often extends well beyond their end. Indeed, even as congressmen met in Washington to discuss the fate of the postwar South, the war raged on in the borough of Gettysburg, Pennsylvania, where residents rebuilt houses and re-dug wells; in Carthage and Goldsboro, in North Carolina's Quaker belt, where poor white women stole food from their wealthy neighbors; on abandoned Confederate plantations, where former slave women worked; and in all the other spaces where war had come either directly or indirectly, drawing women and children into its vortex and leaving them to pick up the pieces in its wake.

So, too, did war proceed in Congress, where U.S. Army veterans and other congressmen came to blows over the fates of freed people and Southern white women. During the war Southern household dependents—slaves, women, and children—acted as independent agents, freeing themselves or becoming breadwinners, smugglers, and saboteurs. The U.S. Army's military success relied on Northern soldiers pursuing a policy of hard war that sought to turn Southern households "inside out."[6] And now as congressional Republicans legislated for the war-torn South, they tried to undo what had been done. This was no easy task. Inasmuch as Southern white women had been treated as individual agents of war, enemy combatants, some in the Northern public had grown uncomfortable seeing them that way. The war of occupation had been based on an inversion of antebellum notions of gender—men rather than women needed protection, and women were political partisans whose loyalties had to be enlisted or coerced. While this construction of gender worked well as a strategy of war, it became untenable as a basis for peace.

In 1867, Benjamin Butler carried considerable baggage with him as he reentered civilian life, including his conviction that Southern white women were not martyrs worthy of sympathy but rather stalwart rebels who should be pacified. Among U.S. Army officers, only Sherman has more of a reputation for mistreating civilians than General Butler, to whom so many Southern women referred only as "Beast."[7] No incident is more representative of Butler's understanding of white women as enemies than his (1862) Woman Order, or General Order No. 28, declaring the (dis)loyal women of New Orleans prostitutes. Butler's order was the opening salvo of the U.S. Army's war on women that relied on the Northern public's consent to rules of engagement that violated antebellum gender norms. Of course, Southern women did not quietly demur to the occupiers but resisted them at every turn.[8] Union troops marching across the occupied South waged war against Southern civilians, expanding the theater of war into Southern homes. This war of occupation did not end in 1865, as Union troops stayed on to oversee emancipation and enlist black voters. But two years later, with famine ravaging the war-torn South, the context had changed.

Despite Butler's angry resistance, John Bingham's measure—titled the Southern Famine Relief Bill—passed, sending food and supplies to Southern civilians.[9] Northern newspapers applauded the bill as an appropriate humanitarian response to the suffering of hapless women and children. Coming on the heels of the Freedmen's Bureau's "war on dependency" in which indigent freedmen and women were ejected from refugee camps and denied aid, Southern white women's rapid reversal of fortunes is worth considering.[10] Taken together, these two initiatives—one aimed at ending the dependency of freed people and the other recognizing the dependency of Southern white women—trace an unraveling of the fates of Southern white women and freed people. Antebellum abolitionists had pitied slaves and slaveholding women as victims of a degenerate Southern slave power, and Republicans had promised to bring Southern domesticity in line with the Northern model. But when slaveholding women in the occupied South failed to welcome U.S. Army soldiers as liberators, the Northern public began to question this pairing of Southern victimhood and learned to embrace hard war against Southern women. As rapidly as the war had changed slaveholding women from victims into she-rebels, some Northern congressmen were eager to imagine them once again contained within the confines of domesticity, to begin forgetting the war on women. For Butler, though, this created a kind of vertigo that left him ill equipped to lead this new Southern campaign.

For freed people and indigent Southern whites trapped in a bleak postwar Southern economy, support from public or private sources of relief meant the difference between life and death. Destruction of homes and loss of property and livestock left Southern families destitute by the end of the war. By January 1867, Northern newspapers carried stories of widespread civilian destitution—entire families dressed in rags and widows and children subsisting on corn husks.[11] Dramatic newspaper headlines such as "Mother and Eight Children Starving to Death" moved readers with stories of the quiet destitution of Southern widows and children displaced by the war.[12]

The 1866 Freedmen's Bureau Bill, passed over Johnson's veto, signaled an ambitious Federal commitment to protecting freed people as the war's principal victims. Although the bill extended relief "to all loyal refugees and freedmen," in practice the bureau was resistant to distributing direct relief to the poor, and many agents were convinced—despite evidence to the contrary—that freedmen and women *wanted* to remain dependent.[13] These concerns informed General Oliver Otis Howard's decision to severely restrict the dispensation of food and shelter to fugitive and homeless Southern blacks in the fall of 1866 and the winter of 1867, at precisely the time when news stories began to reach Northern papers about starvation in the South. While the Southern Famine Relief Bill did not specify that recipients of Federal aid would be poor whites, the news stories that preceded the vote focused in particular on stories describing "poor, hapless widows and orphans in a perishing condition."[14] Shifting money to victims of starvation in the South meant taking money *away* from Southern blacks, who were apparently immune to starvation but highly susceptible to dependence. In contrast, dependence was a welcome condition for Southern white women.

It is ironic that Butler was involved in a conversation about starving civilians. Among the laudatory press coverage Butler had received in New Orleans in 1862 were stories describing his "feeding the starving rebels." *Harper's Weekly* celebrated "General Butler's magnificent success at New Orleans" with a dramatic illustration of his men distributing meat to civilians.[15] As in Northern newspapers' coverage of the Richmond bread riots, Southern women were portrayed in a negative light, animalistic in their grasping for handouts of meat.[16] In the paper's portrait of occupied New Orleans, Butler's absence from the scene as the "starving rebels" were fed highlighted his manly self-restraint and magnanimity toward the South's abandoned dependents. The story behind the story, of course, is an account of the civilians who starved as a result of U.S. Army's policy of hard war. Butler relished playing the part of the patriarch, dispensing harsh discipline with one hand and compassion with the other. Here, too, he rehearsed in wartime the Federal policy of paternalism on which his congressional opponents would hang their hopes of winning the peace.

Butler's Order No. 28 formed the foundation of the Union's hard war policy that would be taken up by soldiers throughout the occupied South. Although he was removed from his command over the Woman Order, Butler never expressed regret about it. Years later, Butler continued to receive fan letters and expressions of support from Northern women and men who thanked him, as Kate Chase did, for keeping "the secession women quiet."[17] When he threatened to treat Southern white women like prostitutes, Benjamin Butler linked their political intransigence with sexual transgression—he declared Southern women abandoned and encouraged prurient and, at times, violent fantasies of retribution.

When Butler mused that Southern women should starve for their war crimes, he invoked a familiar call for retribution against female traitors. In Butler's mind, the landscape of the postwar South remained the same as it had been during the war—populated by unrepentant and unapologetic rebels who had not been called to answer for their crimes. "It would seem as if an avenging Providence had sent this starvation especially upon those parts of the country where the Union prisoners were starved," Butler fumed, "in the vicinity of Richmond and Salisbury, and Andersonville and Millen, and other places in the South where our soldiers underwent so much suffering."[18] In Butler's estimation, Southern white women who had tolerated the neglect of U.S. prisoners in their midst were complicit in their death.[19] Butler continued to fan the flames of this gendered war by comparing Southern women's patriotism unfavorably with Northern women's. The Southern Famine Relief Bill, however, signaled the unraveling of the entangled policy of hard war and the abandonment of Butler's adoring public—at least on this issue. The bill marked the beginning of the end of Southern white women's occupation, leaving in its place a new Federal paternalism. On this measure veterans-turned-congressmen could become self-styled humanitarians.

Though it began with heartrending stories of privation, the debate about the Southern Famine Relief Bill devolved into a defense of the masculinity of veterans who had waged war on women. It all started when Representative Bingham swift-boated Butler, referring to him as the "hero of Fort Fisher not taken," an obvious reference to General Butler's failed attempt to capture a Confederate fortification in the mouth of the Cape Fear River in September 1864, a move that Butler bungled and one for which he was relieved of duty.[20] Butler shot back, citing the approval of the army men in his command and chiding Colonel Bingham for having waged only one battle—and that one against a defenseless woman. "[T]he only victim of the gentleman's prowess that I know of," Butler taunted, "was an innocent woman hung upon the scaffold—one Mrs. Surratt. And I can sustain the memory of Fort Fisher if he and his present associates can sustain him in shedding the blood of a woman tried by military commission."[21] Butler's attack on Bingham's role in the Surratt execution touched a nerve, for Bingham prepared a long statement in his own defense and printed and distributed it to the members of the House. Butler offered no such defense of his own war on women.

Butler was concerned that a hasty and general amnesty would suggest ambivalence about the North's policy of waging war on women. Such a shift would have ramifications not only for his postwar political career but for the understanding of gender on which it rested. Butler had risen through the ranks of the U.S. Army by affecting a careful balance between the restrained middle-class gentility of a legislator and the unrestrained working-class masculinity of a soldier.[22] Pursuing an official policy of punishing women required soldiers like Butler to treat Southern women without restraint. Butler's Order No. 28, Lieber's Code, and the Mary Surratt execution serve as signposts in the progress made on the U.S. Army's second front.[23] In applauding these moves and cheering Benjamin Butler's triumphant homecoming, Northern women indulged in these fantasies, too, casting aside antebellum gender conventions that had held that women and children were inappropriate targets of war.

Underlying congressional efforts to restoring Southern women's dependency were concerns about reaffirming masculinity. The heated exchange that erupted on the House floor between Benjamin Butler and John Bingham evidenced the perfect storm that was brewing in Washington as lawmakers prepared to pass judgment on how the war was waged and won. In three separate but related investigations—the Joint Committee on Reconstruction's prisoner-abuse investigation, the committee investigating the trial of the Lincoln assassins, and the committee drafting the terms of President Andrew Johnson's impeachment— Republican congressmen administering an unstable peace engaged in spasms of self-recrimination and accusation.[24] Overseeing the exchange of prisoners during the critical years when conditions at Southern camps deteriorated rapidly, Benjamin Butler had been unable to effect a system of regular prisoner exchanges.[25] Prisoners starved to death as a result. Two years after the war, public anger over prisoners of war still simmered, and Butler remained deeply sensitive to critics who held him responsible for allowing soldiers to starve to death.[26] Butler's wish for Southern women and men to experience "a little starvation" suggests that, facing some scrutiny, he and other veterans felt they had to publicly defend their war records. In Butler's case, he sought to shift the blame for his own war failures onto others, Southern white women among them. With recriminations and accusations swirling around Washington, the attacks were direct and personal.

In 1867, Americans were still angry about Lincoln's assassination and about the mistreatment of prisoners. But memory can be fickle—anger about prisoners of war, for instance, had just as often focused on Federal officials like Butler as it had on Confederate loyalists. Newspaper accounts of the Southern Famine Relief Bill allowed public anger to begin shifting from Southern white women to those who had waged war against them. The author of the *Harper's Weekly* article on the passage of the Southern Famine Relief Bill angrily dismissed Butler for ignoring the "authentic accounts from the Southern States reveal[ing] the real destitution existing there."[27] As a referendum on the implications of the U.S. Army's war on women, siding with Butler on sentencing women to "a little starvation" would have signaled the public's willingness to persist in waging war alongside the general. Instead Butler found himself standing alone on the issue.

The 40th Congress—not unlike the 110th—was sworn in under the shadow of a scaffold spectacle. In the summer of 1865, newspapers covered the trial and execution of the Lincoln assassins. Photographers Alexander Gardner and

Timothy O'Sullivan recorded the event, splashing blow-by-blow images across the front pages of Northern dailies.[28] The photographs celebrated the executions as the final act of a war that had been waged without mercy and that had consumed soldier and civilian alike. But just as the Union's policy of hard war seemed to reach a climax, regrets and recriminations swirled around the execution. Intended as a testimony to the exercise of legitimate violence against an enemy that had employed violence illegitimately—when Southern women and men protected their homes, refused to feed occupying soldiers, and, finally, when they harbored men and a woman who helped to fell a president—the scene of the hanging instead carried the stain of illegitimacy.[29] After witnessing the execution firsthand, the author of the *Harper's Weekly* article expressed the public's growing sense of regret that Mary Surratt might have been wrongly executed.[30] Indeed, after the executions, the public defense of Surratt's execution quickly faded. Rejecting Congressman Benjamin Butler's call for vengeance against Southern white women and recoiling from the spectacle of the gallows, Northern readers indicated that they, too, could no longer stomach a war on women.[31] In offering food to starving Southern whites, Congress had offered them an exit strategy.

Embracing the new paternalism of the Southern Famine Relief Bill helped to defuse resentments created by the war and to renormalize gender relations in the nation at large. The fates of Southern white women and freed people became entangled in the Union's war of occupation, and as the war came to an end, they traveled parallel paths toward Federal paternalism. Feeding helpless women and children reaffirmed their dependency, and the dependency of both women and freed people precluded their realization of full citizenship. This held true for women both in the South *and* in the North, where hard war had politicized women and enlisted their support for war on Southern households. Politically active Northern women who hoped that their war work would be recognized by the postwar Congress saw their hopes dashed when support for enfranchising women came from moderates—many of whom would support the Southern Famine Relief Bill—who used the measure as a straw-man issue to defeat black enfranchisement.[32] In place of the vote, Northern women received Federal pensions for the loss of their husbands and sons.[33] A welcome source of support, pensions nonetheless reinforced dependency. Indeed, each day as congressmen convened to discuss the fate of the occupied South and to consider how best to bring Southern women into an appropriate dependency, they heard petitions from widows of U.S. Army soldiers who were fighting for their pensions. The daily reading of these petitions—read into the record by congressmen and often filed by women's male acquaintances—served as rituals in which women's dependency was daily rehearsed and confirmed.[34] Seeking to reconstruct antebellum notions of domesticity and dependency, congressmen dispensed paternalism in return for wartime service.

As the essays in this volume attest, the fates of Southern white women and freed people became entangled in the Union's war of occupation. General Benjamin Butler's decision making stood squarely at the center of these concerns, as he had waged war early and eagerly on Southern white women and supported a policy that recognized freedwomen and men who emancipated themselves ahead of advancing U.S. troops. Butler took Southern white women's politics seriously—even though, as Alecia Long reminds us, he subsequently forgot it later—and recognized the value of black women and men as laborers, as we saw in Leslie Schwalm's essay. Butler's gendered war was hard to give up for veterans and others who continued to see enemies around every corner in the postwar South and who were concerned about the reversal of fortunes that might result from a careful assessment of what the Union's hard war policy had wrought. And in the longer chronology that is women's war, peace must have seemed remote to those civilians trying to live in the aftermath of a war that had left them unable to support themselves. In the halls of the Fortieth U.S. Congress, however, it was closer than ever. Lining up behind the Southern Famine Relief Bill allowed congressmen to reclaim one moral high ground even as they relinquished another. Embracing Southern white women once again as the war's unwitting victims served to cover up a record of wartime misdeeds in the occupied South and to salvage women's dependency in the reconstructed nation.

Notes

INTRODUCTION

1. Scholarly discussion of the widespread ideas concerning a short war and quick victory abounds. See, for example, Gerald F. Linderman, *Embattled Courage: The Experience of Combat in the American Civil War* (New York: Free Press, 1987); James McPherson, *Battle Cry of Freedom: The Civil War Era* (New York: Oxford University Press, 1987), 308–38; and Grady McWhiney and Perry D. Jamieson, *Attack and Die: Civil War Military Tactics and the Southern Heritage* (Tuscaloosa: University of Alabama Press, 1982).

2. Many works discuss the hardships civilians faced as a consequence of the long-term absence of so many adult men at the front. See Bell Irvin Wiley, *The Plain People of the Confederacy* (Baton Rouge: Louisiana State University Press, 1943), and Mary Elizabeth Massey, *Ersatz in the Confederacy: Shortages and Substitutes on the Southern Homefront* (Columbia: University of South Carolina, 1952), for two classic discussions.

3. Mary Elizabeth Massey, *Bonnet Brigades: American Women and the Civil War* (New York: Knopf, 1966), and Anne Firor Scott, *The Southern Lady: From Pedestal to Politics, 1830–1930* (Chicago: University of Chicago Press, 1970), were among the first to suggest that the war "opened every door" for women. Drew Gilpin Faust's more recent work, *Mothers of Invention: Women of the Slaveholding South in the American Civil War* (Chapel Hill: University of North Carolina Press, 1996), offers the sharpest counter to this position.

4. For examples of this focus on how the war impacted the status of women, see Catherine Clinton and Nina Silber, eds., *Divided Houses: Gender and the Civil War* (New York: Oxford University Press, 1992) and *Battle Scars: Gender and Sexuality in the American Civil War* (New York: Oxford University Press, 2006); Laura F. Edwards, *Scarlett Doesn't Live Here Anymore: Southern Women in the Civil War Era* (Urbana: University of Illinois Press, 2000); George C. Rable, *Civil Wars: Women and the Crisis of Southern Nationalism* (Urbana: University of Illinois Press, 1989); Nina Silber, *Daughters of the Union: Northern Women Fight the Civil War* (Cambridge: Harvard University Press, 2005); and LeeAnn Whites, *The Civil War as a Crisis in Gender: Augusta, Georgia, 1860–1890* (Athens: University of Georgia Press, 1995).

5. See Nancy Bercaw, *Gendered Freedoms: Race, Rights, and the Politics of Household in the Delta, 1861–1875* (Gainesville: University Press of Florida, 2003), 51–74, and Faust, *Mothers of Invention*, for excellent discussions of the difficulties all women faced, even the most class- and race-privileged.

6. This merger of home front and battlefront in the experience of military occupation has been discussed most extensively from the location of Union military policy. See, for example, Stephen V. Ash, *When the Yankees Came: Conflict and Chaos in the Occupied South* (Chapel Hill: University of North Carolina Press, 1995); Michael Fellman, *Inside War: The Guerrilla Conflict in Missouri During the Ameri-*

can Civil War (New York: Oxford University Press, 1989); and Mark Grimsley, The Hard Hand of War: Union Military Policy Toward Southern Civilians, 1861–1865 (New York: Cambridge University Press, 1995). More recently, historians have given more attention to the agency of the home front in various facets of this merger. See, for example, Joan E. Cashin, ed., The War Was You and Me: Civilians in the American Civil War (Princeton, NJ: Princeton University Press, 2002); Margaret Creighton, The Colors of Courage: Gettysburg's Hidden History: Immigrants, Women, and African-Americans in the Civil War's Defining Battle (New York: Basic Books, 2005); and David Williams, A People's History of the Civil War: Struggles for the Meaning of Freedom (New York: Norton, 2005).

7. On the experience of Unionist women in the Confederacy, see Victoria E. Bynum, Unruly Women: The Politics of Social and Sexual Control in the Old South (Chapel Hill: University of North Carolina Press, 1992), 111–50; Thomas G. Dyer, Secret Yankees: The Union Circle in Confederate Atlanta (Baltimore: Johns Hopkins University Press, 1999); John C. Inscoe and Robert C. Kenzer, eds., Enemies of the Country: New Perspectives on Unionists in the Civil War South (Athens: University of Georgia Press, 2001); and Elizabeth R. Varon, Southern Lady, Yankee Spy: The True Story of Elizabeth Van Lew, a Union Agent in the Heart of the Confederacy (New York: Oxford University Press, 2003). On the experience of African American women in the Confederacy, see Bercaw, Gendered Freedoms, 17–51; Noralee Frankel, Freedom's Women: Black Women and Families in Civil War Era Mississippi (Bloomington: Indiana University Press, 1999); Thavolia Glymph, "'This Species of Property': Female Slave Contrabands in the Civil War," in A Woman's War: Southern Women, Civil War, and the Confederate Legacy, ed. Edward D. C. Campbell Jr. and Kym S. Rice (Charlottesville: University Press of Virginia, 1996), 55–73; Susan Eva O'Donovan, Becoming Free in the Cotton South (Cambridge: Harvard University Press, 2007); and Leslie A. Schwalm, A Hard Fight for We: Women's Transition from Slavery to Freedom in South Carolina (Urbana: University of Illinois Press, 1997), 76–146.

8. Ash, When the Yankees Came, 76–107. For a discussion of Sherman's March as "An Entire Army on a Raid," see Scott Reynolds Nelson and Carol Sheriff, A People at War: Civilians and Soldiers in America's Civil War, 1854–1877 (New York: Oxford University Press, 2007), 157–59.

9. For a classic account of the role of the third front in the Civil War, see Ira Berlin, Barbara Fields, Steven Miller, Joseph Reidy, and Leslie Rowland, Slaves No More: Three Essays on Emancipation and the Civil War (Cambridge: Cambridge University Press, 1992).

10. While some important work has been done recently on the role of women who passed as men on the formal field of battle, such as that of DeAnne Blanton and Lauren M. Cook, They Fought like Demons: Women Soldiers in the American Civil War (Baton Rouge: Louisiana State University Press, 2002), and Elizabeth D. Leonard, All the Daring of the Soldier: Women of the Civil War Armies (New York: Norton, 1999), and women who worked as nurses at the front, such as that of Jane E. Schultz, Women at the Front: Hospital Workers in Civil War America (Chapel Hill: University of North Carolina Press, 2004), we chose to focus here on the majority of women who fought the war at home.

11. See Robert R. Mackey, The Uncivil War: Irregular Warfare in the Upper South, 1861–1865 (Norman: University of Oklahoma Press, 2004), and Fellman, Inside War, 93–230, for a rendering of civilians as primarily inert or victimized in guerrilla warfare.

12. See Nelson and Sheriff, People at War, 148–61, for a useful discussion of the centrality of the issue of supply in Lieber's Code.

13. See Reid Mitchell, The Vacant Chair: The Northern Soldier Leaves Home (New York: Oxford University Press, 1993), 89–144, for a discussion of the Union soldier's response to Southern civilian

women. For examples of the response of Southern civilian women to them, see Varon, *Southern Lady, Yankee Spy,* and LeeAnn Whites, *Gender Matters: Civi War, Reconstruction, and the Making of the New South* (New York: Palgrave Macmillan, 2005), 25–83.

14. See Daniel Sutherland, "Sideshow No Longer: A Historiographical Review of the Guerrilla War," *Civil War History* 46 (March 2000): 5–23, for a persuasive argument for the fundamental role of guerrilla warfare in the Civil War, and see Mark E. Neely Jr., *The Civil War and the Limits of Destruction* (Cambridge: Harvard University Press, 2007), 41–71, for a counter to Sutherland that relies on limiting the frame of guerrilla warfare to a conflict between men. See also Paul D. Escott, *Military Necessity: Civil-Military Relations in the Confederacy* (Westport, CT: Praeger Security International, 2006), for another example of the way that discussions entailing agency on the part of civilians continue to mean men in the most recent literature on the subject.

15. For standard discussions of the Woman Order, see Chester Hearn, *When the Devil Came Down to Dixie: Ben Butler in New Orleans* (Baton Rouge: Louisiana State University, 1997), and Mary P. Ryan, *Women in Public: Between Banners and Ballots, 1825–1880* (Baltimore: John Hopkins University Press, 1990), and for Sherman's March, see Lee Kennett, *Marching Through Georgia: The Story of Soldiers and Civilians During Sherman's Campaign* (New York: HarperCollins, 1995), and Jacqueline Glass Campbell, *When Sherman Marched North from the Sea: Resistance on the Confederate Home Front* (Chapel Hill: University of North Carolina, 2003).

(MIS)REMEMBERING GENERAL ORDER NO. 28

1. For a recent synthetic treatment of Butler's occupation of New Orleans, including a broad range of references to others who have written about Butler in the past, see Chester Hearn, *When the Devil Came Down to Dixie: Ben Butler in New Orleans* (Baton Rouge: Louisiana State University Press, 1997).

2. For interpretations of General Order No. 28 that are focused on women and gender, see Catherine Clinton, "'Public Women' and Sexual Politics During the American Civil War," in *Battle Scars: Gender and Sexuality in the American Civil War,* ed. Catherine Clinton and Nina Silber (New York: Oxford University Press, 2006), 61–77; Drew Gilpin Faust, *Mothers of Invention: Women of the Slaveholding South in the American Civil War* (Chapel Hill: University of North Carolina Press, 1996), 207–14; George Rable, "'Missing in Action': Women in the Confederacy," in *Divided Houses: Gender and the Civil War,* ed. Catherine Clinton and Nina Silber (New York: Oxford University Press, 1992), 137; and Mary P. Ryan, *Women in Public: Between Banners and Ballots, 1825–1880* (Baltimore: Johns Hopkins University Press, 1990), 142–46. Although women and gender are not his focus, Hearn does include a significant amount of data related to women in *When the Devil Came Down to Dixie.*

3. Gerald M. Capers, *Occupied City: New Orleans under the Federals, 1862–1865* (Lexington: University of Kentucky Press, 1965), 60.

4. Transcript of the speech from the *New York Daily Times* (undated), reprinted in James Parton, *General Butler in New Orleans* (New York: Mason Brothers, 1864), 117–19.

5. Joan Elizabeth Doyle, "Civilian Life in Occupied New Orleans, 1862–1865" (Ph.D. diss., Louisiana State University, 1955), 19; Capers, *Occupied City,* 56; Jessie Ames Marshall, ed., *Private and Official Correspondence of Gen. Benjamin F. Butler During the Period of the Civil War,* 5 vols. (Norwood, MA: Plimpton Press, 1917).

6. Parton, *General Butler in New Orleans*, 8.

7. Ibid.; Michael Kammen evokes the quotation by C. Vann Woodward in *Mystic Chords of Memory: The Transformation of Tradition in American Culture* (New York: Knopf, 1991), 31. Over the past two decades, a number of historians have written thoughtfully about how the memory of the Civil War and Reconstruction periods has been shaped. Titles that have had an impact on my own thinking about Butler and memory include David W. Blight, *Race and Reunion: The Civil War in American Memory* (Cambridge: Belknap Press of Harvard University Press, 2001); W. Fitzhugh Brundage, ed., *Where These Memories Grow: History, Memory, and Southern Identity* (Chapel Hill: University of North Carolina Press, 2000); Karen L. Cox, *Dixie's Daughters: The United Daughters of the Confederacy and the Preservation of Confederate Culture* (Gainesville: University Press of Florida, 2003); Alice Fahs and Joan Waugh, eds., *The Memory of the Civil War in American Culture* (Chapel Hill: University of North Carolina Press, 2004); and Gaines M. Foster, *Ghosts of the Confederacy: Defeat, the Lost Cause, and the Emergence of the New South, 1865 to 1913* (New York: Oxford University Press, 1987).

8. David Lowenthal, *Possessed by the Past: The Heritage Crusade and the Spoils of History* (New York: Free Press, 1996), 144.

9. For a recent, careful examination of the practical and theoretical ways that gender politics drove the development of occupation and military policy during the Civil War, see LeeAnn Whites, *Gender Matters: Civil War, Reconstruction, and the Making of the New South* (New York: Palgrave Macmillan, 2005).

10. Benj. F. Butler, *Autobiography and Personal Reminiscences of Major-General Benj. F. Butler,* also known as *Butler's Book* (Boston: A. M. Thayer and Co., 1892), 414 (hereafter cited as *Butler's Book*).

11. The order was widely reprinted in newspapers locally, nationally, and even internationally. See, for example, the *New Orleans Daily Picayune*, May 17, 1862, and the *New York Times*, May 26, 1862.

12. *New York Times*, June 11, 1862.

13. *Butler's Book*, 414–18. Most historians have assumed that this "not very clean water" came from a chamber pot. See also Hearn, *When the Devil Came Down to Dixie*, 101–09.

14. *Butler's Book*, 414–18.

15. Thomas W. Helis, "Of Generals and Jurists: The Judicial System of New Orleans under Union Occupation, May 1862–April 1865," *Louisiana History* 29, no. 2 (1988): 143–62; Parton, *General Butler in New Orleans*, 330.

16. *New York Times*, May 26, 1862.

17. Ibid., June 11, 1862.

18. *Daily Delta*, June 8, 15, 1862.

19. Parton, *Butler in New Orleans*, 328.

20. *Butler's Book*, 419.

21. Clinton, "'Public Women'"; Faust, *Mothers of Invention;* Rable, "'Missing in Action'"; Ryan, *Women in Public*, 142–46.

22. Clinton, "'Public Women,'" 66, 67.

23. Lowenthal, *Possessed by the Past*, 148. For a contemporary account of these events, see Parton, *General Butler in New Orleans*, 322–45.

24. *Butler's Book*, 415. It is likely this event of one of Levy Phillips's sons spitting on a Union officer is true, as Butler includes it in the text of Special Order No. 150 and in his memoir. What is interesting is how he chooses to emphasize it in the memoir.

25. For the full text of Special Order No. 150, see the *Daily Delta* and the *Daily Picayune*, July 2, 1862.

26. *Daily Delta* and the *Daily Picayune,* July 2, 1862.

27. *Butler's Book,* 511.

28. Ibid., 511, 512. Butler sentenced her, like Levy Phillips, to two years at Ship Island, but he released her after three weeks. See also Hearn, *When the Devil Went Down to Dixie,* 169.

29. Parton, *General Butler in New Orleans,* 438. Interestingly, in his version, Parton placed Larue's story before Eugenia Levy Phillips's, also distorting the order of events and their timing.

30. Capers, *Occupied City,* 185–88. Much of Capers's information in this section draws heavily on evidence compiled by Jean Elizabeth Doyle. See Doyle, "Civilian Life in Occupied New Orleans" and "Nurseries of Treason," *Journal of Southern History* 26 (1960): 161–79.

31. "Our New Orleans Correspondence," dateline August 17, 1862, *New York Times,* August 26, 1862.

32. Ibid.

33. *New York Times,* October 4, 1862.

34. Ryan, *Women in Public,* 145, 146. Ryan takes this account from Marion Southwood's *Beauty and Booty: The Watchwords of New Orleans* (New York: published for the author, 1867), 112, 280. For a broadside of the poem believed to have been created shortly after the event, see "The Battle of St. Paul's: Fought in New Orleans, Sunday, October 12, 1862 / sung by a Louisiana soldier," Historic New Orleans Collection, Accession 86–2268-RL. See image of same online at www.//louisdl.louislibraries. org/cdm4/item_viewer.php?CISOROOT=/AAW&CISOPTR=344&REC=5.

35. Ryan, *Women in Public,* 145, 146.

36. Ibid., 146.

37. In 1979, historian Mark Neely cited George Frederickson on Butler, writing that historians "are naturally reluctant to take Ben Butler's word for anything, but some recent scholars have found good reason to accept his account of this conversation." "This conversation" refers to Butler's claim to have discussed the colonization of the freedman with Lincoln shortly before the president's assassination—a claim Neely proves is spurious. See Mark E. Neely, "Abraham Lincoln and Black Colonization: Benjamin Butler's Spurious Testimony," *Civil War History* 25, no. 1 (1979): 77–83.

38. I thank LeeAnn Whites for suggesting the significance of Sherman's simultaneous occupation of Memphis and its relationship to Butler's in New Orleans. For a close examination of Sherman's time in Memphis, see John F. Marszalek, *Sherman: A Soldier's Passion for Order* (New York: Free Press, 1993), 188–201. For the more traditional view that the shift from "soft" to "hard war" on civilians took place later in the conflict—itself an interesting linguistic construct—see Mark Grimsley, *The Hard Hand of War: Union Military Policy Toward Southern Civilians, 1861–1865* (New York: Cambridge University Press, 1995).

39. Cynthia Enloe's work in this area is both invigorating and extensive. See, for example, Enloe, *Bananas, Beaches, and Bases: Making Feminist Sense of International Politics* (Berkeley: University of California Press, 1990); *Manuevers: The International Politics of Militarizing Women's Lives* (Berkeley: University of California Press, 2000); and *Globalization and Militarism: Feminists Make the Link* (Lanham: Rowman and Littlefield, 2007).

BEDROOMS AS BATTLEFIELDS

1. Mother to Daughters, March 8, 1865, Mrs. Albert Rhett (Sallie Coles Green) Heyward Papers, South Caroliniana Library, University of South Carolina, Columbia, South Carolina (hereafter cited as SCL).

2. Anonymous Woman [Fayetteville], March 22, 1865, Emma Mordecai Diary, Mordecai Family Papers, Southern Historical Collection, University of North Carolina, Chapel Hill, North Carolina (hereafter cited as SHC). See also S. McCain to Daughter, March 5, 1865, Mary Amarinthia Snowden Papers, SCL; Elizabeth Collier, April 20, 1865, Elizabeth Collier Diary, SHC; [Laura?] to [?], January 6, 1865, Ferebee, Gregory, and McPherson Family Papers, SHC; and Mrs. E. A. Steele to Tody, February 15, 1865, in Katharine M. Jones, *When Sherman Came: Southern Women and the "Great March"* (Indianapolis: Bobbs-Merrill Co., 1964), 135. Also see E. N. B. to Kate Taylor, April 1, 1865, Edward Smith Tennent Papers, SCL; Elizabeth Palmer Porcher to Philip E. Porcher, March 23, 1865, in *A World Turned Upside Down: The Palmers of South Santee, 1818–1881*, ed. Louis P. Towles (Columbia: University of South Carolina Press, 1996), 450; and Sue Sample, November 29, 1864, in Jones, *When Sherman Came*, 47.

3. Although antebellum gender ideals would have generally prevented men from any assault on white women, the Civil War corrupted these notions and allowed Union men to bring the war to enemy women. On the changes in gender roles and ideas during the war, see LeeAnn Whites, *The Civil War as a Crisis in Gender: Augusta, Georgia, 1860–1890* (Athens: University of Georgia Press, 1995); LeeAnn Whites, *Gender Matters: Civil War, Reconstruction, and the Making of the New South* (New York: Palgrave Macmillan, 2005); Catherine Clinton and Nina Silber, eds., *Divided Houses: Gender and the Civil War* (New York: Oxford University Press, 1992); and Catherine Clinton and Nina Silber, eds., *Battle Scars: Gender and Sexuality in the American Civil War* (New York: Oxford University Press, 2006). On white Southern women's Civil War experiences, see Catherine Clinton, *Tara Revisited: Women, War, and the Plantation Legend* (New York: Abbeville Press, 1995); Drew Gilpin Faust, *Mothers of Invention: Women of the Slaveholding South in the Civil War* (Chapel Hill: University of North Carolina Press, 1996); Laura F. Edwards, *Scarlett Doesn't Live Here Anymore: Southern Women in the Civil War Era* (Urbana: University of Illinois Press, 2000); and George C. Rable, *Civil Wars: Women and the Crisis of Southern Nationalism* (Urbana: University of Illinois Press, 1989).

4. Lee Kennett, *Marching Through Georgia: The Story of Soldiers and Civilians During Sherman's Campaign* (New York: HarperCollins, 1995). See also John Bennett Walters, "General William T. Sherman and Total War," *Journal of Southern History* 14 (November 1948): 447–80; John G. Barrett, *Sherman's March Through the Carolinas* (Chapel Hill: University of North Carolina Press, 1956); John Bennett Walters, *Merchant of Terror: General Sherman and Total War* (Indianapolis: Bobbs-Merrill Co., 1973); Richard Wheeler, *Sherman's March* (New York: Thomas Y. Crowell, 1978); Burke Davis, *Sherman's March* (New York: Random House, 1980); James Lee McDonough and James Pickett Jones, *"War So Terrible": Sherman and Atlanta* (New York: Norton, 1987); Mark A. Smith, "Sherman's Unexpected Companions: Marching Through Georgia with Jomini and Clausewitz," *Georgia Historical Quarterly* 81 (Spring 1997): 1–24; Anne J. Bailey, *The Chessboard of War: Sherman and Hood in the Autumn Campaigns of 1864* (Lincoln: University of Nebraska Press, 2000). Other studies of Sherman delve beneath the political and military but still focus more on military than civilian targets during the march. For examples, see Stanley P. Hirshson, *The White Tecumseh: A Biography of General William T. Sherman* (New York: John Wiley and Sons, 1997); Michael Fellman, *Citizen Sherman: A Life of William Tecumseh Sherman* (New York: Random House, 1995); John F. Marszalek, *Sherman: A Soldier's Passion for Order* (New York: Free Press, 1993); and Lee Kennett, *Sherman: A Soldier's Life* (New York: HarperCollins, 2001).

5. Jacqueline Glass Campbell, *When Sherman Marched North from the Sea: Resistance on the Confederate Home Front* (Chapel Hill: University of North Carolina Press, 2003).

6. On the importance of gender to the study of the Civil War, see Whites, *Civil War as a Crisis in*

Gender; Whites, *Gender Matters;* Clinton and Silber, *Divided Houses;* and Clinton and Silber, *Battle Scars.* Also see Philippa Levine, ed., *Gender and Empire* (New York: Oxford University Press, 2004). Scholars acknowledge the importance of power to the campaign, although they still neglect to discuss its gendered implications. See Mark Grimsley, *The Hard Hand of War: Union Military Policy Toward Southern Civilians, 1861–1865* (New York: Cambridge University Press, 1995); Joseph T. Glatthaar, *The March to the Sea and Beyond: Sherman's Troops in the Savannah and Carolinas Campaigns* (Baton Rouge: Louisiana State University Press, 1995), 39–51; and Charles Royster, *The Destructive War: William Tecumseh Sherman, Stonewall Jackson, and the Americans* (New York: Knopf, 1991), esp. 79–143, 321–404.

7. William T. Sherman to John Sherman, September 22, 1862, in William T. Sherman, *Home Letters of General Sherman,* ed. M. A. DeWolfe Howe (New York: Charles Scribner's Sons, 1909), 162 (emphasis added).

8. William T. Sherman to George H. Thomas, October 20, 1864, in U.S. War Department, *The War of the Rebellion: A Compilation of the Official Records of the Union and Confederate Armies* (Washington, DC: GPO, 1880–1901), ser. 1, vol. 39, pt. 3: 378 (hereafter cited as *OR*).

9. William T. Sherman to Henry Halleck, October 19, 1864, in *OR*, ser. 1, vol. 39, pt. 3: 357–58 (emphasis added).

10. William T. Sherman to Ulysses S. Grant, October 9, 1864, in *OR*, ser. 1, vol. 39, pt. 3: 162.

11. When men left to fight for the Southern nation, their wives, daughters, sisters, and loved ones remained at home to protect family property and support the war effort, materially and spiritually. Consequently the Confederacy's civilian population can be seen as a feminine, or at least feminized, one. Even men on the home front were often seen as emasculated because they were unable to physically fight the invaders and protect their homesteads, as men were expected to do; these men typically hid themselves or fled as soon as enemy soldiers approached. Southern women were left to face the invaders without the accustomed and expected peacetime protection of white men.

12. On the progression of Union war tactics, see Grimsley, *Hard Hand of War.*

13. Lisa Tendrich Frank, "War Comes Home: Confederate Women and Union Soldiers," in *Virginia's Civil War,* ed. Peter Wallenstein and Bertram Wyatt-Brown (Charlottesville: University of Virginia Press, 2005), 123–36.

14. Special Field Orders No. 67, in *OR*, ser. 1, vol. 38, pt. 5: 837–38.

15. William T. Sherman to James M. Calhoun, Mayor, E. E. Rawson and S. C. Wells, representing the City Council of Atlanta, September 12, 1864, in William T. Sherman, *The Hero's Own Story* (New York: Bunce and Huntington, 1865), 60; William T. Sherman to Henry W. Halleck, September 9, 1864, in *OR*, ser. 1, vol. 38, pt. 5: 839.

16. William T. Sherman to Ulysses S. Grant, November 6, 1864, in *OR*, ser. 1, vol. 39, pt. 3: 660. See James Reston Jr., *Sherman's March and Vietnam* (New York: Macmillan, 1984), 93.

17. On the importance of the domestic sphere to nineteenth-century Americans, see, for example, Glenna Matthews, *"Just a Housewife": The Rise and Fall of Domesticity in America* (New York: Oxford University Press, 1987); Anne Firor Scott, *The Southern Lady: From Pedestal to Politics, 1830–1930* (Chicago: University of Chicago Press, 1970); and Barbara Welter, "The Cult of True Womanhood, 1820–1860," *American Quarterly* 18 (Summer 1966): 151–74.

To emphasize Union men's lack of propriety, many Confederate women gave vivid descriptions of their mistreatment by Union soldiers and proudly related their defiant responses to it. These written missives warned others in Sherman's path, stimulated Southern anger against the Northern troops, and highlighted women's roles as protectors of Southern honor and Southern homes. For example, see Eliza Tillinghast to David R. Tillinghast, May 3, 1865, Tillinghast Family Papers, Duke University, Durham, North Carolina (hereafter cited as DU); Caroline Gilman to Eliza, [1865], in "Letters of a Confederate Mother: Charleston in the Sixties," *Atlantic Monthly,* April 1926, 511.

18. Sarah Jane Sams to Randolph Sams, February 4, 1865, Sarah Jane Sams Letter, SCL.

19. Sarah Jane Sams to Randolph Sams, February 5, 1865, Sarah Jane Sams Letter, SCL.

20. Sarah Jane Sams to Randolph Sams, February 4, 1865, Sarah Jane Sams Letter, SCL.

21. Charlotte St. Julien Ravenel to Meta Heyward, February 25, 1865, Charlotte St. Julien Ravenel Diary, Ravenel Family Papers, 1838–1937, South Carolina Historical Society, Charleston, South Carolina. See also Charlotte St. Julien Ravenel to Meta Heyward, February 26, 1865, Charlotte St. Julien Ravenel Diary; Mary Maxcy Leverett to Milton Leverett, February 24, 1865, in *The Leverett Letters: Correspondence of a South Carolina Family, 1851–1868,* ed. Frances Wallace Taylor, Catherine Taylor Matthews, and J. Tracy Power (Columbia: University of South Carolina Press, 2000), 385.

22. Thomas T. Taylor, November 23, 1864, Diary, Taylor Collection, Emory University, Atlanta, Georgia (hereafter cited as EU).

23. William T. Sherman, Special Field Orders No. 120, November 9, 1864, in *OR,* ser. 1, vol. 39, pt. 3: 713.

24. Thomas T. Taylor, November 23, 1864, Diary.

25. For examples, see Belle Boyd, *Belle Boyd in Camp and Prison, Written by Herself,* ed. Curtis Carroll Davis (1865; repr., South Brunswick, NJ: Thomas Yoseloff, 1968); Rose O'Neal Greenhow, *My Imprisonment and the First Year of Abolition Rule in Washington* (London: n.p., 1863); Oscar A. Kinchen, *Women Who Spied for the Blue and the Gray* (Philadelphia: Dorrance and Co., 1972); and Mary Elizabeth Massey, *Women in the Civil War* (Lincoln: University of Nebraska Press, 1994); originally published as *Bonnet Brigades* (New York: Knopf, 1966).

26. Emma LeConte, February 14, 1865, Emma LeConte Diary, SHC. See also Anna Maria Green Cook, November 25, 1864, in *The Journal of a Milledgeville Girl, 1861–1867,* ed. James C. Bonner (Athens: University of Georgia Press, 1964), 62; Mrs. W. K. Bachman to Kate Bachman, March 27, 1865, Mrs. W. K. Bachman Papers, SCL; Mrs. E. A. Steele to Tody, February 15, 1865, in Jones, *When Sherman Came,* 134; Mary Elinor Bouknight Poppenheim, February 27, 1965, in Jones, *When Sherman Came,* 245.

27. Sarah Jane Sams to Randolph Sams, February 4, 1865, Sarah Jane Sams Letter, SCL. Also see Pauline DeCaradeuc Heyward, February 18, 1864, in *A Confederate Lady Comes of Age: The Journal of Pauline DeCaradeuc Heyward, 1863–1888,* ed. Mary D. Robertson (Columbia: University of South Carolina Press, 1992), 97; Nancy Armstrong Furman to Mary Furman, March 8, 1865, in Jones, *When Sherman Came,* 218; and Maria L. Haynsworth to Ma, April 28, 1865, SHC.

28. For examples, see Charlotte St. Julien Ravenel, February 26, 1865, Charlotte St. Julien Ravenel Diary; Dolly Lunt Burge, November 19, 1864, in *The Diary of Dolly Lunt Burge, 1848–1879,* ed. Christine Jacobson Carter (Athens: University of Georgia Press, 1997), 159; Mary Rowe, February 17, 1865, in "A Southern Girl's Diary," *Confederate Veteran* 40 (July 1932): 264–65; Pauline DeCaradeuc Heyward, February 18, 1865, in *Confederate Lady Comes of Age,* 69; Emma LeConte, February 19, 1865, Emma LeConte Diary; Caroline Lamar to Charles Augustus Layfayette Lamar, December 23, 1864, Charles Augustus Layfayette Lamar Family Papers, Georgia Department of Archives and History, Atlanta, Georgia; Mrs. W. K. Bachman to Kate Bachman, March 27, 1865, Mrs. W. K. Bachman Papers.

29. Sister R. to Iverson Louis Harris, [November 30, 1864], Iverson L. Harris Papers, Manuscript

and Rare Book Special Collection Library, DU. Slave women took similar precautions to avoid molestation by Union troops. For example, Mary Jones Mallard describes how her cook hid herself during a Union raid on the house. "From being a young girl she had assumed the attitude and appearance of a sick old woman with a blanket thrown over her head & shoulders & scarcely able to move." Mary Jones Mallard, December 29, 1864, in Mary Sharpe Jones and Mary Jones Mallard, *Yankees a'Coming: One Month's Experience During the Invasion of Liberty County, Georgia, 1864–1865*, ed. Haksell Monroe (Tuscaloosa, AL: Confederate Publishing Co., 1959), 63.

30. Pauline DeCaradeuc Heyward, February 18, 1865, in *Confederate Lady Comes of Age*, 68.

31. Robert Hale Strong, *A Yankee Private's Civil War*, ed. Ashley Halsey (Chicago: H. Regnery Co., 1961), 62–63.

32. Southern women's responses to the invasion of domestic space demonstrate the nineteenth-century belief in the home as women's domain. Although some modern scholars often see women as confined in the domestic sphere, contemporary women saw this as their place of power. They controlled all that happened in the home and therefore fought to protect this realm. The women of the South refused to take the Union invasion of their homes and domestic domain without a fight.

33. Eliza Tillinghast to David R. Tillinghast, May 3, 1865, Tillinghast Family Papers.

34. See Emma LeConte, December 31, 1864, Emma LeConte Diary; Mary Jones Mallard, December 21, 1864, and January 4, 1865, in Jones and Mallard, *Yankees a'Coming*, 53, 66; Loula Kendall Rogers, April 30, 1865, Loula Kendall Rogers Papers, Special Collections Department, Robert W. Woodruff Library, EU; Sarah Jane Sams to Randolph Sams, February 6 and 13, 1865, Sarah Jane Sams Letter, SCL; Sarah to Hattie Taylor Tennent, January 9, 1865, Edward Smith Tennent Papers; Ellen Devereux Hinsdale to Child, March 23, 1865, Hinsdale Family Papers, DU; Kate Crosland to Bea and Nellie, December 28, 1864, Thomas M. McIntosh Papers, DU; Louisa Jane Harllee to Amelia, ca. 1865, Benjamin H. Teague Papers, 1846–1921, South Carolina Historical Society; Susan Bowen Lining to Sister, March 16, 1865, South Carolina Historical Society; Emily Caroline Ellis, February 15, 1865, Mrs. Emily Caroline Ellis Diary, SCL; Catherine Ann Devereux Edmondston, March 14, 1865, in *Journal of a Secesh Lady: The Diary of Catherine Ann Devereux Edmondston, 1860–1866*, ed. Beth G. Crabtree and James W. Patton (Raleigh: North Carolina Division of Archives and History, 1979), 677; Grace Brown Elmore, November 26, 1864, in *A Heritage of Woe: The Civil War Diary of Grace Brown Elmore, 1861–1868*, ed. Marli F. Weiner (Athens: University of Georgia Press, 1997), 81; Fanny Yates Cohen, December 25, 1864, in "Fanny Cohen's Journal of Sherman's Occupation of Savannah," ed. Spencer B. King, *Georgia Historical Quarterly* 41, no. 4 (1957): 413; Mother to Daughters, March 8, 1865, Mrs. Albert Rhett (Sallie Coles Green) Heyward Papers; Mary Rowe, February 17, 1865, in Jones, *When Sherman Came*, 166; Mrs. W. K. Bachman to Kate Bachman, March 27, 1865, Mrs. W. K. Bachman Papers; Dolly Lunt Burge, November 19, 1864, in *Diary of Dolly Lunt Burge*, 159; and Mary Noble to Lelia Montan, November 20, 1864, Mary Noble Papers, SHC.

A few white women expressed outrage when they heard rumors that Union soldiers found their fiery resistance appealing. See [Dorrie] Davis to Brother, December 31, 1865, Confederate Miscellany I, EU.

35. For example, Charles S. Brown described an incident in which an individual soldier asserted his power by forcing Southern women to beg for mercy. Charles S. Brown to Etta, April 26, 1865, Brown Papers, DU.

36. Lieutenant Colonel Jeremiah W. Jenkins as cited in Royster, *Destructive War*, 20.

37. On Southern honor, see Bertram Wyatt-Brown, *Southern Honor: Ethics and Behavior in the Old South* (New York: Oxford University Press, 1982); Bertram Wyatt-Brown, *The Shaping of Southern Culture: Honor, Grace, and War, 1760s–1890s* (Chapel Hill: University of North Carolina Press, 2001).

38. G. S. Bradley, December 28, 1864, in G. S. Bradley, *The Star Corps; Or, Notes of an Army Chaplain During Sherman's Famous "March to the Sea"* (Milwaukee: Jermain and Brightman, 1865), 68 (emphasis in the original).

39. Lieutenant Colonel Jeremiah W. Jenkins as cited in Royster, *Destructive War*, 23. Also see William O. Wettleson to Father and Sisters, November 27, 1864, Wiley Files, EU; Harvey Reid to Homefolk, December 14, 1864, Wiley Files; Samuel B. Crew to Brother and Sister, December 15, 1864, Wiley Files; Jones and Mallard, December 16, 1864, in Jones and Mallard, *Yankees a'Coming;* and Mary Bull Maxcy Leverett to Caroline Pinckney Seabrook, March 18, 1865, SCL.

40. Pauline DeCaradeuc Heyward, February 18, 1865, in *Confederate Lady Comes of Age*, 65–68. Other women felt similar outrage at the insult of having their undergarments taken or displayed. See Mary Maxcy Leverett to Milton Maxcy Leverett, February 24, 1865, in Taylor, Matthews, and Power, *Leverett Letters*, 385; Esther Alden [Elizabeth Allston], March 4, 1865, in *"Our Women in the War": The Lives They Lived, the Deaths They Died, from the Weekly News and Courier, Charleston, S.C.* (Charleston: News and Courier Book Presses, 1885), 359–60; and Mary Sharpe Jones, January 3, 1865, in Jones and Mallard, *Yankees a'Coming*, 65.

41. Mary Sharpe Jones, January 7, 1865, in Jones and Mallard, *Yankees a'Coming*, 73.

42. Mary Sharpe Jones, January 17, 1865, in Jones and Mallard, *Yankees a'Coming*, 81.

43. Historian Michael Fellman recognizes that the invasion of a woman's bedroom is a "symbolic rape." See Fellman, *Inside War: The Guerrilla Conflict in Missouri During the American Civil War* (New York: Oxford University Press, 1989), 207–208.

44. Emma LeConte, December 31, 1864, Emma LeConte Diary (emphasis added).

45. Matilda Montgomery Champion to Sidney S. Champion, June 14, 1864, Sidney S. Champion Papers, EU.

46. Ellen Devereux Hinsdale to Child, March 23, 1865, Hinsdale Family Papers. Also see Sue Sample, November 29, 1864, in Jones, *When Sherman Came*, 48.

47. William T. Sherman to Ellen Sherman, December 25, 1864, in Sherman, *Home Letters*, 319.

48. William T. Sherman to Ellen Sherman, March 12, 1865, in Sherman, *Home Letters*, 332.

49. Loula to Poss, May 22, 1865, Graves Family Papers, SHC (emphasis in the original).

50. Emma LeConte, February 21, 1865, Emma LeConte Diary.

51. Grace Brown Elmore, March 4, 1865, in Weiner, *Heritage of Woe*, 108.

52. Emma LeConte, February 23, 1865, Emma LeConte Diary (emphasis in the original).

53. Grace Brown Elmore, February 21, 1865, in Weiner, *Heritage of Woe*, 102.

54. Eliza Tillinghast to David R. Tillinghast, May 3, 1865, Tillinghast Family Papers.

55. Anne Sarah Rubin explores Confederates' inability to consider a peace treaty with the Union in *A Shattered Nation: The Rise and Fall of the Confederacy, 1861–1868* (Chapel Hill: University of North Carolina Press, 2005), esp. 112–16.

56. Loula Kendall Rogers, May 11, 1865, Loula Kendall Rogers Papers. Also see Emma LeConte, April 20, 1865, Emma LeConte Diary (emphasis in the original).

57. Loula Kendall Rogers, May 11, 1865, Loula Kendall Rogers Papers (emphasis in the original).

"PHYSICAL ABUSE . . . AND ROUGH HANDLING"

1. Testimony of Mary Melissa Kirksey in trial of Charles C. Hunter, NN1921, Record Group 153, Records of the Office of the Judge Advocate General (U.S. Army), National Archives and Records Administration, Washington, D.C. (hereafter, cases from these records will be cited as JAG Trials).

2. For these early mentions, see, for example, Bell I. Wiley, *The Life of Billy Yank: The Common Soldier of the Union* (Garden City, NY: Doubleday, 1971), 114, 205, and Joseph Glatthaar, *Forged in Battle: The Civil War Alliance of Black Soldiers and White Officers* (New York: Free Press, 1990), 118–19. On the broader subject of the history of rape in American society, Catherine Clinton has examined the rape of African American women in the antebellum South (see "Southern Dishonor: Flesh, Blood, Race, and Bondage," in *In Joy and in Sorrow: Women, Family, and Marriage in the Victorian South, 1830–1900*, ed. Carol Bleser [New York: Oxford University Press, 1991], 52–68) and during Reconstruction ("Bloody Terrain: Freedwomen and Violence During Reconstruction," *Georgia Historical Quarterly* 76, no. 2 [1992]: 313–32). See also Diane Miller Sommerville, *Rape and Race in the Nineteenth-Century South* (Chapel Hill: University of North Carolina Press, 2004), and Sharon Block, *Rape and Sexual Power in Early America* (Chapel Hill: University of North Carolina Press, 2006), for a more extended study of the crime.

3. George C. Rable, *Civil Wars: Women and the Crisis of Southern Nationalism* (Urbana: University of Illinois Press, 1989), 161 and 341 n. 25; Victoria E. Bynum, *Unruly Women: The Politics of Social and Sexual Control in the Old South* (Chapel Hill: University of North Carolina Press, 1992), 118; Ervin L. Jordan Jr., "Mirrors beyond Memories: Afro-Virginians and the Civil War," in *New Perspectives on the Civil War*, ed. John W. Simon and Michael E. Stevens (Madison, WI: Madison House, 1998), 158. See also Ervin L. Jordan Jr., "Sleeping with the Enemy: Sex, Black Women, and the Civil War," *Western Journal of Black Studies* 18, no. 2 (1994): 55–63.

4. Drew Gilpin Faust, *Mothers of Invention: Women of the Slaveholding South in the American Civil War* (Chapel Hill: University of North Carolina Press, 1996), 200; see also 296 n. 6.

5. Mark Grimsley, "'Rebels' and 'Redskins': U.S. Military Conduct Toward White Southerners and Native Americans in Comparative Perspective," in *Civilians in the Path of War*, ed. Mark Grimsley and Clifford J. Rodgers (Lincoln: University of Nebraska Press, 2002), 151.

6. Michael Fellman, *Inside War: The Guerrilla Conflict in Missouri During the American Civil War* (New York: Oxford University Press, 1989), 207.

7. Martha Hodes, *White Women, Black Men: Illicit Sex in the Nineteenth-Century South* (New Haven, CT: Yale University Press, 1997); Laura F. Edwards, *Scarlett Doesn't Live Here Anymore: Southern Women in the Civil War Era* (Urbana: University of Illinois Press, 2000); Clinton, "Southern Dishonor" and "Bloody Terrain"; Sommerville, *Rape and Race in the Nineteenth-Century South*; Hannah Rosen, "Rape, Race, and Citizenship in the Postemancipation South" (Ph.D. diss., University of Chicago, 1999). For a useful guide to researching sexual behavior during the American Civil War, see Thomas P. Lowery, *Sexual Misconduct in the Civil War: A Compendium* (Philadelphia: Xlibris Corp., 2006).

8. The most frequently prosecuted military crimes were desertion, being drunk and disorderly, sleeping on post, and the like. Sexual assault and murder were the most frequently prosecuted civilian crimes.

9. For example, in the review of a particularly violent assault by two privates in the Seventy-second New York on a white married mother of two living in Prince George Church, Virginia, in 1864, Commander George G. Meade wrote, "I think it unfortunate for the discipline of this Army and the dignity of our arms, that I am not empowered by law to order the immediate execution of the [death] sen-

tences in these cases. Prompt punishment adds very much to the efficacy of the example, and I request you will take special opportunity to present these cases to the President, at as early a period as possible, that the Army may not be embarrassed by the custody of these prisoners, and that the example may be as striking as a necessary compliance with forms of law may permit." Both were eventually executed. Trials of Daniel Geary and Ransom Gordon, microfilm #M1523, reel 2 (MM1481), JAG Trials.

10. Testimony of David Crutchfield in trial of Charles C. Hunter, JAG Trials.

11. Trial of Charles H. Hunter, JAG Trials.

12. Garrard Glenn, *The Army and the Law,* revised and enlarged by A. Arthur Schiller (New York: AMS Press, 1967), 32. For the 1806 Articles of War, see John F. Callan, *The Military Laws of the United States* (Philadelphia: George W. Childs, 1863), 174.

13. William C. DeHart, *Observations on Military Law and the Constitution and Practice of Courts Martial* (New York: D. Appleton and Co., 1869), 6. *Revised United States Army Regulations of 1861* (Philadelphia: George W. Childs, 1863), 124. Regimental commanders could convene regimental courts-martial, and field commanders had authorization to convene "drumhead" courts-martial, that is, summary justice in the field. Few records of these courts-martial survive.

14. Glenn, *Army and the Law,* 47.

15. No rules governed the role that the judge advocate played in relation to the accused except that it was an "official" relationship. In his capacity as a "minister of justice," the judge advocate would assist in "collecting his proofs and preparing his defence." William Winthrop, *Military Law and Precedents* (Boston: Little, Brown, 1896), 292–93.

16. "Regularly and properly[,] charges can be preferred to a general court martial for trial only by the commander by whom the court has been convened or by his authority." Ibid., 223, 220–24.

17. *Revised United States Army Regulations of 1861,* 125.

18. DeHart, *Observations on Military Law,* 302, 316. A review of judge advocates' service records turned up few who were lawyers prior to their military service.

19. 37th Cong., 2nd sess., July 17, 1862, chap. 201, sec. 6, 12 *Statutes at Large* 597; Callan, *Military Law of the United States,* 532.

20. Winthrop, *Military Law and Precedents* (1896), 265–66.

21. DeHart, *Observations on Military Law,* 309; Article of War 69 in Callan, *Military Law of the United States,* 187.

22. DeHart, *Observations on Military Law,* 315–18; Winthrop, *Military Law and Precedents* (1896), 277–94.

23. Glenn, *Army and the Law,* 49; DeHart, *Observations on Military Law,* 203.

24. Glenn, *Army and the Law,* 47.

25. Joseph Holt to Edwin M. Stanton, December 28, 1863, Correspondence, Letters Sent, entry 1, vol. 4, p. 457, Record Group 153, Records of the Office of the Judge Advocate General (U.S. Army), National Archives and Records Administration, Washington, D.C. (hereafter cited as JAG Correspondence, Letters Sent).

26. Articles of War (1806), Article 99: "All crimes not capital, and all disorders and neglect which officers and soldiers may be guilty of, to the prejudice of military order and military discipline, though not mentioned in the foregoing articles of war, are to be taken cognizance of by a general or regimental court-martial according to the nature and degree of the offense, and be punished at their discretion." *Revised U.S. Army Regulations of 1861,* 501.

27. Joseph W. Bishop Jr., *Justice under Fire: A Study of Military Law* (New York: Charterhouse, 1976), 82–83.

28. A military commission is defined as a "court convened by military authority for the trial of persons not usually subject to military law but who are charged with violations of the laws of war, and in places subject to military government or martial law, for the trial of such persons when charged with violations of proclamations, ordinances, and domestic civil and criminal law of the territory concerned." Edward M. Byrne, *Military Law* (Annapolis, MD: Naval Institute Press, 1981), 752.

29. Lieutenant Colonel Jody Prescott and Major Joanne Eldridge, "Military Commissions, Past and Future," *Military Review,* March–April 2003, 42–43. For the text of General Order No. 20, see William Winthrop, *Military Law and Precedents,* 2nd ed., revised and enlarged (Washington: GPO, 1920), 832. On the Mexican War origins of military commissions, see also K. Jack Bauer, *The Mexican War, 1846–1848* (New York: Macmillan, 1974), 253, 326–27.

30. The crimes enumerated were "[a]ssassination, murder, poisoning, rape, or attempt to commit either, malicious stabbing or maiming, malicious assault and battery, robbery, theft," as well as the crime of property destruction, whether private or religious. Winthrop, *Military Law and Precedents* (1920), 832.

31. Prescott and Eldridge, "Military Commissions, Past and Future," 43.

32. Winthrop, *Military Law and Precedents* (1920), 833. See the extensive discussion of the use of military commissions during the Civil War in Mark E. Neely Jr., *The Fate of Liberty: Abraham Lincoln and Civil Liberties* (New York: Oxford University Press, 1991), esp. 162–75.

33. Judge Advocate J. F. Lee, report of June 8, 1862, vol. 1, pp. 212–13, JAG Correspondence, Letters Sent.

34. Congress created the office of Judge Advocate General of the Army (JAG) in July 1862. "An Act to amend the Act calling forth the Militia to execute the Laws of the Union, suppress Insurrections, and repel Invasions," July 17, 1862, chap. 201, sec. 5, 12 *Statutes at Large* 597, 598 (hereafter cited as "Militia Act").

35. Mary Bernard Allen, "Joseph Holt, Judge Advocate General (1862–1875): A Study in the Treatment of Political Prisoners by the United States Government During the Civil War" (Ph.D. diss., University of Chicago, 1927), 90–94. See also Joseph Holt to Major L. C. Turner, September 9, 1862, vol. 1, p. 358, JAG Correspondence, Letters Sent.

36. Joseph Holt to Major General John E. Wool, December 7, 1862; Holt to Lincoln, February 2, 1863, vol. 1, p. 443; vol. 2, p. 12, JAG Correspondence, Letters Sent.

37. "Militia Act."

38. Joseph Holt to Lincoln, December 9, 1862, vol. 1, p. 455, JAG Correspondence, Letters Sent.

39. Joseph Holt to Henry Wilson, January 14, 1863, vol. 1, 496–98, JAG Correspondence, Letters Sent.

40. "An Act for enrolling and calling out the national Forces, and for other purposes," March 3, 1863, chap. 75, sec. 30, 12 *Statutes at Large* 731, 736

41. Holt to Edwin M. Stanton, April 10, 1863, vol. 2, p. 146, JAG Correspondence, Letters Sent. See also Callan, *Military Laws of the United States,* 562. Section 30 of the Enrollment Act was incorporated in the 1875 revision of the Articles of War as Article 58 and became Articles 92 and 93 in the 1916 overhaul of the articles. Article 92 criminalized murder and rape; Article 93 incorporated the other common-law crimes. *The Army Lawyer* (Buffalo, NY: William S. Hein and Co., 1993), 62. Eugene Wambaugh, *Guide to the Articles of War* (Cambridge: Harvard University Press, 1917), 33. For the 1875 Articles of War, see Lieutenant Colonel William Winthrop, *An Abridgment of Military Law* (Washington, DC: W. H. Morrison, 1887), 361.

42. See Dorothy McBride Stetson, *Women's Rights in the U.S.A: Policy Debates and Gender Roles,* 2nd ed. (New York: Garland, 1997), 307–9.

43. William Blackstone, *Commentaries on the Laws of England* (notes by George Sharswood), bk. 4, chap. 15, sec. 210 (Philadelphia: George W. Childs, 1862), 2:474.

44. See, for instance, *The Statutes of the State of Tennessee*, rev. and digested by John Haywood and Robert L. Cobbs (Knoxville: F. S. Haskell, 1831), 1:245, and *The Code of Virginia, Second Edition, Including Legislation to the Year 1860* (Westport, CT: Negro University Press, 1970), 785.

45. *The Revised Statutes of Louisiana*, comp. U. B. Philips. (New Orleans: John Claiborne, 1856), 50, 136.

46. *A Compilation of the Penal Code of the State of Georgia*, [ed. Howell Cobb] (Macon: J. M. Boordman, 1850), 35, 85.

47. Instructions from the judge advocate general stipulated that "Negroes may testify before a military court, notwithstanding any disqualifying statues or custom in the State where the court is held." *Digest of Opinions of the Judge Advocate General of the Army* (Washington: GPO, 1866), 251.

48. Blackstone said that the rape had to be "against the woman's will." *Commentaries*, bk. 4, chap. 15, sec. 211.

49. Trial of Samuel D. Fitch, OO789; trial of Jacob K. Schuck, OO1185, both in JAG Trials.

50. Trial of Alfred A. Bartholomew, LL2655, and Edward Hays, file E18, no. 31, both in JAG Trials.

51. Martha Hodes, in *White Women, Black Men*, speculates that "most wartime rapes . . . must have gone unreported" (141).

52. *Revised Statutes of Louisiana*, 50, 136; *The Revised Code of the Statute Law of the State of Mississippi* (Jackson: E. Barksdale, 1857), 248, 608; *The Revised Statutes of Kentucky* (by Richard H. Stanton), vol. 1 (Cincinnati: Robert Clark and Co., 1860), 379–80; *Code of Virginia, Second Edition, Including Legislation to the Year, 1860*, 785.

53. Trial of John F. Herd, NN2140JAG Trials.

54. Faust, *Mothers of Invention*, 200, also 296 n. 6; Hodes, *White Women, Black Men*, 141; Stephen V. Ash, *When the Yankees Came: Conflict and Chaos in the Occupied South* (Chapel Hill: University of North Carolina Press, 1995), 197, 200–201.

55. Trial of James Callahan, Jacob Snover, and Thomas Johnson, microfilm #M1523, reel 1 (NN1740), JAG Trials.

56. Trials of John Brennan, William Henry Cahill, Owen Curren, Thomas Hunt, Nicholas Kane, and Edward Pickett, NN2468, and James Halon, LL2252, JAG Trials.

57. Trial of Danbridge (alias Dandridge) Brooks, microfilm #M1523, box #1 (MM1972), and John Sheppard, MM2006, JAG Trials.

58. Trial of Charles Wenz, MM3318, JAG Trials.

59. Trial of Adolph Bork, MM2407, JAG Trials.

60. Four men, all of whom were army teamsters, were tried for assault and battery with intent to rape Harriet Smith, of Little Rock, Arkansas, on March 29, 1865. One, Michael Mackey, was found guilty; the other three men were acquitted. Harriet Smith died the day after the assault. Trial of Michael Mackey, H. H. Wiseman, John Johnson, and Patrick Koloran, OO965, JAG Trials.

61. Trial of Richard Michelson, NN3037, JAG Trials.

62. Trial of Charles Clark, OO654, JAG Trials.

63. Trial of John Lewis, MM2774, JAG Trials.

64. Trial of Thomas Callahan, Jacob Snover, and Thomas Johnson, microfilm #M1523, reel 1 (NN1740), JAG Trials.

65. The literature on Federal occupation has grown in recent years. Stephen Ash broke that ground in *When the Yankees Came*. Many case studies followed in Ash's wake. See, for instance, Daniel

G. Sutherland, *Seasons of War: The Ordeal of a Confederate Community, 1861–1865* (New York: Free Press, 1995); Carol Kettenburg Dubbs, *Defend This Old Town: Williamsburg During the Civil War* (Baton Rouge: Louisiana State University Press, 2002); Brian Steel Wills, *The War Hits Home: The Civil War in Southeastern Virginia* (Charlottesville: University of Virginia Press, 2001); and Michael R. Bradley, *With Blood and Fire: Life behind Union Lines in Middle Tennessee, 1863–65* (Shippensburg, PA: Burd Street Press, 2003). This literature describes situations in which commanders issued general orders to confiscate rebel supplies, confine Confederate sympathizers, and track down and execute rebel guerrillas and partisans. See Sutherland, *Seasons of War*, chap. 5.

66. Proclamation by Governor Thomas O. Moore to the People of Louisiana, May 24, 1862, in U.S. War Department, *The War of the Rebellion: A Compilation of the Official Records of the Union and Confederate Armies* (Washington, DC: GPO, 1880–1901), ser. 1, vol. 15: 743–44 (hereafter cited as *OR*). Ash, in *When the Yankees Came*, says that, inter alia, Butler's order "persuaded many women in the occupied regions that they were in real danger of rape or other physical abuse" (197–98).

67. Trial of Private James Halon, LL2552, JAG Trials.

68. Trial of George O'Malley, MM402, JAG Trials.

69. Richard S. Hartigan, *Lieber's Code and the Law of War* (Chicago: Precedent Publishing, 1983), 14.

70. General Orders No. 100, April 24, 1863, sec. 2, para. 44, ibid., 54.

71. Faust, *Mothers of Invention*, 200. See also Martha Hodes, *White Women, Black Men*; Jacqueline Glass Campbell, *When Sherman Marched North from the Sea: Resistance on the Confederate Home Front* (Chapel Hill: University of North Carolina Press, 2003); and Ash, *When the Yankees Came*. Ash maintains that women "would take any steps necessary to defend their bodies" (201). See also Catherine Clinton and Nina Silber, eds., *Battle Scars: Gender and Sexuality in the American Civil War* (New York: Oxford University Press, 2006).

72. Trials of Lewis Sorg, Lewis Troest, and Jerry Spades, KK207, JAG Trials.

73. Trial of James E. Lee, OO1086, JAG Trials.

74. *Digest of the Opinions of the Judge Advocate General of the Army*, 251.

75. Trial of William L. Hilton, LL3201, JAG Trials. Hilton was sentenced to death, but his case was later overturned on a technicality.

76. Trial of Dudley O. Bravard, OO927, JAG Trials.

77. Trial of Adolph Bork, MM2407, JAG Trials. On review, Bork's sentence was mitigated to five years at hard labor.

78. Trial of Andrew Jackson Smith, NN2099, JAG Trials.

79. Trial of Andrew Jackson Smith, NN2099, JAG Trials.

80. William Johnston to Abraham Lincoln, Trial of Andrew Jackson Smith, NN2099, JAG Trials.

81. Review by Benjamin Butler, June 24, 1864, Trial of Andrew J. Smith, NN2099, JAG Trials (emphasis added).

GETTYSBURG OUT OF BOUNDS

1. See Margaret S. Creighton, "Living on the Fault Line: African American Civilians and the Gettysburg Campaign," in *The War Was You and Me: Civilians in the American Civil War*, ed. Joan E. Cashin (Princeton, NJ: Princeton University Press, 2002), 209–36.

2. For more details on Gettysburg's first day of battle, see Stephen Sears, *Gettysburg* (Boston: Houghton Mifflin, 2003), and Margaret Creighton, *The Colors of Courage: Gettysburg's Hidden History: Immigrants, Women, and African-Americans in the Civil War's Defining Battle* (New York: Basic Books, 2005).

3. John Rupp to Anne Rupp, July 19, 1863, Adams County Historical Society, Gettysburg, Pennsylvania (hereafter cited as ACHS); Annie Young letter, July 5, 1863, ACHS; Jennie Croll, attrib., "Days of Dread," *Philadelphia Weekly Press*, November 16, 1887; Lieutenant Colonel W. W. Blackford, *War Years with Jeb Stuart* (New York: Charles Scribner's Sons, 1945), 231.

4. Sallie Myers to "Mr. Russel," August 19, 1863, ACHS.

5. Elizabeth McClean, "The Rebels Are Coming," *Gettysburg Compiler*, July 8, 1908, ACHS; C. M. W. Foster, *Gettysburg Compiler*, January 20, 1917.

6. [Carrie Sheads] in Frank Moore, *Women of the War: Their Heroism and Self-Sacrifice* (Hartford: S. S. Scranton and Co., 1867), 241–42; Mary McAllister, *Philadelphia Inquirer*, June 26–29, 1938.

7. [Carrie Sheads] in Moore, *Women of the War*, 241–42; John Chisolm Horn, trans., "A Vivid Story of the Mighty Conflict from the Lips of Rev. Dr. Jacobs, Who Was a Gettysburg Boy," *Baltimore American*, June 29, 1913.

8. "Gettysburg Heroine," *Gettysburg Compiler*, July 29, 1884; "Experience During Battle: A Woman's Thrilling Experiences of the Battle," *Gettysburg Compiler*, July 26, 1905; "Mrs. Thorn's War Story," *Gettysburg Times*, July 2, 1938.

9. "Wymorean Recalls Battle of Gettysburg," *Arbor State* (Nebraska), ca. May 30, 1944; Emma Yount Stumpf to Raymond Neff Stumpf, February 17, 1943, Civilian File, Gettysburg National Military Park Library, Gettysburg, Pennsylvania (hereafter cited as GNMP).

10. Sarah Barrett King, "A Mother's Story of [the] Battle of Gettysburg," *The Compiler Scrapbook*, vol. 1, no. 2 (July 4, 1906), 46, GNMP; Mrs. Jacob A. Clutz [Liberty Augusta Hollinger], "Some Personal Recollections of the Battle of Gettysburg" (privately printed, ca. 1925), 9, ACHS; Louie Dale Leeds and Nellie Aughinbaugh, "Personal Experiences of a Young Girl" (privately printed, ca. 1926–38), 13, ACHS.

11. Fannie Buehler, "Recollections of the Rebel Invasion" (privately printed, 1896), 19, 22, Huntington Library, San Marino, California.

12. Alice Powers, "Dark Days of the Battle Week," *Gettysburg Compiler*, July 1, 1903; William Hamilton Bayly, "William Hamilton Bayly's Stories of the Battle," *The Compiler's Scrapbook*, n.d., 14, GNMP.

13. King, "Mother's Story"; Annie Young to Annie ———, July 5, 1863, ACHS.

14. Clutz, "Some Personal Recollections," 9; Leeds and Aughinbaugh, "Personal Experiences."

15. Leeds and Aughinbaugh, "Personal Experiences," 7; King, "Mother's Story."

16. Clutz, "Some Personal Recollections," 6; comments on the Eleventh Corps can be found in Shriver to Myer, July 2, 1863; Salome Myers also makes an equivocal remark about the "gallant" Eleventh Corps crowding into her basement. Myers to "Mr. Russel," August 19, 1863, ACHS.

17. See Nina Silber, *The Romance of Reunion: Northerners and the South, 1865–1900* (Chapel Hill: University of North Carolina Press, 1993).

18. For the ways in which women of means were advantaged during the battle, see Harriet Bayly, "Mrs. Joseph Bayly's Story," *The Compiler Scrapbook*, n.d., ACHS, and Buehler, "Recollections of the Rebel Invasion."

19. Sarah M. Broadhead, *Diary of a Lady of Gettysburg* (privately printed, 1864; repr., Hershey, PA: Gary J. Hawbaker, n.d.), 14; Catherine Mary White Foster, "The Story of the Battle by a Citizen," *Gettysburg Compiler*, June 29, 1904; Annie Young to Annie ———, July 5, 1863, ACHS.

20. Harriet Bayly, "A Woman's Story," *Gettysburg Star and Sentinel*, September 25, 1888, and "Mrs. Joseph Bayly's Story."

21. King, "Mother's Story."

22. Croll, "Days of Dread," 2; Jennie McCreary to her sister, July 22, 1863, in "Girl Saw Street Filled with Dead and Wounded at Gettysburg," *Philadelphia Evening Bulletin*, July 2, 1938; Leander H. Warren, "Recollections of the Battle of Gettysburg," n.d., 5–7, ACHS; Bayly, "Stories of the Battle"; Lavinia Bollinger to Susan White, September 9, 1863, ACHS; Elma Epley Gerbeling, ed., "Account of Sophia Culp Epley," n.d., GNMP.

23. Sue King Black to Belle Miller Willard, n.d., ACHS; G. F. Minter to "Dear Cousin," July 27, 1863, ACHS; Albertus McCreary, "Gettysburg: A Boy's Experience of the Battle," *McClure's Magazine*, July 1909, 250.

24. Broadhead, *Diary of a Lady of Gettysburg*, 11, 14, 15; Bayly, "Stories of the Battle."

25. Mary Hunt Carson to her mother, July 12, 1863, private collection.

26. *Lancaster Daily Evening Express*, July 2, 1863. This is a rare public report of an incident of rape during the Gettysburg campaign. Thanks to Tim Smith for bringing it to my attention.

27. May Garlach Hoffman and Mary McAllister, "Rebels at Gettysburg Ate Molasses in Hunger," *Philadelphia Inquirer*, June 28, 1938; Jennie McCreary to her sister, July 22, 1863, in "Girl Saw Street Filled with Dead"; Leeds and Aughinbaugh, "Personal Experiences"; Bayly, "Woman's Story" and "Mrs. Joseph Bayly's Story"; King, "Mother's Story."

28. Gerald F. Linderman describes how Federal soldiers in the South also sought to punish "unwomanly" behavior. See *Embattled Courage: The Experience of Combat in the American Civil War* (New York: Free Press, 1987), 195.

29. Lydia Meals Panebaker, "Reminiscences of the Battle of Gettysburg," ca. 1926, ACHS.

30. Alice Powers, "Dark Days of the Battle Week"; Hoffman and McAllister, "Rebels at Gettysburg"; "Burning of M'Lean Home on the First Day's Battle of Gettysburg Told by a Young Girl Driven from the House When Set on Fire," *Gettysburg Compiler*, July 15, 1915; Caroline S. Sheads, "Scenes of the Battle of Gettysburg," *National Republican* (Washington), November 28, 1863.

31. Jane Smith, "An Echo of the Battle," *Gettysburg Star and Sentinel*, July 2, 1913, ACHS.

32. Bayly, "Woman's Story; Bayly, "Stories of the Battle."

33. E. D. McSwain, ed., *Crumbling Defenses: Memoirs and Reminiscences of John Logan Black, Colonel CSA* (Macon, GA: privately published, 1960), 45, clipping, ACHS; *Gettysburg Star and Sentinel*, July 16, 1913; Hoffman and McAllister, "Rebels at Gettysburg." See also William McClean, "The Days of Terror in 1863," *Gettysburg Compiler*, June 1, 1908.

34. Anna Garlach Kitzmiller, "Mrs. Kitzmiller's Story: Battle Days Between Union and Confederate Lines," *Gettysburg Compiler*, August 23m 1905, ACHS; Sheads, "Scenes of the Battle of Gettysburg."

35. Clutz, "Some Personal Recollections"; "Nonagenarian Buys Bond Thursday," *Gettysburg Times*, September 10, 1943; King, "Mother's Story"; Widow Mary Thompson also refused to make meals for the Confederate officer in her house. When asked about it later, in fact, she grew "indignant." "No," she recollected, "I guess I didn't cook for any Rebel. They had to do their own cooking." In this case the "Rebel" was Robert E. Lee, who used her house as his headquarters. See Timothy H. Smith, *The Story of Lee's Headquarters: Gettysburg, Pennsylvania* (Gettysburg: Thomas Publications, 1995), 48–49.

36. Gerbeling, "Account of Sophia Culp Epley"; Bayly, "Woman's Story"; Buehler, "Recollections of the Rebel Invasion," 20.

37. "Grand Army Corner: Jennie Wade, Heroine," in *Madison (Wis.) Democrat*, n.d., clipping,

Special Collections, Rochester Museum and Science Center, Rochester, New York (hereafter cited as RMSC); J. W. Johnston, *The True Story of "Jennie" Wade: A Gettysburg Maid* (Rochester, NY: privately printed, 1917), 13, ACHS.

38. Georgia Wade McClellan, "Response" in "Dedication Ceremonies of the Jennie Wade Monument," September 16, 1901, RMSC; Georgia Wade McClellan to "Dear Comrade," in untitled, *Madison (Wis.) Democrat*, n.d., RMSC.

39. Johnston, *True Story*, 21–22.

40. Ibid., 22–23.

41. ——— *Times*, June 25, 1911, clipping in Historian's Office, GNMP; *Gettysburg Star and Sentinel*, September 9, 1890.

42. "Native of Adams County Writes of Experiences of Parents During '63 Battle," *Gettysburg Compiler*, April 26, 1941; *Gettysburg Star and Sentinel*, July 18, 1903; "Memories of Gettysburg: Recalled by Maj.-Gen. O. O. Howard before His Death," *Gettysburg Compiler*, March 23, 1910.

43. "Gettysburg's Fight: The Part That a Brave Little Girl Played During the Battle," *Gettysburg Compiler*, January 12, 1892. On the popular currency of the "angel of mercy" image of Civil War women, see Elizabeth D. Leonard, *Yankee Women: Gender Battles in the Civil War* (New York: Norton, 1994), 171.

44. "Gettysburg's Fight: The Part That a Brave Little Girl Played."

45. "Mrs. Jungerman's Story," *San Francisco Bulletin*, March 9, 1902; Ilza Veith, "Hygeia by the Bay—A City of Health," *Western Journal of Medicine* 127 (November 1977): 442–49. Thanks to Dr. David Steinhardt for information on Dr. Lyford.

46. "Mrs. Jungerman's Story." There is some confusion as to the date that Lyford picked up Sadie Bushman's story. The story seems to have first circulated in San Francisco in late 1891 (according to the January 12, 1892, *Gettysburg Compiler*), but the reunion was featured in a San Francisco paper ten years later.

47. *Gettysburg Star and Sentinel*, September 29, 1891; see also Timothy H. Smith, "Josephine Miller: A Heroine of the Battle," *Blue and Gray Magazine*, Holiday 2002, 21–24.

48. "Pickett's Men Listen to Heroine of Battle," *Philadelphia Press*, July 4, 1913.

49. *Gettysburg Star and Sentinel*, September 1, 1891.

50. *Gettysburg Star and Sentinel*, July 8, 1903.

51. *New York Herald*, July 1, 1913.

52. "Story of a Brig. General," *Gettysburg Compiler*, August 9, 1905; Creighton, *Colors of Courage*, 190–93.

53. Perhaps the most popular battle story to avoid civilian experience is the legendary Electric Map show, offered in the Visitor's Center. This show uses lights on a large map to show the progression of the battle, but the borough itself is left largely in the dark.

54. On dominant gender ideals, see E. Anthony Rotundo, *American Manhood: Transformations in Masculinity from the Revolution to the Modern Era* (New York: Basic Books, 1993), 232–39, and Gail Bederman, "Civilization, the Decline of Middle-Class Manliness, and Ida B. Well's Anti-Lynching Campaign (1892–94)," in *Gender and American History since 1890*, ed. Barbara Melosh (London: Routledge, 1993), 213. On the application of these ideals to Gettysburg, see Creighton, *Colors of Courage*, 202–4.

55. On means and ends in American warfare, from the Civil War to the late twentieth century, see James Reston Jr., *Sherman's March and Vietnam* (New York: Macmillan, 1984); on invisible civilian casualty accounts more recently, see "A Year in Iraq," www.nytimes.com/2008/01/06/opinion/06chart.html?scp=4&sq=iraq+count.

"SHE-REBELS" ON THE SUPPLY LINE

1. Brigadier General Commanding to Lieutenant T. J. Hardin, Midway, Ky., June 15, 1864; vol. 62, bk. 119, Department of Kentucky (hereafter cited as Dky); Part 1, Geographical Divisions and Departments and Military (Reconstruction) Districts (hereafter cited as Part 1); General Records, entry 2168, "Telegrams Sent. Jan. 1864–Feb. 1865"; Preliminary Inventory of the Records of United States Army Continental Commands, 1821–1920, Record Group 393 (hereafter cited as RG 393); National Archives and Records Administration, Washington, D.C. (hereafter cited as NA).

2. Elizabeth Varon, *We Mean to Be Counted: White Women and Politics in Antebellum Virginia* (Chapel Hill: University of North Carolina Press, 1998), 4–5.

3. LeeAnn Whites, "The Civil War as a Crisis in Gender," in *Divided Houses: Gender and the Civil War,* ed. Catherine Clinton and Nina Silber (New York: Oxford University Press, 1992), 15–16.

4. Jeanie Attie, "Warwork and the Crisis of Domesticity in the North," in Clinton and Silber, *Divided Houses,* 31, 251–52; LeeAnn Whites, *The Civil War as a Crisis in Gender: Augusta, Georgia, 1860–1890* (Athens: University of Georgia Press, 1995), 15–16; Drew Gilpin Faust, *Mothers of Invention: Women of the Slaveholding South in the American Civil War* (Chapel Hill: University of North Carolina Press, 1996), 24, 90; Arlie Hochschild, *The Managed Heart: Commercialization of Human Feeling* (Berkeley: University of California Press, 1983).

5. Whites, *Civil War as a Crisis in Gender,* 53; Bertram Wyatt-Brown, *Southern Honor: Ethics and Behavior in the Old South* (New York: Oxford University Press, 1982), 248; Mary P. Ryan, *Women in Public: Between Banners and Ballots, 1825–1880* (Baltimore: Johns Hopkins University Press, 1990), 142; Laura F. Edwards, *Scarlett Doesn't Live Here Anymore: Southern Women in the Civil War Era* (Urbana: University of Illinois Press, 2000), 28.

6. Faust, *Mothers of Invention,* 10, 23.

7. Glenna Matthews, *"Just a Housewife": The Rise and Fall of Domesticity in America* (New York: Oxford University Press, 1987), 7; see also xiii, 92–93, 110; Jeanne Boydston, *Home and Work: Housework, Wages, and the Ideology of Labor in the Early Republic* (New York: Oxford University Press, 1990), 33; Jeanie Attie, *Patriotic Toil: Northern Women and the American Civil War* (Ithaca, NY: Cornell University Press, 1998), 22–23, 25, 36; Attie, "Warwork," 254; Varon, *We Mean to Be Counted,* 143.

8. Wyatt-Brown, *Southern Honor,* 59; Paula Baker, "The Domestication of Politics: Women and American Political Society, 1780–1920," *American Historical Review* 89 (June 1984): 622; Attie, *Patriotic Toil,* 37; Varon, *We Mean to Be Counted,* 2; Matthews, *"Just a Housewife,"* 26.

9. Amelia Bourne, diary, February 3, 1863, Amelia Bourne (Mrs. Henry Lane Stone) Papers, MS A B775, Filson Historical Society, Louisville, Kentucky (hereafter cited as FHS) (emphasis in original).

10. Whites, *Civil War as a Crisis in Gender,* 57–58.

11. Faust, *Mothers of Invention,* 202; Randall C. Jimerson, *The Private Civil War: Popular Thought during the Sectional Conflict* (Baton Rouge: Louisiana State University Press, 1988), 153.

12. Thomas D. Clark, *The Kentucky* (New York: Farrar and Rinehart, 1942), 304–5. Union officials also imprisoned her daughter Kate, who, with her mother, "kept up their knitting of long gray socks, and the clicking of their needles added to the monotonous sounds of the tramping and heel clicking of the handsome sentry" (305).

13. Special Orders No. 60, Headquarters Military Commander, Provost Marshal's Office, May 17, 1865; vol. 145½, Dky; Part 4, Military Installations, 1821–81 (hereafter cited as Part 4); Louisville, KY.,

1861–66, entry 1638, "Special Orders Issued. Feb. 1862–July 1865"; RG 393; NA. See also Special Order No. 59, May 16, 1865, ibid.

14. General Order No. 5, October 7, 1861, in U.S. War Department, *The War of the Rebellion: A Compilation of the Official Records of the Union and Confederate Armies* (Washington: GPO, 1880–1901), ser. 2, vol. 2: 91–92 (hereafter cited as *OR*); McClellan to Buell, November 12, 1861, in *OR*, ser. 2, vol. 2: 136.

15. Josephine Covington [Wells] [Mrs. Albert Covington] to Robert Wells, March 2, 1862, MS C C, FHS.

16. Ibid.

17. Jimerson, *Private Civil War*, 129.

18. Bvt. Maj. General Burbridge to Brig. General Hugh Ewing, July 7, 186[?]; vol. 62, bk. 105, DKy, p. 108; Part 1; General Records, entry 2164, "Letters Sent. May–Sept 1863 and Sept 1864–Mar 1869"; RG 393; NA. Munfordville was a strategic town during the war in Kentucky, serving as a significant stop along the Louisville and Nashville Railroad line and containing the Green River Bridge, which spanned a large gorge along that line. This rail line "was a most important transportation and communication artery. For Union forces holding Kentucky, the Louisville and Nashville was their principal means of supply and reinforcements. . . . For the Confederates to retake Kentucky would require them being supplied by rail from Nashville." Kent Masterson Brown, "Munfordville: The Campaign and Battle along Kentucky's Strategic Axis," in *The Civil War in Kentucky: Battle for the Bluegrass State*, ed. Kent Masterson Brown (Mason City, IA: Savas Publishing Co., 2000), 138–40.

19. F. Meacham [?] to Surgeon Gen G Shermard, March 10, 1864; Part 4; Louisville, KY., 1861–66, entry 1636, "Letters Received, 1862–65"; RG 393, NA.

20. Burbridge's order contained in a communication from J. Bates Dickson to Lt. Col. William B. Fairleigh, June 28, 1864; vol. 52, bk. 363, DKy, p. 51; Part 4; Louisville, Ky., 1862–73, entry 735, "Telegrams Received. May 1864–June 1865"; RG 393, NA.

21. Mary Scott to Rebecca, October 23, 1862, Susan Preston (Shelby) Grigsby Papers, MS A.G857, file 173, FHS.

22. Nancy Isenberg, *Sex and Citizenship in Antebellum America* (Chapel Hill: University of North Carolina Press, 1998), 104.

23. Wyatt-Brown, *Southern Honor*, 14.

24. George C. Rable, *Civil Wars: Women and the Crisis of Southern Nationalism* (Urbana: University of Illinois Press, 1989), 173.

25. Martha McDowell Buford Jones, *Peach Leather and Rebel Gray: Bluegrass Life and the War, 1860–1865: Farm and Social Life, Famous Horses, Tragedies of War: Diary and Letters of a Confederate Wife*, ed. Mary E. Wharton and Ellen F. Williams (Lexington: Helicon Co., 1986), March 11, 1863, April 9, 1863, pp. 107, 109; Mary to Brother, April 1862, Bush-Beauchamp Family Papers, MS A B978, file 27, Beauchamp-Crockett Family Correspondence, 1861–64, FHS; Mr. Irvine to Susan Grigsby, December 17, 1862, Susan Preston (Shelby) Grigsby Papers, MS A.G857, file 175, FHS; Ellen Kenton McGaughey Killebrew, 1988, Wallace-Starling Family Diaries, Kentucky Historical Society, Frankfort, Kentucky (hereafter cited as Wallace, journal, date, KHS).

26. Wallace, journal, December 20, 1864, KHS.

27. Frances Peter, diary, September 22, 1863, Evans Papers: Frances (Dallam) Peter material, 72M15, box 7, file 85, University of Kentucky Archives and Special Collections, M. I. King Library, Lexington, Kentucky.

28. Linda K. Kerber, "'History Can Do It No Justice': Women and the Reinterpretation of the

American Revolution," in *Women in the Age of the American Revolution*, ed. Ronald Hoffman and Peter J. Albert (Charlottesville: University of Virginia Press, 1989), 40.

29. Captain and AAG John Boyle to Lt. Col. Dent, July 18, 1862; Part 4; Louisville, KY., 1861–66, entry 1636, "Letters Received, 1862–65"; RG 393; NA.

30. Lt. Col. and Provost Marshal Henry Dent to Capt Dillard, July 18, 1862; vol. 220, p. 61; Part 4; Louisville, KY., 1861–66, entry 1632, "Letters Sent by the Provost Marshal. Jan. 1862–Apr. 1863"; RG 393; NA.

31. Special Order No. 18, July 20, 1862; Part 4; Louisville, KY., 1861–66, entry 1636, "Letters Received, 1862–65"; RG 393; NA.

32. Brig. General Boyle to Major Fitch, May 8, 1863; Part 4; Louisville, KY., 1861–66, entry 1636, "Letters Received, 1862–65"; RG 393; NA. See also Maj. Selby Hamey to Capt HG Dillard, June 26, 1862; vol. 220; Part 4; Louisville, KY., 1861–66, entry 1632, "Letters Sent by the Provost Marshal. Jan. 1862–Apr. 1863"; RG 393; NA.

33. Lowell Harrison, *The Civil War in Kentucky* (Lexington: University Press of Kentucky, 1975), 57; James A. Ramage, "General John Hunt Morgan and His Great Raids into Kentucky," in Brown, *Civil War in Kentucky*, 243–70.

34. *OR*, ser. 1, vol. 23, pt. 2: 237.

35. Report from J. Holt, Judge Advocate General, to Secretary of War E. M. Stanton, October 8, 1864, in *OR*, ser. 2, vol. 7: 945.

36. James C. Scott, *Domination and the Arts of Resistance: Hidden Transcripts* (New York: Yale University Press, 1990), 11, 115.

37. First quotation from ibid., 205; second quotation from Attie, *Patriotic Toil*, 51; Victoria E. Bynum, *Unruly Women: The Politics of Social and Sexual Control in the Old South* (Chapel Hill: University of North Carolina Press, 1992), 14, 50; Isenberg, *Sex and Citizenship*, 73; Earl J. Hess, *Liberty, Virtue, and Progress: Northerners and Their War for the Union* (New York: New York University Press, 1988), 88.

38. Linda K. Kerber, "The Meanings of Citizenship," *Journal of American History* 84 (December 1997): 834. Kerber also offers these early national era definitions: "'Treason—the act of aiding the enemy—and misprison of treason—the knowledge of and concealment of an enemy plot. . . . Treason and misprison of treason were understood throughout the nation to be crimes that either sex might commit." Kerber, *No Constitutional Right to Be Ladies: Women and the Obligations of Citizenship* (New York: Hill and Wang, 1998), 16.

39. Concern came to Hardin from friends and family alike; two friends came "to warn us," one of the Hardins' slaves "begged us to save ourselves by flight," and even "Grandma begged us to hush [about laughing about the rumors] for 'we might talk about such things until they became true.'" Lizzie [Elizabeth Pendleton] Hardin, *The Private War of Lizzie Hardin: A Kentucky Confederate Girl's Diary of the Civil War in Kentucky, Virginia, Tennessee, Alabama, and Georgia*, ed. G. Glen Clift (Frankfort: Kentucky Historical Society, 1963), 101. James A. Ramage, *Rebel Raider: The Life of John Hunt Morgan* (Lexington: University Press of Kentucky, 1986).

40. Hardin, *Private War*, 125. Lewis Collins notes on August 2, 1862, "Three ladies, of Harrodsburg, brought to Louisville by one Capt. Jack Mann, and put in the military prison." Collins, *History of Kentucky*, rev. Richard H. Collins, vol. 1 (Frankfort: Kentucky Historical Society, 1966), 105.

41. Hardin, *Private War*, 122–23.

42. Ramage, *Rebel Raider*, 64–68.

43. Boyle quoted in Hardin, *Private War*, 153.

44. Ibid., 125.

45. Ramage, *Rebel Raider*, 158–82.

46. Vol. 21, pp. 102, 103; Part 1; Provost Marshal, entry 2241, 1 of 2, "Register of Letters Received and Endorsements Sent by Capt. Stephen E. Jones, Provost Marshal and Aide-de-Camp, May 1863-Dec. 1864"; RG 393; NA.

47. Frances Peter diary, May 23, 1863, Evans Papers, file 86, pp. 202–3.

48. *National Unionist*, July 12, 1864. See also other examples in "The Genus Copperhead," *National Unionist*, April 22, 1864, and "Union Officers and Rebel Crinoline," *National Unionist*, June 28, 1864.

49. George Browder, June 23, 1863, in *The Heavens Are Weeping: The Diaries of George Richard Browder, 1852–1886*, ed. Richard L. Troutman (Grand Rapids, MI: Zondervan, 1987), 157; Thomas D. Clark, *A History of Kentucky*, rev. 6th ed. (Ashland: Jesse Stuart Foundation, 1988), 346.

50. Faust, *Mothers of Invention*, 198, 205; Bynum, *Unruly Women*, 143–44.

51. Faust, *Mothers of Invention*, 201, 214.

52. Special Orders No. 111; vol. 149, bk. 353, p. 102; Part 4; Louisville, Ky., 1862–73, entry 739, 2 of 6, "Special Orders Issued, Jan. 1862–June 1873"; RG 393; NA. A Captain E. P. Byrne is listed as leading the Kentucky artillery unit attached to John Hunt Morgan's cavalry division in 1863. See Ramage, "General John Hunt Morgan," 267. In both this order and a subsequent directive, limits were placed on the amount of luggage allowed: "Rebel families ordered South may take with them their ordinary wearing apparel, not to exceed one hundred pounds to each woman, and the clothing in use for a child. money enough to defray traveling expenses." William Hoffman to Capt. SE Jones, March 1, 1864; Part 4; Louisville, KY., 1861–66, entry 1636, "Letters Received. 1862–65"; RG 393; NA.

53. For an analysis of conflicting loyalties between husbands and wives and within families in border states, see Amy Murrell Taylor, *The Divided Family in Civil War America* (Chapel Hill: University of North Carolina Press, 2005).

54. Vol. 149, bk. 353, p. 102, DKy; Part 4; Louisville, Ky., 1862–73, entry 739, 2 of 6, "Special Orders Issued, Jan. 1862–June 1873"; RG 393; NA.

55. Dent to Boyle, August 1, 1862; vol. 220, bks. 523, 524, DKy, p. 76; Part 4; Louisville, KY., 1861–66, entry 1632, "Letters Sent by the Provost Marshal, Jan. 1862–Apr. 1863"; RG 393; NA.

56. Vol. 269, bk. 509, DKy; Part 1; Provost Marshal, entry 2237, 5 of 5, "Miscellaneous Records of the Provost Marshal, 1863–66"; RG 393; NA.

57. Vol. 269, bk. 589, DKy; Part 1; Provost Marshal, entry 2237, 5 of 5, "Miscellaneous Records of the Provost Marshal, 1863–66"; "Special Orders No. 21" Feb. 11, 1865; RG 393; NA. Vol. 145½, DKy; Part 4; Louisville, KY., 1861–66, entry 1638, "Special Orders Issued. Feb. 1862–July 1865"; RG 393; NA.

58. "Affidavits in the Cases of Miss Hutchinson, Mr. Bridgeford, Mrs. Wilson, Mr. Miller and Mrs. Henderson." April 13, 1865; Part 1; Provost Marshal, entry 2229, "Correspondence, Affidavits and Oaths relating to Civilians Charged with Illegal or Disloyal Acts, 1863–65"; RG 393; NA.

59. Ibid.

60. Report from J. Holt, Judge Advocate General, to Secretary of War E. M. Stanton, October 8, 1864, in *OR*, ser. 2, vol. 7: 946.

61. Jones, *Peach Leather and Rebel Gray*, 90; see also Hardin, *Private War*, 96–97n. Several other state histories make references to Boyle's attention to Confederate women. See Collins, *History of Kentucky*, 103; E. Merton Coulter, *Civil War and Readjustment in Kentucky* (Gloucester, MA: Peter Smith,

1966), 152; Lowell H. Harrison and James C. Klotter, *A New History of Kentucky* (Lexington: University Press of Kentucky, 1997), 205–6.

62. Hardin, *Private War*, 157. Collins also confirms this story: on July 28, 1862, "By order of Gen. Boyle, a prison prepared at Newport for 'rebel females'—where they will be required to sew for the Federal soldiers." Collins, *History of Kentucky*, 105.

63. Mrs. M. M. Givens, *Minutes of the Fourteenth Annual Convention of the Kentucky Division Daughters of the Confederacy. Held in Louisville, Kentucky, October 12, 13 and 14, 1910* (Lexington: Press of Transylvania Printing Co., 1910), 75.

64. Halleck to Burbridge, June 25, 1864, in *OR*, ser. 1, vol. 39, pt. 2: 144–45. On July 19, 1864, Abraham Lincoln issued General Orders No. 233 from the War Department in Washington, D.C., officially declaring martial law in Kentucky. See *OR*, ser. 1, vol. 39, pt. 2: 180.

65. Ramage, *Rebel* Raider, 208–25; vol. 219, bk. 517, pp. 5, 28, 72, and 107, respectively; Part 1, Provost Marshal, entry 2237, "Miscellaneous Records of the Provost Marshal, 1863–66"; RG 393; NA.

66. Burbridge's order contained in communication from Col. S. D. Rance [?] to Major Fitch, Mar. 19, 1864; Part 4; Louisville, KY., 1861–66, entry 1636, "Letters Received, 1862–65"; RG 393; NA.

67. "Genus Copperhead," *National Unionist*, April 22, 1864 (emphasis in original).

68. Brig. General Burbridge to Major, March 7, 1864; Part 4; Louisville, KY., 1861–66, entry 1636, "Letters Received, 1862–65"; RG 393; NA.

69. "Papers in the case of Miss Jennie Mann," Capt. W. H. Ward to Lt. Col. Fairleigh, Oct. 17, 1864; Part 1; Provost Marshal, entry 2229, "Correspondence, Affidavits, and Oaths Relating to Civilians Charged with Illegal or Disloyal Acts, 1863–65"; RG 393; NA. Upon investigation by the Provost Marshal's Office, Union officials found "that this lady is rather light headed & made use of these expressions more to attract attention than with the intention of being disloyal & recommend that she be required to take the oath of allegiance." Note from Major Henry Plessnor, October 19, 1864, in "Papers in the Case of Miss Jennie Mann," ibid. The oath was administered and Mann released.

70. Respectively, "Papers in the Case of McDowell Son and Wife," April 17, 1865; "Papers in the Case of Smith, Mrs. Francis," April 18, 1865; and "Papers in the Case of Atwell, Alice," April 21, 1865; all in Part 1; Provost Marshal, entry 2229, "Correspondence, Affidavits, and Oaths Relating to Civilians Charged with Illegal or Disloyal Acts, 1863–65"; RG 393; NA.

"CORRESPONDING WITH THE ENEMY"

1. *St. Louis Republican*, May 14, 1863, June 22, 1863. Thomas P. Lowry discusses the difficulties of locating the larger historical significance of particular cases like this one; see Lowry, *Confederate Heroines: 120 Southern Women Convicted by Union Military Justice* (Baton Rouge: Louisiana State University Press, 2006), 179–87. Fortunately, one of the largest relevant military records, The Union Provost Marshal's File of Papers Relating to Individual Citizens, is now partially indexed; see http://www.sos.mo.gov/archives/provost. A search of this site indicates the pivotal significance of this mass 1863 St. Louis banishment in initiating a new policy of "hard war," as more than 90 percent of all women noted as banished were banished in its aftermath. Certainly this new policy of mass banishment was immediately applied to the western border of Missouri by the commanding general Thomas Ewing in July 1863, when he ordered the arrest and banishment of a similarly large number of women in

NOTES TO PAGES 104–106

Order No. 10. This policy failing, General Ewing turned to an even more drastic extension of mass banishment in the infamous Order No. 11, which banished all the largely female population from a three-county area. See Albert Castel, "Order #11 and the Civil War on the Border," *Missouri Historical Review* 57 (1963): 357–68. A similar policy of mass banishment was applied later by Ewing's foster brother, William T. Sherman, in Atlanta in September 1864, when the entire civilian population was again banished, rendering both areas nothing but military posts. See Mark Grimsley, *The Hard Hand of War: Union Military Policy Toward Southern Civilians, 1861–1865* (New York: Cambridge University Press, 1995), 186–90, and Thomas G. Dyer, *Secret Yankees: The Union Circle in Confederate Atlanta* (Baltimore: Johns Hopkins University Press, 1999), 191–212.

2. Information about many of these women can be found in their Provost Marshal files. See Jane Cleveland (file 1239); Sarah Dorsey (1304); Lily Frost (1469); Margaret McLure (1197); Mary Louden (1195); Marion Vail (1273); and Lucy Welch (1414), Records of Individual Disloyal Citizens, Missouri State Archives, Jefferson City, Missouri (hereafter cited as Provost Marshal Files). For Mrs. Gen. David (Lily) Frost, see Harriet Lane Cates Hardaway, "The Adventures of General Frost and His Wife Lily During the Civil War," *Florissant Valley Historical Society Quarterly* 14, no. 2 (1972): 1–7. Some of the banished women left their own account of their experiences in *Reminiscences of Women of Missouri During the Sixties*, comp. Missouri Division, United Daughters of the Confederacy (Jefferson City: n.p., 1912).

3. For an overview of St. Louis during the Civil War, see Louis Gerteis, *Civil War St. Louis* (Lawrence: Kansas University Press, 2001).

4. Priscilla Thomas Ingram Patton Journal, Patton-Scott Family Papers, C. 3710, 64–66, Western Historical Manuscripts, University of Missouri–Columbia, Columbia, Missouri. On the experience of women during the Civil War in Missouri in general, see Rebecca Weber Bowen, "The Changing Role of Protection on the Border: Gender and the Civil War in Saline County," in *Women in Missouri History: In Search of Power and Influence*, ed. LeeAnn Whites, Mary Neth and Gary Kremer (Columbia: University of Missouri Press, 2004), 119–33; Michael Fellman, *Inside War: The Guerrilla Conflict in Missouri During the American Civil War* (New York: Oxford University Press, 1989), 193–230; and LeeAnn Whites, *Gender Matters: Civil War, Reconstruction, and the Making of the New South* (New York: Palgrave Macmillan, 2005), 25–89, 95–112.

5. Grimsley, *Hard Hand of War*; Fellman, *Inside War*.

6. Much of the recent scholarship on women and the Civil War has stressed the way that for white women the war was a matter of discovering that they were not able or willing to act like men particularly in relation to their slaves; see George C. Rable, *Civil Wars: Women and the Crisis of Southern Nationalism* (Urbana: University of Illinois Press, 1989); Drew Gilpin Faust, *Mothers of Invention: Women of the Slaveholding South in the American Civil War* (Chapel Hill: University of North Carolina Press, 1996); and Nancy Bercaw, *Gendered Freedoms: Race, Rights, and the Politics of Household in the Delta, 1861–1875* (Gainesville: University of Florida Press, 2003). This essay suggests that for Southern sympathizing women in Missouri, the salient issue was their position as women itself, which they certainly had the necessary social standing to defend in the terms that most mattered to them, their relations to their kin. See Lisa Tendrich Frank, "Bedrooms as Battlefields: The Role of Gender Politics in Sherman's March," and Kristen L. Streater, "'She-Rebels' on the Supply Line: Gender Conventions in Civil War Kentucky," in this volume.

7. The numbers of prisoners who went through the two St. Louis military prisons were derived from Joanne Chiles Eakin, *Missouri Prisoners of War from Gratiot Street Prison and Myrtle Street Prison,*

NOTES TO PAGES 107–118

St. Louis, Missouri and Alton, Illinois (Independence, MO: Print America, 1995); *Reminiscences of Women of Missouri During the Sixties,* 44.

8. U.S. War Department, *The War of the Rebellion: A Compilation of the Official Records of the Union and Confederate Armies* (Washington: GPO, 1880-1901), ser. 2, vol. 5: 48 (hereafter cited as *OR*); *Reminiscences of Women of Missouri During the Sixties,* 45.

9. *OR,* ser. 2, vol. 3: 379–80, 315.

10. Ibid., 379–80.

11. Ibid., 281; *Reminiscences of Women of Missouri During the Sixties,* 46.

12. *Reminiscences of Women of Missouri During the Sixties,* 46. *St. Louis Democrat,* March 11, 1862; see also April 29, 1862.

13. *Reminiscences of Women of Missouri During the Sixties,* 47–48.

14. *St. Louis Republican Daily,* June 18, 23, 24, 1862.

15. Absalom Grimes, *Confederate Mail Runner,* ed. M. M. Quaife (New Haven, CT: Yale University Press, 1926). See also Absalom Grimes, file 1334, Provost Marshal Files, and Leonard V. Huber, "The Saga of Captain Absalom Grimes, Confederate Mail Carrier Extraordinary," *American Philatelist* 65, no. 10 (1952): 761–67. For a fictionalized account, see James Bradley, *The Confederate Mail Carrier* (Mexico, MO: privately printed, 1894).

16. *St. Louis Globe-Democrat,* September 10, 1862; Anne Ewing Lane to Sarah Lane Glasgow, September 6, 1862, William Carr Lane Papers, Missouri Historical Society, St. Louis, Missouri.

17. John Crosswhite, file 1245, Provost Marshal Files (emphasis in original); Lizzie Ivins, file 1346, Provost Marshal Files; Mary S. F. Cleveland, file 1239, Provost Marshal Files.

18. John Crosswhite, file 1245, Provost Marshal Files.

19. B. F. Parker to Rebel General Sterling Price, February 9, 1863, box 10, e. 2593, Record Group 393, National Archives, Washington, D.C.

20. *OR,* ser. 2, vol. 5: 99–100.

21. Ibid., 319–21.

22. Ibid., 515.

23. *Reminiscences of Women of Missouri During the Sixties,* 78–84; Margaret McLure, file 1197, Provost Marshal Files.

24. Margaret McLure, file 1197, Provost Marshal Files.

25. For example, in the Provost Marshal file of Mrs. Haynes (file 1341), a regular U.S. mail carrier, Thomas Cramer, testified on July 25, 1862, that he delivered "a good many letters to Mrs. McLure, on Chesnut Street. Mostly from Nashville and from prisoners of war."

26. In the course of the war, 47 women were sent to Gratiot and Myrtle prisons, 26 of those from St. Louis. Of those 26, 7 were sent in 1862, 2 in 1863, and 13 in 1864; mostly these arrests were a matter of holding and releasing the women to the provost marshal for questioning and, after 1863, releasing them to the Female Military Prison. Compiled from Eakin, *Missouri Prisoners of War from Gratiot Street Prison and Myrtle Street Prison.*

THE PRACTICAL LADIES OF OCCUPIED NATCHEZ

1. For a discussion of the increasing emphasis on manners in Victorian America, see John F. Kas-

son, *Rudeness and Civility: Manners in Nineteenth-Century Urban America* (New York: Hill and Want, 1990), and Karen Halttunen, *Confidence Men and Painted Women: A Study of Middle-Class Culture in America, 1830–1870* (New Haven, CT: Yale University Press, 1982).

2. For the history of the "Pilgrimage" and the pageant, see Jack E. Davis, *Race Against Time: Culture and Separation in Natchez since 1930* (Baton Rouge: Louisiana State University Press, 2001), 51–82. A few years ago, Pilgrimage organizers changed the name of the Confederate Pageant to the Historic Natchez Pageant and added a performance by African American singers celebrating their heritage.

3. For example, see Catharine Van Court, *The Old House* (Richmond, VA: Dietz Press, 1950). Two works written for a popular audience that do discuss the impact of Unionism in Natchez are William Banks Taylor, *King Cotton and Old Glory: Natchez, Mississippi, in the Age of Sectional Controversy and Civil War* (Hattiesburg, MS: William Banks Taylor, 1977), and David G. Sansing, Sim C. Callon, and Carolyn Vance Smith, *Natchez: An Illustrated History* (Natchez, MS: Plantation Publishing Co., 1992).

4. See, in particular, Michael Wayne, *The Reshaping of Plantation Society: The Natchez District, 1860–1880* (Baton Rouge: Louisiana State University Press, 1983), 31–39, and William Kauffman Scarborough, *Masters of the Big House: Elite Slaveholders of the Mid-Nineteenth-Century South* (Baton Rouge: Louisiana State University Press, 2003), 316–72.

5. Anthony E. Kaye, "Slaves, Emancipation, and the Powers of War: Views from the Natchez District of Mississippi," in *The War Was You and Me: Civilians in the American Civil War*, ed. Joan E. Cashin (Princeton, NJ: Princeton University Press, 2002), 60–84; Derrick S. Ward, "Military Justice in Occupied Natchez," in *Natchez on the Mississippi: Journey Through Southern History, 1870–1920*, ed. Ronald L. F. Davis and Joyce L. Broussard (Northridge: California State University, 1995); Noralee Frankel, *Freedom's Women: Black Women and Families in Civil War Era Mississippi* (Bloomington: University of Indiana Press, 1999), 28–55; Ronald L. F. Davis, *The Black Experience in Natchez, 1720–1880* (Natchez National Historical Park, MS: Eastern National Park and Monument Association, ca. 1994), 131–65; Ira Berlin et al., *Freedom: A Documentary History of Emancipation, 1861–1867*, ser. 1, vol. 3: *The Wartime Genesis of Free Labor: The Lower South* (New York: Cambridge University Press, 1990), 635–37, 648–49, 722–23, 808–11, 814–18, 838–39; and Vernon Lane Wharton, *The Negro in Mississippi, 1865–1890* (New York: Harper Torchbook, 1965), 22–47.

6. Lawrence Powell and Michael Wayne, "Self-Interest and the Decline of Confederate Nationalism," in *The Old South in the Crucible of War*, ed. Harry P. Owens and James J. Cooke (Jackson: University Press of Mississippi, 1983), 29–45.

7. Giselle Roberts, *The Confederate Belle* (Columbia: University of Missouri Press, 2003); Steven V. Ash, *When the Yankees Came: Conflict and Chaos in the Occupied South, 1861–1865* (Chapel Hill: University of North Carolina Press, 1995), 218, 222; Drew Gilpin Faust, *Mothers of Invention: Women of the Slaveholding South in the American Civil War* (Chapel Hill: University of North Carolina Press, 1996), 197–98, 206–7.

8. See, for example, Anne Sarah Rubin, *A Shattered Nation: The Rise and Fall of the Confederacy, 1861–1868* (Chapel Hill: University of North Carolina Press, 2005), 93–94; Drew Gilpin Faust, "Introduction: Writing the War," in *Brokenburn: The Journal of Kate Stone, 1861–1868*, ed. John Q. Anderson (Baton Rouge: Louisiana State University Press, 1995); and George C. Rable, *Civil Wars: Women and the Crisis of Southern Nationalism* (Urbana: University of Illinois Press, 1989), 164, 166.

9. Faust, *Mothers of Invention*, 207.

10. The wealth of this elite came from their investments in cotton and sugar plantations between Memphis and southern Louisiana, in slaves counted by each owner in the hundreds, and in Northern

stocks and bonds. Historians have usually defined the Natchez region as including not only Adams County but also several other nearby Mississippi counties and Louisiana parishes where a number of the wealthiest planters with their home bases in Natchez owned cotton plantations. The specifics for this essay deal with the experiences of females in families that, during the occupation of Natchez, were living inside the town or close enough to it to make day trips there.

11. August 16, 1863, in James Witford Garner, *Reconstruction in Mississippi* (New York: Macmillan, 1901), 53.

12. For more information on divisions over secession among the Natchez-region elite, see Catherine Minor, Testimony to the Southern Claims Commission, April 9, 1879, East excerpts, Historic Natchez Foundation; Testimony of William F. Martin, December 12, 1877, in the case of Catherine S. Minor, C. of C. No. 7960, GAO files in Frank W. Klingberg, *The Southern Claims Commission* (Berkeley: University of California Press, 1955), 11–12; Percy Lee Rainwater, *Mississippi: Storm Center of Secession, 1856–1861* (Baton Rouge: Claitor's, 1938); Glover Moore, "Separation from the Union, 1854–1861," in *A History of Mississippi*, ed. Richard Aubrey McLemore (Hattiesburg, MS: University and College Press of Mississippi, 1973), 420–46; William L. Barney, *The Secessionist Impulse: Alabama and Mississippi in 1860* (Princeton, NJ: Princeton University Press, 1974); and Bradley G. Bond, *Political Culture in the Nineteenth-Century South: Mississippi, 1830–1900* (Baton Rouge: Louisiana State University Press, 1995), 94–122. For more information on Unionist planters, see James L. Roark, *Masters without Slaves: Southern Planters in the Civil War and Reconstruction* (New York: Norton, 1977), 25–28, 31, 55–58; Ted Tunnell, *Crucible of Reconstruction: War, Radicalism, and Race in Louisiana, 1862–1877* (Baton Rouge: Louisiana State University Press, 1984), 16–18; Randall C. Jimerson, *The Private Civil War: Popular Thought During the Sectional Conflict* (Baton Rouge: Louisiana State University Press, 1988), 22–23, 210–12; Daniel W. Crofts, *Reluctant Confederates: Upper South Unionists in the Secession Crisis* (Chapel Hill: University of North Carolina Press, 1989); Steven V. Ash, *Conflict and Chaos in the Occupied South, 1861–1865* (Chapel Hill: University of North Carolina Press, 1995), 108–30; and Drew Gilpin Faust, *Mothers of Invention: Women of the Slaveholding South in the American Civil War* (Chapel Hill: University of North Carolina Press, 1996), 11–12.

13. Garner, *Reconstruction in Mississippi*, 11.

14. Sansing, Callon, and Smith, *Natchez*, 114–15; *Natchez Daily Courier*, May 14, 1862 and various later issues; Taylor, *King Cotton*, 43, 47.

15. *Natchez Daily Courier*, June 19, 1863

16. Randall Lee Gibson to Cora Bell Gibson [n.d., wartime], Gibson-Humphreys Papers, University of North Carolina, quoted in Roark, *Masters without Slaves*, 65.

17. An infantryman from Iowa, for example, had written in May after his unit had attacked communities in Mississippi, "We burnt every thing. . . . At Jackson we had a fine old time. The soldiers were allowed to take whatever they wanted." R. Hoadley to Cousin Em, May 29, 1863, Hoadley Papers, Duke University, Durham, North Carolina, in Ash, *When the Yankees Came*, 55.

18. Rose Ker to Mary Ker, July 1, 1862, Mary Ker Papers, Southern Historical Collection, University of North Carolina, Chapel Hill, North Carolina (hereafter cited as SHC).

19. Brigadier General Thomas E. G. Ransom, U.S. Army, report, July 16, 1863, Natchez, in U.S. War Department, *The War of the Rebellion: A Compilation of the Official Records of the Union and Confederate Armies* (Washington: GPO, 1880–1901), ser. 1, vol. 24, pt. 2: 680–82 (hereafter cited as *OR*). Ransom did not consider the confiscation of horses and cattle to be "pillaging."

20. "Dan," "About Natchez, Etc.," August 23, 1863, report to the *Chicago Tribune*, reprinted in the *Natchez Daily Courier*, September 18, 1863.

21. U. S. Grant to Maj. Gen. H. W. Halleck, July 18, 24, 1863, *OR*, ser. 1, vol. 24, pt. 3: 529–30, 547. Special Orders No. 205, By order of Maj. Gen. U. S. Grant, July 29, 1863, *OR*, ser. 1, vol. 24, pt. 3: 549. See also General James B. McPherson to Brigadier General T. E. G. Ransom, July 17, 1863, *OR*, ser. 1, vol. 24, pt. 3: 521.

22. For some correspondence concerning these skirmishes, see *OR*, ser. 1, vol. 31, pt. 1: 594–600.

23. For some discussion of the rosewater policy, see Ash, *When the Yankees Came*, 25–32, 34–37. U. S. Grant to Salmon P. Chase, July 21, 1863, *OR*, ser. 1, vol. 24, pt. 3: 538; U. S. Grant to Maj. Gen. Stephen A. Hurlbut, August 4, 1863, *OR*, ser. 1, vol. 24, pt. 3: 575.

24. Brig. Gen. Thomas E. G. Ransom to Lt. Col. W. T. Clark, July 16, 1863, *OR*, ser. 1, vol. 24, pt. 2: 680–81.

25. Kate Foster, diary, July 16, 1863, Manuscript Department, William R. Perkins Library, Duke University, Durham, North Carolina (hereafter cited as WRPL).

26. By the end of 1863, the population of Natchez was at least as twice as large as it had been in June. Sansing, Callon and Smith, *Natchez*, 120.

27. Foster diary, July 25, 1863, WRPL.

28. [Ellen Shields], "Account of One of the Many Atrocities to Which Our Family Was Subjected by Federal Officials & Men," 1903, in Shields Family Genealogical File, Mississippi Department of Archives and History, Jackson, Mississippi (hereafter cited as MDAH). Shields did not mention the race of the men who harrassed her, but she probably would have if any of them had been black.

29. *Natchez Daily Courier*, November 13, 1864.

30. Joseph Dunbar Shields had been so opposed to secession that he stopped eating South Carolina rice after that state seceded. Elizabeth Dunbar Murray, *My Mother Used to Say: A Natchez Belle of the Sixties* (Boston: Christopher Publishing House, 1959), 171–73.

31. Ibid.

32. Fanny Conner to Captain Ellis, October 3, 1863, Lemuel P. Conner Papers, Department of Archives and Manuscripts, Louisiana State University, Baton Rouge, Louisiana (hereafter cited as AMLSU).

33. Fanny Conner to Lemuel P. Conner, October 13, 1863, Lemuel P. Conner Papers, AMLSU.

34. Walter Quintin Gresham, *The Life of Walter Quintin Gresham, 1832–1895* (Chicago: Rand McNally, 1919), 262–63.

35. Reid Smith and John Owens, *The Majesty of Natchez* (Gretna, LA: Pelican Publishing Co., 1986), 38; Gresham, *Life of Walter Quintin Gresham*, 243–44, 250–51.

36. Ash, *When the Yankees Came*, 76–77.

37. Scarborough, *Masters of the Big House*, 348.

38. Katherine Minor, Testimony to the Southern Claims Commission, "The Digest of the Minor Case," in Klingberg, *Southern Claims Commission*, 223–24.

39. For more information on women's reaction to the oath in various occupied communities, see Rubin, *Shattered Nation*, 94–100, 271 n. 26.

40. Records of requests by plantation lessees for permission to pass through the picket lines to and from Natchez, Mississippi, January–March 1854, Record Group 393 (hereafter cited as RG 393), National Archives and Records Administration, Washington, D.C. (hereafter cited as NA).

41. "Lady Pedlars," *Natchez Daily Courier,* September 16, 1863.

42. Fanny Conner to Lemuel P. Conner, October 13, 1864, and May 25, 1864, Lemuel P. Conner Papers, AMLSU.

43. Louisa Lovell to Joseph Lovell, August 17, 1863, Quitman Family Papers, SHC.

44. Louisa Lovell to Joseph Lovell, February 7, 1864, quoted in Robert May, "Southern Elite Women, Sectional Extremism, and the Male Political Sphere: The Case of John A. Quitman's Wife and Female Descendants, 1847–1931," draft in possession of author, 16.

45. Louisa Lovell to Joseph Lovell, February 7, 1864, Quitman Family Papers, SHC.

46. Janet Sharp Hermann, *The Pursuit of a Dream* (New York: Oxford University Press, 1981), 49–50.

47. Annie Harper, *Annie Harper's Journal: A Southern Mother's Legacy* (Denton, TX: Flower Mound Writing Co., 1983), 22–23.

48. John E. Stanchak, "James Madison Tuttle," in *Historical Times Illustrated Encyclopedia of the Civil War,* ed. Patricia L. Faust (New York: Harper and Row, 1986), 766–77.

49. N. J. T. Dana to General O. O. Howard from the headquarters of the Sixteenth Army Corps in Vicksburg, November 12, 1864, *OR,* ser. 1, vol. 52, pt. 1: 652–55.

50. General Lorenzo Thomas to Edwin Stanton, October 24, 1863, quoted in Klingberg, *Southern Claims Commission,* 112 n.72.

51. John Stanford Coussons, "The Federal Occupation of Natchez, Mississippi, 1863–1865 " (master's thesis, Louisiana State University, 1958), 66–68. See also *OR,* ser. 39, vol. 2: 186–87, 193–94.

52. Shields, "Account," MDAH; Harper, *Annie Harper's Journal,* 21.

53. Judge William Burnet to Garrett Davis, in *Natchez Daily Courier,* March 26, 1866.

54. [?] to John Jenkins, December 11, 1864, Jenkins Family Papers, Louisiana State University.

55. Taylor, *King Cotton,* 52.

56. Shields, "Account," MDAH.

57. Harper, *Annie Harper's Journal,* 23.

58. Testimony of Sidney Collins, Records of the U.S. Military Commission in Natchez, pt. 2, 2245, p. 23, RG 393, NA.

59. Records of the U.S. Military Commission in Natchez, n.d., pt. 2, 2245, RG 393, NA.

60. Special Orders No. 126, November 24, 1864, By Order of Genl. Brayman, pt. 2, 2241, RG 393, NA.

61. General Orders No. 60, November 25, 1864, By Order of General Brayman, pt. 2, 292, RG 393, NA.

62. S. A. Hurlbut, December 2, 1864, pt. 2, 2246, p. 74, RG 393, NA.

63. General Orders No. 44, October 13, 1864, By Order of Brig. Gen. M. Brayman, pt. 2, p. 292, RG 393, NA.

64. General Orders No. 14, August 19, 1864, By Command of Brig. Gen'l M. Brayman, pt. 2, p. 292, RG 393, NA.

65. J. W. Davidson to C. T. Christensen, January 17, 1865, *OR,* ser. 1, vol. 48, pt. 1: 562.

66. "Dan," "About Natchez, Etc.."

67. Murray, *My Mother Used to Say,* 170–71.

68. Harper, *Annie Harper's Journal,* 20.

69. Elizabeth Christie Brown, diary, August 18, 19, 20, September 3, 7, 1863, Historic Natchez Foundation.

70. Foster diary, July 14, 16, August 16, 1863, and scattered references, WRPL.

71. Ibid., September 10, 1863.

72. Ibid., July 16, 1863, .

73. Gresham, *Life of Walter Quintin Gresham*, 243.

74. *Natchez Daily Courier*, October 9, 1863.

75. Richard A. Hall to his parents, November 4, 1863, August 4 and November 26, 1864, Richard A. Hall Correspondence, quoted in Taylor, *King Cotton*, 49.

76. Harper, *Annie Harper's Journal*, 20.

77. Theodora Britton Marshall and Gladys Crail Evans, *They Found It in Natchez* (New Orleans: Pelican Publishing Co., 1939).

78. This quotation is from a later letter by the widow of Willie Ker in which she summarizes what he had said, possibly in his own words. Josie Ker to Mr. Rogers, April 2, 1914, Ker Family Papers, SHC (emphasis in original).

79. Lt. Richard A. Kent to Mary Ker, June 19, 1865, Mary Ker Papers, SHC.

80. George McKee to Mary Ker, August 23, December 15, 1864; Loren Kent to Mary Ker, October 27, 1864, Mary Ker Papers, SHC. For more information on this social set, see Dick Bozman to Mary Ker, May 15 and November 17, 1864; Alice Jenkins to Mary Ker, December 25, 1864, Mary Ker Papers, SHC.

81. Leonie Varennes to Mary Ker, April 29, 1865, Mary Ker Papers, SHC.

82. Loren Kent to Doctor [Surgeon S. L. Chaunch Mann?], June 21, 1864, Mary Ker Papers, SHC.

83. Official papers, Mary Ker Papers, SHC.

BETWEEN SLAVERY AND FREEDOM

1. Drew Gilpin Faust, *Mothers of Invention: Women of the Slaveholding South in the American Civil War* (Chapel Hill: University of North Carolina Press, 1996), 60.

2. C. Vann Woodward, ed., *Mary Chesnut's Civil War* (New Haven, CT: Yale University Press, 1981), 44; C. Vann Woodward, ed., *The Private Mary Chesnut: The Unpublished Civil War Diaries* (New York: Oxford University Press, 1984), 74–75, 181. See also Faust, *Mothers of Invention*, 56, 59; Daniel W. Stowell, "A Family of Women and Children: The Fains of East Tennessee During Wartime," in *Southern Families at War: Loyalty and Conflict in the Civil War South*, ed. Catherine Clinton (New York: Oxford University Press, 2000), 165; Leslie A. Schwalm, *A Hard Fight for We: Women's Transition from Slavery to Freedom in South Carolina* (Urbana: University of Illinois Press, 1997), chap. 3; and Armstead L. Robinson, *Bitter Fruits of Bondage: The Demise of Slavery and the Collapse of the Confederacy, 1861–1865* (Charlottesville: University of Virginia Press, 2005), 11.

3. Schwalm, *Hard Fight*, 104–7; see Sylvia R. Frey, *Water from the Rock: Black Resistance in a Revolutionary Age* (Princeton, NJ: Princeton University Press, 1991), and Simon Schama, *Rough Crossings: Britain, the Slaves, and the American Revolution* (New York: HarperCollins, 2006), chap. 3, on slave flight during American Revolution.

4. Consider, for example, the Virginia planter who begged his runaway slaves to return during the war, promising not to punish them for their flight, willing to bargain for the laborers he so desperately needed; see Ervin L. Jordan Jr., *Black Confederates and Afro-Yankees in Civil War Virginia* (Charlottesville: University of Virginia Press, 1995), 70–71.

5. Bell Irvin Wiley, *Southern Negroes, 1861–1865* (New Haven, CT: Yale University Press, 1938), chap. 7. See also Schwalm, *Hard Fight*, chap. 3, and Robinson, *Bitter Fruits of Bondage*.

6. Enslaved women were also subject to forced displacement by slave owners, Confederate guerrillas, and advancing Union forces; see Schwalm, *Hard Fight*, 108–14; Faust, *Mothers of Invention*, 53–79; Cashin, "Into the Trackless Wilderness: The Refugee Experience in the Civil War," 42–43, and Thavolia Glymph, "'This Species of Property': Female Slave Contrabands in the Civil War," both in *A Woman's War: Southern Women, Civil War, and the Confederate Legacy*, ed. Edward D. C. Campbell Jr. and Kym S. Rice (Charlottesville: University of Virginia Press, 1996), 55–71.

7. The Freedmen and Southern Society Project at the University of Maryland estimates some 474,000 former slaves and free blacks taking part in Federally sponsored free labor arrangements in the Union-occupied South by spring of 1865. Of that number, 93,542 were soldiers. Deducting that number, as well as 61,364 (the 6.2 percent of the black population estimated to consist of free blacks), leaves an estimated 319,094 Southern slaves who, in choosing to abandon homes in slavery, joined the population of displaced people at some point during the war. See Ira Berlin et al., eds., *Freedom: A Documentary History of Emancipation, 1861–1867*, ser. 1, vol. 3: *The Wartime Genesis of Free Labor: The Lower South* (Cambridge: Cambridge University Press, 1990), 77–80 (hereafter cited as *Wartime Genesis, Lower South*); Ira Berlin, Leslie S. Rowland, and Joseph Reidy, eds., *Freedom: A Documentary History of Emancipation, 1861–1867*, ser. 2: *The Black Military Experience* (Cambridge: Cambridge University Press, 1982), 12; and John B. Boles, *Black Southerners, 1619–1869* (Lexington: University Press of Kentucky, 1984), 135.

8. See, for example, Nancy Bercaw, *Gendered Freedoms: Race, Rights, and the Politics of Household in the Delta, 1861–1875* (Gainesville: University Press of Florida, 2003), 24–33.

9. Gregory J. W. Urwin and Cathy Kunzinger Urwin, eds., *History of the 33d Iowa Infantry Volunteer Regiment 1863–6, by A. F. Sperry* (1866; repr., Fayetteville: University of Arkansas Press, 1999), 309–10 n 7.

10. Schwalm, *Hard Fight*, 314 n. 17.

11. Faust, *Mothers of Invention*, 198–200.

12. Louise Michelle Newman, *White Women's Rights: The Racial Origins of Feminism in the United States* (New York: Oxford University Press, 1999), 10.

13. For a description of Union soldiers' mistreatment of fugitive slave women, see William Ault to "My Dear Wife," February 23, 1865, p. 6, box 3, William Ault, Civil War Papers, 1864–1865, the State of Wisconsin Collection, University of Wisconsin Digital Collections, www.digital.library.wisc.edu/1711.dl/WI.WillAult (last accessed 9/14/2006); James McPherson, *Battle Cry of Freedom: The Civil War Era* (New York: Oxford University Press, 1988), 497; Carol Faulkner, *Women's Reconstruction: The Freedmen's Aid Movement* (Philadelphia: University of Pennsylvania Press, 2004), 19.

14. Drew Gilpin Faust, who has closely studied white women's experience as refugees, has argued for a further distinction that the term "refugee" was reserved in fact for elite Southern whites and carried a pejorative meaning, implying lack of patriotism in the decision to flee. Southern whites with fewer resources, she suggests, might more accurately be termed displaced persons; see Faust, *Mothers of Invention*, 40–45. On social constructions of the role of noncombatants in war, see Jean Bethke Elshtain, *Women and War* (New York: Basic Books, 1987), 180–93. For another critique of the passivity implied in the term "contraband," see Glymph, "'This Species of Property,'" 55–71.

15. Union commanders in Florida, western Virginia, and Missouri demonstrated their willingness to abide by Lincoln's instructions in the spring of 1861; see Silvana R. Siddali, *From Property to Person: Slavery and the Confiscation Acts, 1861–1862* (Baton Rouge: Louisiana State University Press, 2005), 50–51.

16. Barbara Jeanne Fields, *Slavery and Freedom on the Middle Ground: Maryland During the Nineteenth Century* (New Haven, CT: Yale University Press, 1985), 95.

17. Several contemporary newspaper reports and private correspondence on the approach of enslaved people to Fortress Monroe are included in the *Liberator*, June, 7, 1861.

18. There were extensive debates in Congress about the legality of confiscation and about whether enslaved people themselves—or their labor—was subject to confiscation; see Siddali, *From Property to Person*, chap. 4.

19. *Liberator*, June 7, 1861. The *Richmond Whig* described Butler as "a Massachusetts Democrat—warmly in favor of Southern rights" (quoted ibid.), an assessment supported by his endorsement of the Dred Scott decision (Chester G. Hearn, *When the Devil Came Down to Dixie: Ben Butler in New Orleans* [Baton Rouge: Louisiana State University Press, 1997], 20).

20. Only after he informed his commander, General Winfield Scott, of his actions, after the Lincoln cabinet discussed his policy, and after Secretary of War Simon Cameron's cautious message on May 30, 1861, approved of his actions did Butler's approach gain official sanction. Louis S. Gerteis, *From Contraband to Freedman: Federal Policy Toward Southern Blacks, 1861–1865* (Westport, CT: Greenwood Press, 1973), 14–15; Jessie Ames Marshall, ed., *Private and Official Correspondence of Gen. Benjamin F. Butler during the Period of the Civil War* (Norwood, MA: Plimpton Press, 1917), 1:119. Butler's description of able-bodied men and women comes from his letter to General Scott, quoted in the *Liberator*, June 7, 1861; see also Ira Berlin, Barbara J. Fields, Thavolia Glymph, Joseph P. Reidy, and Leslie S. Rowland, eds., *Freedom: A Documentary History of Emancipation, 1861–1867*, ser. 1, vol. 1: *The Destruction of Slavery*, 71 (hereafter cited as *Destruction of Slavery*).

21. See Butler's order of May 30, 1861, instructing a Mr. Cram to keep careful account of those "negroes acting in the hospitals as servants," and other lists of women's employment, in Marshall, *Private and Official Correspondence*, 1:120, 186.

22. Ibid., 186–87. By July 29, 1861, the Fortress Monroe contraband included 288 able-bodied men, 47 elderly men; 140 able-bodied women, 29 elderly women; 200 children under the age of 10, and 150 between 10 and 18 years (ibid., 1:183). Butler's ideas about the Federal government's role in relation to these fugitive slaves continued to evolve; by July 30, 1861, he had communicated to Secretary of War Simon Cameron his belief that the fugitive slaves should be regarded as free, although he continued to carefully distinguish between the slaves of loyal owners and the "contraband" he accepted into his lines (ibid., 180–81; 185–88). The humanitarian issues Butler engaged while at Fortress Monroe became less personally compelling when he assumed command of the Department of the Gulf during the Union occupation of New Orleans. Rejecting the wholesale confiscation of fugitive slaves ("It is a physical impossibility" to take all the enslaved people seeking refuge with the occupying Union Army, he wrote to Secretary of War Edwin Stanton in May 1862), Butler instead admitted only male fugitives useful for military labor, excluding those fugitive slave women incapable of self-support or service to the Union Army (Berlin et al., *Destruction of Slavery*, 203–8).

23. See Siddali, *From Property to Person*, 62–63.

24. On the gender-specific practices of slave impressment, see Schwalm, *Hard Fight*, 81–86, and Michelle Ann Krowl, "Dixie's Other Daughters: African-American Women in Virginia, 1861–1868" (Ph.D. diss., University of California, Berkeley, 1998), 11–12.

25. *Independent*, July 18, 1861.

26. Thomas Montgomery to Dear Parents and Brothers, March 23, 1864, Thomas Montgomery Papers, 1862–67 (MF), Minnesota Historical Society, St. Paul, Minnesota (hereafter cited as MHS).

27. Lucius Hubbard to Aunt Mary, September 8, 1862, Lucius F. Hubbard and Family Papers, A.H875,

MHS; Judson Wade to My Dear Sister, February 26, 1863, Judson Wade Papers, box 1, P1922, MHS.

28. John Eaton, *Grant, Lincoln and the Freedmen: Reminiscences of the Civil War* (1907; repr., New York: Negro Universities Press, 1969), 47–49.

29. While this was a developing policy driven most immediately by the pressing context of war, any contemplation of removing African Americans from the wartime South was likely influenced by the antebellum and wartime public debates over black colonization and emigration movements, whose advocates had long asserted that white supremacy presented an impossibly powerful obstacle to coexistence, let alone black political and civic equality. President Lincoln would continue to advocate the colonization of emancipated slaves to a location outside the borders of the United States until 1864, and this alternative continued to find high-level endorsement after the war had ended. On antebellum and wartime colonization and emigration advocates as well as their dissenters, see Floyd J. Miller, *The Search for a Black Nationality: Black Emigration and Colonization, 1783–1863* (Urbana: University of Illinois Press, 1975); David W. Blight, *Frederick Douglass' Civil War: Keeping Faith in Jubilee* (Baton Rouge: Louisiana State University Press, 1989), 122–34, 141–46; and Eric Foner, *Reconstruction: America's Unfinished Revolution* (New York: Harper and Row, 1988), 222–23.

30. Marshall, *Private and Official Correspondence*, 1:199–201.

31. Leslie A. Schwalm, "'Overrun with Free Negroes': Emancipation and Wartime Migration in the Upper Midwest," *Civil War History* 50, no. 2 (March 2004): 155–57.

32. There were occasional examples of organized relocation, attempted by civilians, prior to 1862, but they were quite secretive; see, for example, W. H. Hicks to Dear Bro. Salter, July 18, 1861; P. B. Bell to William Salter, October 28, 1861, File: Race Relations, Burlington Public Library, Burlington, Iowa.

33. Quoted in Berlin et al., *Destruction of Slavery*, 294, 291.

34. The number is reported in the *Burlington (Iowa) Hawk-Eye*, September 1, 1862; see also the *St. Paul Pioneer*, September 23, 1862. On Secretary of War Stanton's authority, see U.S. War Department, *The War of the Rebellion: A Compilation of the Official Records of the Union and Confederate Armies* (Washington: GPO, 1880–1901), ser. 2, vol. 2: 569 (hereafter cited as *OR*). Large numbers of contrabands similarly gathered by the fall of 1862 at Helena, Arkansas; Jackson, Tennessee; and Corinth, Mississippi. They added cumulatively to the pressure on General Grant and Stanton to authorize their relocation to Northern employers; see Ira Berlin, Steven F. Miller, Joseph P. Reidy, and Leslie S. Rowland, eds., *Freedom: A Documentary History of Emancipation, 1861–1867*, ser. 1, vol. 2: *The Wartime Genesis of Free Labor: The Upper South* (Cambridge: Cambridge University Press, 1993), 27–29, 665–70 (hereafter cited as *Wartime Genesis, Upper South*). See also Schwalm, "'Overrun with Free Negroes.'"

35. *OR*, ser. 3, vol. 2: 569; *New York Times*, November 2, 1862.

36. Lucius Hubbard to My Dear Aunt Mary, September 8, 1862, and October 13, 1862, Lucius F. Hubbard and Family Papers, AH875, MHS.

37. On the army's response to the numbers of fugitive slaves gathering behind Union lines, see Maj. Gen. B. M. Prentiss to Maj. Gen. J. Schofield, Helena, Ark., June 16, 1863, ser. 2593, Letters Received, Dept. of the Missouri (hereafter cited as Dept. of the MO), RG 393, pt. 1.

38. Carl H. Moneyhon, "From Slave to Free Labor: The Federal Plantation Experiment in Arkansas," *Arkansas Historical Quarterly* 53 (1994): 138.

39. Quoted in Berlin et al., *Wartime Genesis, Lower South*, 659–60; on the arrival of women and children, see also p. 665.

40. On the estimated population at Helena, see Berlin et al., *Wartime Genesis, Lower South*, 665,

and the Emancipation League, *Facts Concerning the Freedmen: Their Capacity and Destiny* (Boston: Press of Commercial Printing House, 1863), 7. On the impact of the Emancipation Proclamation, see *OR*, ser. 1, vol. 22, pt. 2: 39 (Col. Cyrus Bussey to Maj. Gen. Samuel R. Curtis, from Helena, January 13, 1863).

41. In September 1862 the post commander at Helena was directed by one superior officer to feed contraband with army rations but warned by another that in so doing he was violating official policy; see Berlin et al., *Wartime Genesis, Lower South*, 665.

42. Maria R. Mann to Rev. Ropes, April 13, 1863, Mary Peabody Tyler Mann Collection, Library of Congress.

43. The contraband camp at Corinth, Mississippi, had to be closed early in 1864 because of the inability of the Union Army to protect it from Confederate raids; see Noralee Frankel, *Freedom's Women: Black Women and Families in Civil War Era Mississippi* (Indianapolis: Indiana University Press, 1999), 37.

44. Berlin et al., *Wartime Genesis, Lower South*, 674–75.

45. Samuel Sawyer, Supt. of Contrabands, to Maj. Gen. Curtis, from St. L., April 18, 1863, ser. 2593, Letters Received, Dept. of the MO, RG 393, pt. 1.

46. Berlin et al., *Wartime Genesis, Lower South*, 674–76.

47. *Weekly Gazette and Free Press* (Janesville, Wis.), January 16, 1863.

48. *New York Times*, October 27, 1862.

49. Berlin et al., *Wartime Genesis, Upper South*, 677–80, 686; Maj. R. E. Lawder, 2nd OH Cav. and Supt. & Pro Mar. R & F (St. Louis), to Brig. Gen. J. Sprague, Assist. Comr. (Freedmen's Bureau), September 4, 1865, ser. 2593, Letters Received, Dept. of the MO, RG 393, pt. 1; *First Annual Report of the Educational Commission for Freedmen, May 1863* (Boston: Prentiss and Deland, 1863), 9.

50. Rev. J. B. Rogers, *War Pictures: Experiences and Observations of a Chaplain in the U.S. Army* (Chicago: Church and Goodman, 1863), 211–13.

51. Berlin et al., *Wartime Genesis, Upper South*, 684–98.

52. Maj. R. E. Lawder to Brig. Gen. J. Sprague, September 4, 1865, ser. 2593, Letters Received, Dept. of the MO, RG 393, pt. 1.

53. *Douglass' Monthly*, November 1862.

54. Samuel Sawyer to Maj. Gen. Curtis, March 16, 1863, ser. 2593, Letters Received, Dept. of the MO, RG 393, pt. 1.

55. Curtis informed Prentiss, "I have more of these, unfortunately, than I know what to do with. The State of Missouri must not be made the depot for the paupers of Arkansas . . . the subject is troublesome and perplexing, but I respectfully suggest that you only transfer it by sending the negroes to my command. . . . I will have to send back if you repeat the shipments." *OR*, ser. 1, vol. 22, pt. 2: 147.

56. Samuel Sawyer to Brig. Genl. Prentiss, March 16, 1863, ser. 2593, Letters Received, Dept. of the MO, RG 393, pt. 1; see also Maj. Gen. B. M. Prentiss to Maj. Gen. J. Schofield, June 16, 1863, ser. 2593, LR, Dept. of the MO, RG 393, pt. 1.

57. Samuel Sawyer to Brig. Genl. Prentiss, March 16, 1863, ser. 2593, Letters Received, Dept. of the MO, RG 393, pt. 1; *Daily Missouri Democrat*, March 20, 1863.

58. *The Annual Report of the Freedmen's Relief Society, of Saint Louis, Missouri, for 1863* (St. Louis: St. Louis Missouri Democrat, 1864); *Daily Missouri Democrat*, January 23, 1863, March 9, 1863, and June 15, 1863; Lucien Eaton to Major General Schofield, May 30, 1863, ser. 2593, Letters Received, Dept. of the MO, RG 393, pt. 1. Later reports indicate the higher number (Berlin et al., *Wartime Genesis, Upper South*, 581–84.).

59. *New York Evangelist*, April 2, 1863.

60. *Douglass' Monthly,* August 1863; *Daily Missouri Democrat,* September 30, 1865.

61. Gerteis, *Civil War St. Louis,* 273–93.

62. Ibid., 279–80; see also Berlin et al., *Destruction of Slavery,* 408–9.

63. Berlin et al., *Wartime Genesis, Upper South,* 581–84.

64. Ibid., 597–98.

65. Ibid., 204–7; Carol Faulkner, *Women's Radical Reconstruction: The Freedmen's Aid Movement* (Philadelphia: University of Pennsylvania Press, 2004), 117–31; William Cohen, *At Freedom's Edge: Black Mobility and the Southern White Quest for Racial Control, 1861–1915* (Baton Rouge: Louisiana State University Press, 1991), 78–108.

66. *Keokuk (Iowa) Daily Gate City,* October 29, 1862, March 25, 1863; *St. Paul Pioneer Press,* March 26, 1863. For an amplified discussion of the relocation and migration of African Americans to the North during the war, see my book *Emancipation's Diaspora: The Politics of Race and Relocation on a Northern Home Front* (forthcoming).

67. Orrin Densmore Jr. to Daniel Densmore, October, 27, 1864, Densmore Family Papers, MHS.

68. For a more in-depth discussion of white opposition to relocation, see. Schwalm, "'Overrun with Free Negroes,'" 145–74.

69. On Elizabeth Estell, see Thomas Montgomery to Mother, May 27, June 14, August n.d., August 22, August 31, October 12, October 27, November 27, 1864, January 1, January 14, 1864 [1865], June 11, January 16, May 29, December 5, 1866; Thomas Montgomery to Parents and Brothers, October 22, 1864, September 5, September 23, 1866; Thomas Montgomery to Charles, October 26, December 17, 1864, February 21, 1865, March 29, 1866; Thomas Montgomery to Father, March 22, 1865, February 23, 1866, all in Montgomery Papers, MHS.

70. V. Jacque Voegeli, *Free but Not Equal: The Midwest and the Negro During the Civil War* (Chicago: University of Chicago Press, 1967), 13–20, 34–35, 60–63; Berlin et al., *Wartime Genesis, Upper South,* 28–29.

71. "Contrabands Arriving from the South: Extraordinary Demand for their Service," reported one St. Louis observer (*New York Evangelist,* April 2, 1863).

72. Rev. J. B. Rogers, *War Pictures: Experiences and Observations of a Chaplain in the U.S. Army* (Chicago: Church and Goodman, 1863), 125–27, 132; *Fond du Lac (Wis.) Commonwealth Reporter,* October 13, 1933, October 25, 1862; H. G. Shane to Annie Wittenmyer, March 20, 1863, folder 5, box 2, Annie Turner Wittenmyer Papers, State Historical Society of Iowa, Des Moines, Iowa.

73. Berlin et al., *Wartime Genesis, Upper South,* 189.

74. Berlin et al., *Destruction of Slavery,* 265–66, 249–51.

75. Berlin et al., *Wartime Genesis, Lower South,* 786–87.

OCCUPIED AT HOME

1. Franny Jordan's confrontation with Confederate troops is detailed in a letter from Moore County resident Thomas W. Ritter to Governor Zebulon B. Vance (January 25, 1864, Governors' Papers, Vance, North Carolina Division of Archives and History, Raleigh, North Carolina (hereafter cited as NCDAH). Ritter identified Franny only as "Mrs. Jordan"; he did not identify her female companions by name. I deduced Franny's first name by using clues in Ritter's letter, such as the surnames of her neighbors and the age of her son, to find the only Jordan family living in the Moore County town of

Carthage that matched Ritter's descriptions. See U.S. Bureau of the Census, Eighth Census of the United States, 1860, Manuscript Schedules of Free Population, Moore County, N.C., National Archives and Records Administration, Washington, D.C. (hereafter cited as NA), M653, roll 906. My thanks to LeeAnn Whites, Brian S. Willis, and Greg Andrews for their helpful comments.

2. Ritter to Vance, January 25, 1864, Governors' Papers, Vance, NCDAH.

3. On the North Carolina Civil War home front, see Bess Beatty, *Alamance: The Holt Family and Industrialization in a North Carolina County, 1837–1900* (Baton Rouge: Louisiana State University, 1999), 72–105; Victoria E. Bynum *Unruly Women: The Politics of Social and Sexual Control in the Old South* (Chapel Hill: University of North Carolina Press, 1992), 111–50; Wayne Durrill, *War of Another Kind: A Southern Community in the Great Rebellion* (New York: Oxford University Press, 1990); William Thomas Auman, "Neighbor Against Neighbor: The Inner Civil War in the Central Counties of Confederate North Carolina" (Ph.D. diss., University of North Carolina, 1988); Robert Kenzer, *Kinship and Neighborhood in a Southern Community: Orange County, North Carolina, 1849–1881* (Knoxville: University of Tennessee Press, 1987), 71–96; and Paul Escott, *Many Excellent People: Power and Privilege in North Carolina, 1850–1900* (Chapel Hill: University of North Carolina Press, 1985).

4. The fact that Franny Jordan is only referred to as "Mrs. Jordan" by her defender, Thomas Ritter, signifies his equation of her identity with her status as a wife and mother. Likewise, the first name of guerrilla leader Bill Owen's wife, who was tortured by Confederate militia, was not provided by Thomas Settle when he reported the abuse to Governor Zebulon Vance. On Southern women's behavior on the Civil War home front, see especially LeeAnn Whites, *Gender Matters: Civil War, Reconstruction, and the Making of the New South* (New York: Palgrave Macmillan, 2005); Margaret M. Storey, *Loyalty and Loss: Alabama's Unionists in the Civil War and Reconstruction* (Baton Rouge: Louisiana University Press, 2004); Victoria Bynum, *Free State of Jones: Mississippi's Longest Civil War* (Chapel Hill: University of North Carolina Press, 2001); David Williams, Teresa Crisp Williams, and David Carlton, *Plain Folk in a Rich Man's War: Class and Dissent in Confederate Georgia* (Gainesville: University Press of Florida, 2002); John C. Inscoe and Robert C. Kenzer, *Enemies of the Country: New Perspectives on Unionists in the Civil War South* (Athens: University of Georgia Press, 2001); and Laura F. Edwards, *Scarlett Doesn't Live Here Anymore: Southern Women in the Civil War Era* (Urbana: University of Illinois Press, 2000).

5. Daniel W. Crofts, *Reluctant Confederates: Upper South Unionists in the Secession Crisis* (Chapel Hill: University of North Carolina Press, 1989), 133, 147, 154.

6. On slaveholders' opposition to secession in the Upper South, see especially ibid.; on policing of slaves and free blacks in Civil War North Carolina, see Escott, *Many Excellent People,* 41–43.

7. Petition from citizens of Goldsboro (Wayne County) to Governor Jonathan Worth, October 1867, Governors' Papers, Worth, NCDAH.

8. Paul Escott, "Poverty and Governmental Aid for the Poor in Confederate North Carolina," *North Carolina Historical Review* 61 (October 1984): 462–80; Bynum, *Unruly Women,* 127–29.

9. Kenzer, *Kinship and Neighborhood,* 8–9, 66–96.

10. According to Robert Kenzer, by April 1861 Confederate forces had assumed control over the levers of Orange County government (ibid., 66–70); Crofts, *Reluctant Confederates,* 334–47; quoted material from Abner Dixon, Claim, 12791, March 1877; Joseph Ivey, Claim 37087, March 25, 1875, both in Claims of Loyal Citizens for Supplies furnished during the Rebellion, Southern Claims Commission, Orange County, N.C., NA.

11. Nancy Brewer purchased her husband, Green Brewer, a slave, sometime before 1858, when

she bought a home and lot in the town of Chapel Hill. Nancy Brewer, Claim 11545, Southern Claims Commission, Orange County, N.C., NA.

12. Female-headed households constituted 16.7 percent of total households in Orange County, compared with 12 percent and 11.5 percent in Granville and Montgomery. Their per capita wealth equaled only 63 percent of male-headed households, compared with 80 percent and 94 percent in Granville and Montgomery. Bynum, *Unruly Women*, 27–33; on similar conditions in neighboring Alamance County, see Beatty, *Alamance*, 86–88.

13. *State v. Rebecca Davis (or Carson), Nancy Bowers, and Nancy Carroll*, May 1864; *State v. Elizabeth Gilbert and Hawkins Browning*, January 1865, all in Criminal Action Papers, Orange County, NCDAH.

14. U.S. Bureau of the Census, Seventh Census of the United States, 1850, Manuscript Schedules of Free Population, Orange County, N.C., NA, M432, roll 639; Orange County Wardens of the Poor, vol. 1, 1832–56, vol. 2, 1856–79, NCDAH.

15. U.S. Bureau of the Census, Seventh Census of the United States, 1850, Manuscript Schedules of Free Population, Orange County, N.C., NA, M432, roll 639; Orange County Wardens of the Poor, vol. 1, 1832–56, vol. 2, 1856–79, NCDAH; Bastardy Bonds, Orange County, NCDAH; Charges of fornication and adultery are from Criminal Action Papers, Orange County, NCDAH.

16. U.S. Bureau of the Census, Seventh Census of the United States, 1850, Manuscript Schedules of Free Population, Orange County, N.C., NA, M432, roll 639; Orange County Wardens of the Poor, vol. 1, 1832–56, vol. 2, 1856–79, NCDAH; Charge against Penny Gilbert for operating a Disorderly House, [April] 1862, Criminal Action Papers, NCDAH.

17. Martha A. [Cranford] Sheets to Sheriff Aaron H. Sanders, January 27, 1865, Criminal Action Papers, Montgomery County, NCDAH (see also Bynum, *Unruly Women*, 148). Sheriff A. H. Sanders owned twenty-eight slaves in 1860 (U.S. Bureau of the Census, Eighth Census of the United States, 1860, Manuscript Schedules of Slave Population, Montgomery County, N.C., NA, M653, roll 924). Martha Adeline Cranford Sheets was the daughter of Leonard Cranford, a non-slaveholding farmer who claimed property worth $550 in 1850 (U.S. Bureau of the Census, Seventh Census of the United States, 1850, Manuscript Schedules of Free Population, Randolph County, N.C., NA, M432, roll 641). She married Lewis Sheets, a non-slaveholding miller, on January 6, 1859 (North Carolina Marriage Bonds, 1741–1868, Randolph County). Indicative of the manner in which communities overlapped county borders in the Randolph County area, Sheets threatened the Montgomery County sheriff even though she lived near Lassiter's Mill, on the Randolph County side of her community (U.S. Bureau of the Census, Eighth Census of the United States, 1860, Manuscript Schedules of Free Population, Randolph County, N.C., NA, M653, roll 910).

18. I have found no evidence that Aaron H. Sanders obtained exemptions for adult sons Jesse A., Romulus F., or Aaron T. Sanders. In the fall of 1864, he served as state's witness against widow Sarah Atkins for harboring her son James Atkins, who failed to report for Confederate duty. Aaron H. Sanders's son Romulus F. Sanders served as state's witness against James Meachum, James Blake, and John Yarbrough, all charged with harboring Confederate deserters or evaders who shared their surnames (all from Criminal Action Papers, Miscellaneous Records, Desertion, box 2, Montgomery County, Fall 1864, NCDAH). Romulus Sanders was charged that same court term with stealing Malinda Beaman's horse (Criminal Action Papers, Fall 1864, Montgomery County, NCDAH).

19. B. Craven to Governor Clark, March 13, 1862, Governors' Papers, Clark, NCDAH. Braxton Craven was the president of Trinity College, located in Randolph County; the school was later moved

to Durham, where it became Duke University. Montgomery County was estimated in June 1864 to have about two hundred deserters (Lt. T. H. Haughton, Enrolling Officer of Montgomery County, to Capt. D. C. Pearson, Chief Enrolling Officer, Confederate Conscript Papers, Southern Historical Collection, University of North Carolina, Chapel Hill, North Carolina [hereafter cited as SHC]). Randolph County's desertion figures are from Auman, "Neighbor Against Neighbor," 454. Other Central Piedmont "Quaker Belt" counties with high levels of opposition to the Confederacy were Chatham, Davidson, Forsyth, Guilford, Wilkes, and Yadkin.

20. Escott, *Many Excellent People*, 64-65; Crofts, *Reluctant Confederates*, 133, 154.

21. Kenzer, *Kinship and Neighborhood*, 29-51. On the demise of Quaker antislavery views, see Auman, "Neighbor Against Neighbor, 15-16; 64-66. On the Moravians' gradual movement away from a more humane form of slavery that recognized individual rights during the period of the early Republic to one more in line with that of traditional Southern slaveholders, see Jon F. Sensbach, "Interracial Sects: Religion, Race, and Gender among Early North Carolina Moravians," in *The Devil's Lane: Sex and Race in the Early South*, ed. Catherine Clinton and Michele Gillespie (New York: Oxford University Press, 1997), 154-67. In 1852, Wesleyan leader Daniel Wilson reported eleven Wesleyan Methodist churches in four Quaker Belt counties: five in Guilford, one in Chatham, three in Randolph, and two in Montgomery (Auman, "Neighbor Against Neighbor," 48-49). Martha Sheets's cousin, Malinda Cranford Beaman, and Malinda's husband, John Beaman, belonged to the same Wesleyan Methodist circle as did Martha Sheets. On Adam Crooks's address before the Lovejoy Church and genealogical links between the Cranford family and the Wesleyan Methodist Beaman, Hulin, Moore, and Hurley families, see Bynum, *Unruly Women*, 135-40; Ray S. Nicholson, *Wesleyan Methodism in the South* (Syracuse, NY: Wesleyan Methodist Publishing House, 1933), 53-76, 106-13; and Mrs. E. W. Crooks, *Life of Reverend Adam Crooks A.M.* (Syracuse, NY: Wesleyan Methodist Publishing House, 1871), 28-105.

22. Crofts, *Reluctant Confederates*, 133, 154; David Brown, "Attacking Slavery from Within: The Making of *The Impending Crisis of the South*," *Journal of Southern History* 70, no. 3 (2004): 541-76; The Heroes of America, also called the "Red Strings," were estimated by newspaper editor and future governor William W. Holden to have had ten thousand members in Civil War North Carolina. See William T. Auman and David D. Scarboro, "The Heroes of America in Civil War North Carolina," *North Carolina Historical Review* 58 (October 1981): 327-63.

23. Hinton Rowan Helper, *The Impending Crisis of the South and How to Meet It* (New York: Burdick Brothers, 1857), vi. For a reexamination of Helper's racial views and the depth of his antislavery convictions, see especially Brown, "Attacking Slavery from Within," 552-61.

24. For an analysis of the gender divisions among Northern abolitionists and free soil reformers and politicians, see especially Michael D. Pierson, *Free Hearts, Free Homes: Gender and American Antislavery Politics* (Chapel Hill: University of North Carolina Press, 2003).

25. Over the course of the war, North Carolina's desertion rate averaged 12.2 percent; Randolph County's 22.8 percent. Richard Reid, "A Test Case of the 'Crying Evil' Desertion among North Carolina Troops During the Civil War," *North Carolina Historical Review* 58 (July 1981): 235; Bynum *Unruly Women*, 130.

26. Auman, "Neighbor Against Neighbor," 142-43; Capt. N. A. Ramsey, Commander of Co. D, 61st regiment, NCT, to Governor Vance, February 1, 1863, Governors' Papers, Vance, NCDAH.

27. Federal Manuscript Census, 1860, Randolph County, Moore County. On Bryan Tyson's career as a Southern Unionist political agitator, see Auman, "Neighbor Against Neighbor."

28. Ritter to Vance, January 25, 1864, Governors' Papers, Vance, NCDAH.

29. See Bynum, *Unruly Women*, 132–33, for one example of a woman who delivered a "hearty blow" to an officer who had shot and wounded her son. All of the men quoted above lived near Adams Brewer in 1860. H. K. Trogden to Bryan Tyson, April 23, 1864; Alexander K. Pearce to Bryan Tyson, October 24, 1864; Israel Lowdermilk to Bryan Tyson, October 20, 1864, all in Bryan Tyson Papers, Special Collections, Duke University. I have found no record of Brewer in the 1870 census (U.S. Bureau of the Census, Ninth Census of the United States, 1870, Manuscript Schedules of Free Population for Randolph, Montgomery, and Moore counties, N.C., NA, M593, rolls 1149 and 1156), but his indictment for the murder of George Moon (Moore?) in 1866 indicates he survived the war. See Auman, "Neighbor Against Neighbor," 277.

30. H. W. Ayer to Governor Vance, March 10, 1863, Governors' Papers, Vance, NCDAH.

31. Ibid.; First Lieutenant Wm. A. Pugh to Major Archer Anderson, A. A. General, March 21, 1863, Governors' Papers, Vance, NCDAH. Henry W. Ayer is identified as state agent for contracts in Christopher M. Watford, *The Civil War in North Carolina: Soldiers' and Civilians' Letters and Diaries, 1861–1865*, vol. 1: *The Piedmont* (Jefferson, NC: McFarland and Co., 2003), 79. I did not find Loton Williams in either the population or slave schedules for 1860. He is listed as a non-slaveholding farmer in the 1850 Federal Manuscript Census for Alamance County and as a farmer with combined real and personal property valued at nine hundred dollars in the 1870 Randolph County Federal Manuscript Census (U.S. Bureau of the Census, Seventh Census of the United States, 1850, Manuscript Schedules of Free Population, Alamance County, N.C., NA, M432, roll 619; U.S. Bureau of the Census, Ninth Census of the United States, 1870, Manuscript Schedules of Free Population, Randolph County, N.C., NA, M593, roll 1156.

32. Ayer to Vance, March 10, 1863, Governors' Papers, Vance, NCDAH.

33. Ibid.; Pugh to Anderson, March 21, 1863, Governors' Papers, Vance, NCDAH. For a description of Nancy Hoover's losses, estimated at $197.15, and Pugh's grudging payment to her of $100, see letter from her lawyer, Thomas M. Moore, to Maj. Gen'l D. H. Hill, June 25, 1863, Governors' Papers, Vance, NCDAH.

34. Z. B. Vance to General D. H. Hill, April 22, 1863; Pugh to Anderson, March 21, 1863, both in Governors' Papers, Vance, NCDAD.

35. Auman and Scarboro, "Heroes of America," 347. D. C. Pearson's remarks came in response to Thomas Morris's petition for exemption (February 22, 1864, Office of the Enrolling Officer, Seventh North Carolina Congressional District, Confederate Conscript Papers, SHC).

36. P. H. Williamson to D. C. Pearson, August 5, 1864, Confederate Conscript Papers, SHC; Auman, "Neighbor Against Neighbor," 226, 368.

37. J. M. Worth to Governor Vance, August 9, 1864 (emphasis added); Iver D. Patterson to Governor Vance, December 24, 1864, both in Governors' Papers, Vance, NCDAH. Patterson's personal estate, which included nine slaves in 1860, was valued at ten thousand dollars (U.S. Bureau of the Census, Eighth Census of the United States, 1860, Manuscript Schedules of Free and Slave Populations, Randolph County, N.C., NA, M653, rolls 910 and 920).

38. On the torture of Bill Owens's wife, see Bynum, *Unruly Women*, 143–44. On Confederate policy in regard to millers providing services for deserters' wives, see J. S. Patterson to Governor Vance, June 15, 1863, and Wm. Thomas to Governor Vance, August 11, 1864, both in Governors' Papers, Vance, NCDAH.

39. Clarinda Hulin to Governor Vance, November 20, 1863, Governors' Papers, Vance, NCDAH. Clarinda Crook Hulin and Phebe Crook were the daughters of William and Rachel Crook of Montgomery County (U.S. Bureau of the Census, Seventh Census of the United States, 1850, Manuscript Schedules of Free Population, Montgomery County, N.C., NA, M653, roll 905). Clarinda married Nelson Hulin on January 15, 1855 (Marriage Records, Montgomery County, NCDAH). Although the couple lived in Montgomery County in 1860, Clarinda's letter was addressed from Randolph County.

40. Phebe Crook to Governor Vance, September 15, 1864, Governors' Papers, Vance, NCDAH. Crook's letter was addressed from Davidson County, although she advised Governor Vance to direct his response to Salem Church in Randolph County.

41. Ibid.

42. Hiram Hulin and sons Nelson and Jesse were charged with circulating "seditious publications" in March 1860 (Minutes, Superior Court, Montgomery County). On the Hulin family's conversion to Wesleyan Methodism, membership in the Lovejoy Methodist Church, support for Wesleyan antislavery leaders Adam Crooks and Daniel Wilson, and their harassment by neighbors and militia during the war, see Bynum, *Unruly Women*, 24–25, 142–49.

43. The Hulin brothers and Atkins were reportedly killed early on the morning of January 28, after being tied down in a "cold basement," presumably in the jail. It is also possible that Sheets's letter was misdated and written in response to the executions (narrative of Thoburn M. Freeman, in Winnie Richter, ed. *The Heritage of Montgomery County, North Carolina* [Troy, NC: Montgomery County Historical Society, 1981], 316–17).

44. Hiram Hulin to Colonel M. Cogwell, Commanding the Post of Fayetteville, N.C., September 28, 1867, printed in Elizabeth Gregory McPherson, ed., "Letters from North Carolina to Andrew Johnson," *North Carolina Historical Review* 39 (January 1952): 118–19. My thanks to William Auman for bringing this letter to my attention.

45. Charges against Sarah Atkins for harboring James Atkins are in Criminal Action Papers, Montgomery County, Fall 1864, Spring 1865, Miscellaneous box 2, NCDAH. As late as 1980, a Hulin descendant recounted that one "Aaron Saunders" was among the "officers in charge" (quoted from narrative of Thoburn M. Freeman, in Richter, *Heritage of Montgomery County*, 316–17). The story of the Hulin brothers' murder was revisited on October 22, 2003, by the *Montgomery Herald*, which printed a photograph of the shoe, cap, and sock worn by Jesse Hulin at the time of his murder. My thanks to Allen Green of Star, N.C., for providing me with a copy of the article.

46. A. C. McAlister's orders were quoted by Jno. M. Waddill on March 6, 1865, Alexander Carey McAlister Papers, SHC.

47. For an indication that Confederate soldiers may have aimed guns at women to force compliance or achieve arrest, see an Iredell County letter to Governor Vance that claimed military forces had "presented their guns at a lady in Alexander County" (Auman, "Neighbor Against Neighbor," 287).

48. Thomas Settle to Gov. Z. B. Vance, October 4, 1864, quoted in W. Buck Yearns and John G. Barrett, eds., *North Carolina Civil War Documentary* (Chapel Hill: University of North Carolina Press, 1980), 104.

49. Maj. J. G. Harris, Commander, 7th NCT, Headquarters, to Lt. Col. McAlister, Asheboro, March 27, 1865, McAlister Papers, SHC.

50. Letter of Lt. Col. McAlister, March 16, 1865, contained in Report to General Lee, March 30, 1865; Lt. Jno. M. Waddell to Maj. J. G. Harris, Commander, 7th NCT, March 30, 1865, both in McAlister Papers, SHC.

51. U.S. Bureau of the Census, Ninth Census of the United States, 1870, Manuscript Schedules of Free Population, Orange County, N.C., NA, M593, roll 1153.

52. Kenzer, *Kinship and Neighborhood*, 128–47; Escott, *Many Excellent Men*. On the gendered nature of Civil War rhetoric and mythmaking, before and after the war, see LeeAnn Whites, *The Civil War as a Crisis in Gender: Augusta, Georgia, 1860–1890* (Athens: University of Georgia Press, 1995).

53. Ramsey not only ignored Southern Unionists but refused even to credit Northern soldiers for the Union's victory, insisting that the Confederacy was "crushed not by the people of the North but by the hundreds of thousands of foreign trash, who fought for money and not for the love of the union." N. A. Ramsey, "61st North Carolina Infantry," Durham, N.C., 1901, http://members.aol.com/jweaver301/nc/61ncinf.htm. On the gendered nature of Civil War rhetoric and mythmaking, before and after the war, see especially LeeAnn Whites, *The Civil War as a Crisis in Gender: Augusta, Georgia, 1860–1890* (Athens: University of Georgia Press, 1995).

54. Ramsey, "61st North Carolina Infantry."

WIDOW IN A SWAMP

1. Ann Mew, case 6659, South Carolina, box 237, Record Group 217, Records of the Accounting Officers of the Department of the Treasury, Records of the Land, Files, and Miscellaneous Division, Settled Case Files for Claims Approved by the Southern Claims Commission, 1871–80, National Archives and Records Administration, College Park, Maryland (hereafter cited as SCC). I wish to thank LeeAnn Whites, Vikki Bynum, and Robert Farrell for their helpful comments on drafts of this article.

2. Margaret M. Storey, *Loyalty and Loss: Alabama's Unionists in the Civil War and Reconstruction* (Baton Rouge: Louisiana State University Press, 2004); Daniel E. Sutherland, ed., *Guerrillas, Unionists, and Violence on the Confederate Home Front* (Fayetteville: University of Arkansas Press, 1999); Richard Nelson Current, *Lincoln's Loyalists: Union Soldiers from the Confederacy* (New York: Oxford University Press, 1992); Daniel Crofts, *Reluctant Confederates: Upper South Unionists in the Secession Crisis* (Chapel Hill: University of North Carolina Press, 1989); Elizabeth R. Varon, *Southern Lady, Yankee Spy: The True Story of Elizabeth Van Lew, a Union Agent in the Heart of the Confederacy* (New York: Oxford University Press, 2003); Thomas G. Dyer, *Secret Yankees: The Union Circle in Confederate Atlanta* (Baltimore: Johns Hopkins University Press, 1999); Kirsten E. Wood, *Masterful Women: Slaveholding Widows from the American Revolution Through the Civil War* (Chapel Hill: University of North Carolina Press, 2005), 1–14; Robert Kenzer, "The Uncertainty of Life: A Profile of Virginia's Civil War Widows," in *The War Was You and Me: Civilians in the American Civil War*, ed. Joan E. Cashin (Princeton, NJ: Princeton University Press, 2002), 112–35; Drew Gilpin Faust, *Mothers of Invention: Women of the Slaveholding South in the American Civil War* (Chapel Hill: University of North Carolina Press, 1996), 148–50; Victoria E. Bynum, *Unruly Women: The Politics of Social and Sexual Control in the Old South* (Chapel Hill: University of North Carolina Press, 1992), 59–62, 146; George C. Rable, *Civil Wars: Women and the Crisis of Southern Nationalism* (Urbana: University of Illinois Press, 1989), 248–52, 267–88.

3. Lawrence S. Rowland, Alexander Moore, and George C. Rogers Jr., *The History of Beaufort County, South Carolina*, vol. 1: *1514–1861* (Columbia: University of South Carolina Press, 1996), 63, 88, 91, 113, 161, 198–203, 215–42, 277, 280–83, 1; Peter A. Coclanis, *The Shadow of a Dream: Economic Life and Death in the South Carolina Low Country, 1670–1920* (New York: Oxford University Press, 1989),

47; Theodore Rosengarten, *Tombee: Portrait of a Cotton Planter, with the Plantation Journal of Thomas B. Chaplin (1822–1890)* (New York: William Morrow, 1986), 40–41, 37–38, 88–89; *The Complete Civil War Journal and Selected Letters of Thomas Wentworth Higginson*, ed. Christopher Looby (Chicago: University of Chicago Press, 2000), 215; Nancy Rhyne, *Touring the Coastal South Carolina Backroads* (Winston-Salem, NC: John F. Blair, 1992), 208; Thomas Wentworth Higginson, *Army Life in a Black Regiment*, intro. and a new preface by Howard N. Meyer (New York: Norton, 1984), 164, 171–72.

4. Coclanis, *Shadow of a Dream*, 126, 128; Edward A. Miller Jr., *Gullah Statesman: Robert Smalls from Slavery to Congress, 1839–1915* (Columbia: University of South Carolina Press, 1995), 8; Rosengarten, *Tombee*, 25, 27–28, 88, 90, 116, 133–34, 298, 62, 177; "Port Royal and Beaufort, S.C.," *Miscellaneous Readings* (Amherst, NH), November 22, 1861, 1; "Beaufort," *New Hampshire Sentinel*, November 21, 1861, 2; C. Vann Woodward, ed., *Mary Chesnut's Civil War* (New Haven, CT: Yale University Press, 1981), 547; Rowland, Moore, and Rogers, *Beaufort County*, 381–82, 284.

5. Rowland, Moore, and Rogers, *Beaufort County*, 299, 333–45, 420–41, 416–17.

6. Ibid., 297–302, 387, 311; James Smith's testimony, SCC; 1850 U.S. Federal Census, South Carolina, Beaufort, roll M432, p. 64; 1860 U.S. Federal Census, South Carolina, Beaufort, S.C., roll M653, p. 56; Ann Mew's testimony, SCC; Rebecca Lowe, "Crum-Everett & Ingram-Ray Family," OneWorldTree, www.ancestry.com, accessed July 1, 2007; Revolutionary War Rolls, 1775–83, South Carolina, Continental Regiment of Artillery, National Archives and Records Administration, M246, folder 6, ancestry. com, accessed July 1, 2007; *F. Crossby & others v. Abram Smith & others*, January Term, 1851, 3 Rich. Eq. 244, 1851 WL (2583), WestLaw Web site, accessed July 11, 2007. The records give several birthdates for Ann Smith Mew in the 1780s, but the most reliable date, in the records of the Southern Claims Commission, is 1785. The spelling for the place-name varies, but the most common is Coosawhatchie.

7. Rowland, Moore, and Rogers, *Beaufort County*, 215, 220–21, 232–42, 254, 289; Lucius W. Barber, *Army Memoirs of Lucius W. Barber, Company "D," 15th Illinois Volunteer Infantry, May 24, 1861 to Sept. 30, 1865* (Chicago: J. M. W. Jones Stationery and Printing Co., 1894), 193.

8. Lowe, "Crum-Everett"; *Crossby & others v. Abram Smith & others*, WestLaw Web site; 1810 U.S. Federal Census, South Carolina, Beaufort, St. Peter's Parish; Ann Mew's testimony, SCC; *War of 1812 Service Records* (Provo, UT: Generations Network, 1999), n.p. www.ancestry.com, accessed July 2, 2007; Thomas O. Lawton Jr., *Upper St. Peter's Parish and Environs* (Garnett, SC: by the author, 2001), 176; Rowland, Moore, and Rogers, *Beaufort County*, 303–4, 309–11, 335–40, 385; Wood, *Masterful Women*, 31. The Mews' wedding date is not recorded.

9. Lowe, "Crum-Everett"; 1860 U.S. Federal Census, South Carolina, Beaufort, M653; Henry Newton's testimony, SCC; *Crossby & others v. Abram Smith & others*, WestLaw Web site; Harvey S. Teal and Robert J. Stets, *South Carolina Postal History and Illustrated Catalog of Postmarks, 1760–1860* (Lake Oswego, OR: Raven Press, 1989), 58–59; *Beaufort County, South Carolina, Revised and Corrected from the Surveys of Vignoles and Ravenel by Law and Kirk, Civil Engineers, 1873*, Beaufort District Collection, Beaufort County Library; Rowland, Moore, and Rogers, *Beaufort County*, 1, 371, 259, 385; Harriet McDonald's testimony, Ann Mew's testimony, SCC; U.S. War Department, *The War of the Rebellion: A Compilation of the Official Records of the Union and Confederate Armies* (Washington: GPO, 1880–1901), ser. 1, vol. 44: 445 (hereafter cited as *OR*); *OR*, ser. 1, vol. 47, pt. 1: 252; *Soldiering: The Civil War Diary of Rice C. Bull, 123rd New York Volunteer Infantry*, ed. K. Jack Bauer (San Rafael, CA: Presidio Press, 1995), 205, 208–9.

10. 1860 U.S. Federal Census, South Carolina, Beaufort, M653, for Ann Mew, John Mew, Samuel

Mew; Rowland, Moore, and Rogers, *Beaufort County*, 255, 256, 350; Rosengarten, *Tombee*, 118, 119; Hannah Mew's testimony, Henry Newton's testimony, SCC.

11. David Harman, *Illiteracy: A National Dilemma* (New York: Cambridge, the Adult Education Co., 1987), 3, 11, 19, 25, 27; National Assessment of Adult Literacy, www.nces.ed.gov/naal/ (accessed October 25, 2006); Jonathan Kozol, *Illiterate America* (Garden City, NY: Anchor Press/Doubleday, 1985), 4, 11–12, 26; *Illiteracy in America*, ed. Gary E. McCuen (Hudson, WI: Gary E. McCuen Publications, 1988); Jonathan Kozol, *Prisoners of Silence: Breaking the Bonds of Adult Illiteracy in the United States* (New York: Continuum, 1980), 8, 11.

12. Mary Beth Norton, *Liberty's Daughters: The Revolutionary Experience of American Women, 1750–1800*, with a new preface (Ithaca, NY: Cornell University Press, 1980), 265–72; Rowland, Moore, and Rogers, *Beaufort County*, 287–88; Rosengarten, *Tombee*, 177; Ann Mew's testimony, SCC; Paulo Freire, *Pedagogy of the Oppressed*, trans. Myra B. Ramos, intro. by Donald Macedo (New York: Continuum, 2007), 47–48; Harman, *Illiteracy*, 73, 92, 10. Ann Mew's illiteracy may explain why she evidently did not apply for a pension for her husband's service in the War of 1812.

13. Rowland, Moore, and Rogers, *Beaufort County*, 424, illustration opposite 456, 428–31, 438–41; Woodward, *Chesnut's Civil War*, 275 n. 2, 155 n. 4, 71; Rhyne, *Coastal South Carolina*, 240; "The Right Man for Collector of Beaufort," *New York Times*, November 17, 1861, 4. On similar divisions in other communities, see Noel C. Fisher, *War at Every Door: Partisan Politics and Guerrilla Violence in East Tennessee, 1860–1869* (Chapel Hill: University of North Carolina Press, 1997).

14. Ann Mew's testimony, Harriet McDonald's testimony, James R. Smith's testimony, SCC; 1860 U.S. Federal Census, South Carolina, Beaufort, roll M653, p. 56; WPA Slave Narratives, Federal Writers' Project, South Carolina, vol. 14, pt. 2, narrator Willis Gillison, p. 117, American Memory, African American History, Library of Congress Web site; Current, *Lincoln's Loyalists*, 107; National Archives and Records Administration, *Civil War Service Records*, online database, box 381, extraction 22, record 2560, www.ancestry.com, accessed July 1, 2007; 1860 U.S. Federal Census, Beaufort, S.C., roll M653–1214, p. 56; National Archives and Records Administration, *Civil War Service Records*, online database, box 381, extraction 22, record 2558, www.ancestry.com, accessed July 20, 2007. For similar ideas among slave-owning women, see *Our Common Affairs: Texts from Women in the Old South*, ed. Joan E. Cashin (Baltimore: Johns Hopkins University Press, 1996), 267–68, 286.

15. 1860 U.S. Federal Census, South Carolina, Beaufort, roll M653, p. 56; 1850 U.S. Federal Census, South Carolina, Beaufort, roll M432, p. 77; James R. Smith's testimony, SCC; National Park Service, *U.S. Civil War Soldiers, 1861–1865*, online database, M381, roll 22, www.ancestry.com, accessed July 1, 2007; *OR*, ser. 1, vol. 47, pt. 2: 1087. Because of the repetition of names in the Mew family, it is difficult to identify all the nephews, uncles, and brothers-in-law with certainty.

16. Rosengarten, *Tombee*, 214, 165, 218; "Beaufort, South Carolina," *Chicago Tribune*, October 8, 1861, 1; Rowland, Moore, and Rogers, *Beaufort County*, 456–57; "Port Royal and Beaufort," *Chicago Tribune*, November 13, 1861, 1; "Planters Burning Their Cotton," *Macon (Ga.) Telegraph*, November 16, 1861, n.p.; "A Traitor," *Columbus (Ga.) Ledger-Enquirer*, November 14, 1861, n.p. (name given as Chapman); "Our Beaufort Correspondence," *New York Times*, January 3, 1863, 12; Rhyne, *Coastal South Carolina*, 185–86; "Contrabands with the Naval Expedition," *Chicago Tribune*, November 12, 1861, 2; *Sherman's Civil War: Selected Correspondence of William T. Sherman, 1860–1865*, ed. Brooks S. Simpson and Jean V. Berlin (Chapel Hill: University of North Carolina Press, 1999), 545; Looby, *Journal and Selected Letters*, 112, 135–36, 93.

17. Miller, *Gullah Statesman*, 1–10; Looby, *Journal and Selected Letters*, 329, 183, 348; "The Happy New Year," *Chicago Tribune*, January 10, 1863, 2; "The Abolition Missionaries at Beaufort, South Carolina," *Macon Weekly Telegraph*, April 25, 1862, 1; Rosengarten, *Tombee*, 254; Higginson, *Army Life*, 164, 170; "Our South Carolina Correspondence," *Philadelphia Inquirer*, January 14, 1863, n.p.

18. Rosengarten, *Tombee*, 221–25; Douglas Southall Freeman, *Lee: An Abridgment in One Volume by Richard Harwell of the Four-Volume R. E. Lee*, with a new foreword by James M. McPherson (New York: Collier Books, 1991), 154–60; "Multiple News Items," *Savannah Daily Morning News*, April 10, 1863, col. b; *OR*, ser. 1, vol. 6: 435; ser. 1, vol. 14: 146; ser. 1, vol. 14: 183, 188; ser. 1, vol. 14: 182.

19. Higginson, *Army Life*, 164–65; Henry Newton's testimony, Hannah Mew's testimony, Ann Mew's testimony, Harriet McDonald's testimony, SCC.

20. Harriet McDonald's testimony, James W. Grimes's testimony, SCC; Rosengarten, *Tombee*, 212; 1850 U.S. Federal Census, South Carolina, Beaufort, roll M432, p. 57; 1870 U.S. Federal Census, South Carolina, Beaufort, roll M593, p. 323.

21. Lowe, "Crum-Everett"; Ann Mew's testimony, SCC; *Regulations for the Army of the Confederate States* (Richmond, VA: J. W. Randolph, for the War Department, 1863); William T. Sherman, *Memoirs* (1866), with an intro. by Ian M. Cuthbertson (New York: Barnes and Noble, 2005), 645; Rosengarten, *Tombee*, 229n; Woodward, *Chesnut's Civil War*, 680; *OR*, ser. 1, vol. 47, pt. 2: 1015–17; Barber, *Army Memoirs*, 192.

22. WPA Slave Narratives, Federal Writers' Project, South Carolina, vol. 14, pt. 1, narrator Silvia Chisolm, p. 199, American Memory, African American History, Library of Congress Web site; Bauer, *Soldiering*, 207, 209; Rowland, Moore, and Rogers, *Beaufort County*, 385–86; "General Sherman's Route," *Daily Cleveland Herald*, February 15, 1865, col. b; *OR*, ser. 1, vol. 47, pt. 1: 618–26.

23. Summary Report by Commissioners, Ann Mew's testimony, Harriet McDonald's testimony, Rebecca DeWitt's testimony, Hannah Mew's, SCC; Articles of War, chap. 20, Article 52, www.freepages.military.rootsweb.com, accessed January 18, 2007; Rosengarten, *Tombee*, 265; Sherman, *Memoirs*, 565–66; Bynum, *Unruly Women*, 112; Wood, *Masterful Women*, 179. Union and Confederate regulations on this score were identical. On foraging during the war, see Storey, *Loyalty and Loss*, 124–29, and Stephen V. Ash, *When the Yankees Came: Conflict and Chaos in the Occupied South, 1861–1865* (Chapel Hill: University of North Carolina Press, 1995).

24. *OR*, ser. 1, vol. 47, pt. 2: 1087; Sherman, *Memoirs*, 646; Rowland, Moore, and Rogers, *Beaufort County*, 371; OneWorldTree, www.ancestry.com, accessed July 19, 2007.

25. Eric Foner, *Reconstruction: America's Unfinished Revolution, 1863–1877* (New York: Harper and Row, 1988); Miller, *Gullah Statesman*, 93, 36.

26. Rosengarten, *Tombee*, 267, 270; Miller, *Gullah Statesman*, 23, 53, 67–68; OneWorldTree, www.ancestry.com, accessed July 20, 2007; Kenzer, "Uncertainty of Life," 129, 131.

27. Elizabeth Allston Pringle, *A Woman Rice Planter* (Columbia: University of South Carolina Press, 1992), 6–7, 335–36; Rosengarten, *Tombee*, 284; Hannah Mew's testimony, SCC; 1860 U.S. Federal Census, South Carolina, Beaufort, M653.

28. Summary Report, December 4, 1876, Statement by Special Commissioner J. P. M. Epping, March 3, 1875, SCC.

29. Summary Report, December 4, 1876, SCC; Description of records, SCC, www.footnote.com; Storey, *Loyalty and Loss*, 51–54, 146; South Carolina, Beaufort, J. P. Mew, Claim Number 6799, Claim Date May 31, 1878, p. 6, M1407, SCC, footnote.com.

30. Foner, *Reconstruction*; Rosengarten, *Tombee*, 714 n. 7; Lowe, "Crum-Everett"; Probate Judge Sheila Odom, Hampton County Courthouse, to the author, June 29, 2007; Rose D. Reedy, Division Chief, Decedent Estates, Beaufort County, to the author, March 27, 2007; 1900 U.S. Federal Census, South Carolina, Hampton, T623 1531, p. 5A.

31. Kozol, *Illiterate America*, 11; Kozol, *Prisoners*, 11, 13.

EPILOGUE

1. Republicans passed a law authorizing Federal funding to the Freedmen's Bureau in February 1866. In his veto message, President Johnson characterized the bureau as "class legislation" designed to falsely raise the expectations of and encourage the dependency of freedmen and women. For the complete text of Johnson's veto, see Edward McPherson, *The Political History of the United States of America During the Period of Reconstruction* (New York: Negro Universities Press, 1875), 149.

2. *Debate in the House of Representatives Between Mr. Butler, of Massachusetts, and Mr. Bingham, of Ohio, on the Million Appropriation Bill of the Senate for the Relief of the Southern Rebels* (Washington, DC: n.p., 1867).

3. Congressman John Covode (R-PA), for instance, agreed with Butler's objections to the bill, remembering the slow death of his youngest son, "who suffered the torments of the damned for 20 months at Andersonville." Covode agreed with Butler that the idea of provisioning Southern white civilians was a slap in the face to those who still mourned U.S. Army soldiers who died in Southern prisons. "Southern Relief Bill," *New York Tribune*, March 14, 1867, n.p., clipping file, Southern Famine Relief Commission Collection (hereafter cited as SFRC), Newspaper Extracts, reel 4, New-York Historical Society, New York, N.Y..

4. One New York veteran who signed his name "Inkgall, from Andersonville," wrote an angry editorial dismissing the Southern Famine Relief Commission (see n. 9 below) as "a hollow heartless mockery of the mutilated saviors of the country" brought about by "a few impractical women . . . who are dying for something to do." "The Southern Relief Fund: Charity Should Begin at Home," *Brooklyn Daily Union*, March 12, 1867, n.p., SFRC.

5. See Damien Cave's article on U.S. Marines weathering the abrupt transition from war to peace in Falluja in "A Tall Order for a Marine: Feeding the Hand That Bit You," *New York Times*, Week in Review, December 30, 2007, 3.

6. LeeAnn Whites, *Gender Matters: Civil War, Reconstruction, and the Making of the New South* (New York: Palgrave Macmillan, 2005), 5.

7. In his study of Union military policy toward Southern civilians, Mark Grimsley characterizes Butler as a pragmatist. Mark Grimsley, *The Hard Hand of War: Union Military Policy Toward Southern Civilians, 1861–1865* (New York: Cambridge University Press, 1995), 52.

8. See Alecia Long's essay, "(Mis)Remembering General Order No. 28: Benjamin Butler, the Woman Order, and Historical Memory," in this volume.

9. The passage of the Southern Famine Relief Bill was in part the result of a lobbying campaign launched by members of a private relief organization, the Southern Famine Relief Commission. The commission collected corn, bread, and other supplies from private donations. "Immediate Aid for the South," *New York Times*, February 25, 1867, 4. "An Appeal by the Ladies New York Southern Relief

Association," *New York Times*, March 12, 1867, 5. "The Southern Famine—The Relief Commission," *New York Times*, April 25, 1867, 5.

In "A Marshall Plan for the South?" Heather Cox Richardson argues that poverty was at the heart of white resistance to black civil rights. Richardson, "A Marshall Plan for the South? The Failure of Republican and Democratic Ideology During Reconstruction," *Civil War History* 51 (2005): 4, 378–87.

10. Eric Foner, *A Short History of Reconstruction* (New York: HarperCollins, 1990), 152.

11. "Living on Corn Husks," *New York Post*, March 9, 1867, n.p., SFRC. "The Southern Famine," *New York Times*, March 10, 1867, 4. "The Cry of Anguish," *New York Times*, March 16, 1867, 5.

12. "A Mother and Eight Children Starving to Death (Chattanooga, Tennessee)—Three Children Already Dead," *New York Times*, November 11, 1866, 3.

13. McPherson, *Political History*, 149. Foner, *Short History*, 152.

14. "The Southern Famine," *New York Times*, June 5, 1867, 1. In contrast, the appeals for famine relief that mentioned Southern blacks referred not to their starvation but to their inability to work. "There are a number of freedmen," an April 1867 appeal in the *New York Times* read, "under contract with employers who have not agreed, nor in fact are able, to furnish them with food." "The Southern Famine—The Relief Commission," *New York Times*, April 25, 1867, 5.

15. During the debate on the Southern Famine Relief Bill, Butler insisted that he had managed to feed "the starving wives and children of Rebel soldiers" for many months in New Orleans without having to draw "a dollar from the Government" by taxing "the rich of the South to feed the poor of the South." "Southern Relief Bill," *New York Tribune*, March 14, 1867, n.p., SFRC.

16. "Feeding the Rebels," *Harper's Weekly*, June 14, 1862, 383.

17. Kate Chase quoted in Michael Smith, "The Beast Unleashed: Benjamin F. Butler and Conceptions of Masculinity in the Civil War North," *New England Quarterly* 79 (June 2006): 249. Smith also notes that the women of New York held a reception for Butler after New Orleans (249).

18. *Debate*, 2.

19. That Northern women had tolerated similar neglect of Confederate POWs at camps in their midst did not impress the lawmaker. William Hesseltine estimates that POWs at the Elmira (New York) camp suffered a 24 percent fatality rate, a rate comparable to that of some Confederate prisons. William Hesseltine, ed., *Civil War Prisons* Kent, OH: Kent State University Press, 1962), 86, 88.

20. *Debate*, 3. For a discussion of the siege of Fort Fisher, see Chester G. Hearn, *When the Devil Came Down to Dixie: Ben Butler in New Orleans* (Baton Rouge: Louisiana State University Press, 1997), 235.

21. *Debate*, 4.

22. Smith, "Beast Unleashed," 255–58.

23. U.S. Army actions against Southern civilians received official sanction with General Order No. 100 (1863)—commonly known as Lieber's Code—which, among other things, held that "[t]he law of war makes no difference on account of the difference of sexes, concerning the spy, the war-traitor, or the war-rebel." Grimsley, *Hard Hand of War*, 148–51.

24. When Butler came to Washington, the Joint Committee on Reconstruction was investigating the death of Union prisoners. U.S. Congress, House, *Report on the Treatment of Prisoners of War by the Rebel Authorities, During the War of the Rebellion*, 40th Cong., 3rd sess., 1869, H. Rept, 45, 7.

25. In 1863–65, Butler had served as commissioner of prisoner exchanges, a position he had lobbied for aggressively but in which he experienced little success. Both Secretary of War Edwin Stanton and General Ulysses S. Grant strongly resisted returning Confederate POWs who would be conscripted

into the Confederate Army. Butler's Confederate counterpart was not authorized to deal with Butler because President Jefferson Davis had a reward on Butler's head in response, in part, to Order No. 28. Charles W. Sanders Jr., *While in the Hands of the Enemy: Military Prisons of the Civil War* (Baton Rouge: Louisiana State University Press, 2005), chap. 8.

26. Ibid., 161–275. Grant, too, had been called to testify in the investigation. "General Grant's Testimony before the Committee on the Conduct of the War, on Exchange of Prisoners, February 11, 1865," in McPherson, *Political History,* 296.

27. "The Southern Relief Bill," *Harper's Weekly,* April 6, 1867, 210.

28. Mary Surratt, David Herold, Lewis Powell, and George Atzerodt. Franny Nudelman refers to this episode as the birth of photojournalism. Nudleman, *John Brown's Body: Slavery, Violence, and the Culture of War* (Chapel Hill: University of North Carolina Press, 2004), 172.

29. D. Mark Katz, *Witness to an Era: The Life and Photographs of Alexander Gardner* (New York: Viking Press, 1991), 182–87. As historian Franny Nudelman has noted, William Coxshall, a U.S. Army soldier who assisted at the execution, vomited over the side of the platform. One of Gardner's photographs shows Coxshall leaning over the trap door. Nudleman, *John Brown's Body,* 173.

30. Elizabeth Leonard argues that in the postassassination climate of vengeance Mary Surratt was executed as an example to other women who would conspire against the nation. Elizabeth Leonard, "Mary Surratt and the Plot to Assassinate Abraham Lincoln," in *The War Was You and Me: Civilians in the American Civil War,* ed. Joan E. Cashin (Princeton, NJ: Princeton University Press, 2002), 300–305.

31. Katz notes that the *cartes de visite* did not sell well. Katz, *Witness to an Era,* 187.

32. For two days in December 1866 and January 1867, lawmakers argued about voting rights in the capital after Representative Edgar Cowan (R-PA), who opposed black enfranchisement, proposed an amendment to enfranchise women. Rep. Edgar Cowan to House, December 11, 1866, *Congressional Globe,* 39th Cong., 2nd sess., 57–60. See also February 1866 debates about the Fourteenth Amendment: Rep. Andrew Rogers (R-NJ) to House, January 11, 1866, *Congressional Globe,* 39th Cong., 2nd sess., 202–3. Congressman Benjamin Wade (R-OH), a strong proponent of black enfranchisement, endorsed Cowan's amendment enfranchising women out of principle. Rep. Benjamin Wade to House, December 11, 1866, *Congressional Globe,* 39th Cong., 2nd sess., 62–63.

For all his talk and his reliance on an active, politicized, female citizenry in his war against Southern women, Congressman Benjamin Butler turned out to be an unreliable ally in postwar feminists' fight for suffrage. Though he encouraged their lobbying, he frustrated them by refusing to extend his public support. Robert Holzman, *Stormy Ben Butler* (New York: Collier Books, 1961), 196–97.

33. See discussion of pensions in Nina Silber, *Daughters of the Union: Northern Women Fight the Civil War* (Cambridge: Harvard University Press, 2005), 82–86.

34. See, for instance, the petition filed by "Mr. Darling" on behalf of Christina Elder, "for payment to her of pension due Jesse Elder, deceased," February 20, 1866, *Congressional Globe,* 39th Cong., 1st sess., 951, or the petition filed by Mr. Yates, "for the relief of Mary Stanley," December 11, 1867, *Congressional Globe,* 40th Cong., 2nd sess., 55.

Notes on Contributors

E. SUSAN BARBER is an associate professor of history at the College of Notre Dame of Maryland, where she teaches courses in U.S. and women's history and is coauthoring a book with Charles Ritter on the issue of sexual justice in the American Civil War.

VICTORIA E. BYNUM is a professor of history at Texas State University. She is the author of numerous articles and two books, *Unruly Women: The Politics of Sexual and Social Control in the Old South* (University of North Carolina Press, 1992) and *The Free State of Jones: Mississippi's Longest Civil War* (University of North Carolina Press, 2001). She has a new book in progress examining southern dissent during the Civil War era.

JOAN E. CASHIN is an associate professor at Ohio State University, where she teaches U.S. history, specializing in social history, including the antebellum, Civil War, and Reconstruction eras. In addition to many articles on social and cultural history, she has published *A Family Venture: Men and Women on the Southern Frontier* (Oxford University Press, 1991); *Our Common Affairs: Texts from Women in the Old South* (Johns Hopkins University Press, 1996); an edition of William Wells Brown's novel *Clotel* (M. E. Sharpe, 1996); and a biography, *First Lady of the Confederacy: Varina Davis's Civil War* (Harvard University Press, 2006). She has also edited a book of essays on civilians in the American Civil War, *The War Was You and Me: Civilians in the American Civil War* (Princeton University Press, 2002).

CITA COOK is an associate professor of history at the State University of West Georgia, where she teaches courses on U.S., women's, and southern history. Cook has published articles in various journals and is writing a book on the young women of Natchez, 1835–1915.

MARGARET CREIGHTON is a professor of history at Bates College, where she teaches courses on American social history and cultural geography. She has written on the social history of seafaring, notably in *Rites and Passages: The Experience of American Whaling* (Cambridge University Press, 1995) and in a collection she coedited with Lisa Norling, *Iron Men, Wooden Women: Gender and Seafaring in the Atlantic World, 1700–1920* (Johns Hopkins University Press, 1996). Her recently published work on women, immigrants, and people of color in the Gettysburg campaign, *The Colors of Courage: Gettysburg's Hidden History* (Basic Books, 2005), was a runner-up for the Lincoln Prize in 2006.

LISA TENDRICH FRANK is an independent scholar living in Tallahassee, Florida. Her study that explores a gendered interpretation of Sherman's March to the Sea is forthcoming from Louisiana State University Press. She is the author of various articles on southern women's history and the editor of *Women in the American Civil War* (ABC-CLIO, 2008) and *The Civil War: People and Perspectives* (ABC-CLIO, forthcoming).

JUDITH GIESBERG is an assistant professor of history at Villanova University. She is the author of two books, *Civil War Sisterhood: The U.S. Sanitary Commission and Women's Politics in Transition* (Northeastern University Press, 2000) and *"Army at Home": Women and the Civil War on the Northern Home Front* (University of North Carolina Press, 2009).

ALECIA P. LONG is an assistant professor in the Department of History at Louisiana State University, where she teaches courses on Louisiana history, women's history, and the history of sexuality. She is the author of *The Great Southern Babylon: Sex, Race, and Respectability in New Orleans, 1865–1920* (Louisiana State University Press, 2004), which won the Julia Cherry Spruill Prize for the best book in southern women's history in 2005.

CHARLES F. RITTER is a professor of history and director of the Elizabeth Morrissy Honors Program at the College of Notre Dame of Maryland. He is the coauthor (with Jon L. Wakelyn) of two books, *American Legislative Leaders, 1850–1910* (Greenwood Press, 1989) and *Leaders of the American Civil War* (Greenwood Press, 1998), and is coauthoring a book on sexual justice in the American Civil War with E. Susan Barber.

LESLIE A. SCHWALM is an associate professor of history, women's studies, and African American studies at the University of Iowa. She is the author of numerous articles and two books, *A Hard Fight for We: Women's Transition from Slavery to Freedom in South Carolina* (University of Illinois Press, 1997), which received the Willie Lee Rose Book Award from the Southern Association of Women Historians, and *Emancipation's Diaspora: Race and Reconstruction in the Upper Midwest* (University of North Carolina Press, 2009).

KRISTEN L. STREATER is an associate professor of history at Collin Community College in Plano, Texas, where she teaches courses on the Civil War, women, and the nineteenth-century United States. She is working on a book concerning the experiences of women in Kentucky during the Civil War, and is the author of "'No Friend to Traitors No Matter How Beautiful': The Union Military and Confederate Women in Civil War Kentucky," in *The Civil War in Tennessee and Kentucky*, edited by Calvin Dickson, Kent Dollar, and Larry Whiteaker (forthcoming, University of Kentucky Press).

LEEANN WHITES is a professor of history at the University of Missouri, where she teaches courses in the Civil War and Reconstruction and the history of sexuality and gender relations. She is the author of *The Civil War as a Crisis in Gender: Augusta, Georgia, 1860–1890* (University of Georgia Press, 1995) and *Gender Matters: Civil War, Reconstruction, and the Making of the New South* (Palgrave, 2005) and coeditor of *Women in Missouri History: In Search of Power and Influence* (University of Missouri Press, 2004).

Index